# LIFE *in a* FISHBOWL

# LIFE in a FISHBOWL

## Confessions of an
## Aquarium Director

## MURRAY NEWMAN

Douglas & McIntyre
Vancouver/Toronto

94 95 96 97 98  5 4 3 2 1

Douglas & McIntyre
1615 Venables Street
Vancouver, British Columbia
V5L 2H1


**Canadian Cataloguing in Publication Data**

Newman, Murray A., 1924-
  Life in a fishbowl

  ISBN 1-55054-125-0

  1. Vancouver Aquarium—History.  2. Aquariums, Public—British
Columbia—Vancouver.  3. Newman, Murray A., 1924-  I. Title.
QL79.C32V364 1994     597'.0074'71133     C94-910097-8

Design by Rose Cowles
Front cover photograph by Philippe Martin-Morice
Typeset by Vancouver Desktop Publishing Centre
Printed and bound in Canada
Printed on acid-free paper ∞

# CONTENTS

# Foreword

When a leader retires from a distinguished career, it is the custom to present him with a gift. The givers, beneficiaries of his life work, thereby acknowledge their respect and appreciation for his accomplishments and contributions. After almost four decades as a leader in marine education, research and management innovation, Murray Newman has reversed the tradition. With this book, he gives to *us* a gift—the splendid, candid and useful recounting of his complex and influential career as director of the Vancouver Public Aquarium.

At the end of this century, a period so filled with environmental episode and human struggle, our communities are blessed with a multitude of public aquariums. Their distinct missions combine education, research, recreation and interpretation into a specific will. It is their fervent intent to inspire appreciation and stewardship for wild and natural places and their systems of life, especially in aquatic habitats. Tens of millions of people attend aquariums each year. Although they have their critics, responsibly run aquariums—the kind for which Murray Newman has helped to set the model—are a positive force in education and environmental conservation.

In the past half-century, curiosity and concern about life in oceans, bays, lagoons, lakes, rivers, streams and adjacent terrestrial habitats have increased markedly. Some observers—I among them—will argue that public aquariums have stimulated that concern and whetted that curiosity. Aquariums teach us that our stewardship and active advocacy for marine systems are vital for the survival of life on earth.

It was not always so. For most of history, we looked at the ocean as an immense, mysterious expanse. It seemed big enough to dilute all of our wastes and rich enough to feed everyone our families produced. We are learning in hard ways that the watery environments of the world and the lives they support are sensitive, finite and increasingly at risk. Aquariums are an easier, enjoyable way to learn these lessons.

The 1950s, when Murray began his career in Vancouver, was a time of both beginning and renewal. The decade following World War II saw an acceleration in the study of the seas, stimulated in part by the peacetime enthusiasm of scientists whose disciplines had been challenged, and in some cases invented, during the war by the need for oceanographic information for beach landings and naval operations. Expanding research centres, such as the University of California's Scripps Institution, widened their studies. At the University of California's related campuses, in Berkeley and Los Angeles, the student Murray Newman benefited from this growing enterprise. He shared a deepening interest in marine biology and its interpretation with young men who would later invent their own institutions of influence— among them Kenneth Norris at Marineland of the Pacific and Sea Life Park, and John Prescott at the New England Aquarium.

There must have been some spark in that time around the 1950s that fired ambition and achievement in the discovery and teaching about aquatic life. Maybe it came from an earlier time, perhaps in part from William Beebe's writings of his pioneering dives, *A Half Mile Down,* and his well-publicized explorations in the twenties and thirties, *Galapagos–World's End.* We know Beebe's work influenced Rachel Carson in her best-selling and stirring book *The Sea around Us* (1950). Cousteau's invention of the aqualung literally had opened the sea to young naturalists. Early diving forays with scuba and homemade apparatus inspired such popular books as Cousteau's own *The Silent Sea* (1950), Eugenie Clark's *Lady with a Spear* (1953) and Hans Hass's *Manta* (1952). Public interest in the seas was awakening, and the stage was being set for an expansion of marine displays and education.

At the same time, concern, even worry, was spreading about the state of the environment and human effects on natural systems. Today we take for granted the green movements and laws such as the U.S. Marine Mammal Protection Act and Canadian marine mammal regulations. Marine biologist Rachel Carson raised the level of concern first in the 1950s and later with *Silent Spring* in 1960. The burgeoning environmental movement may have first centred on the land (for example, Aldo Leopold's *Sand County Almanac,* 1948), but during Murray's tenure, it spread to include the waters and the seas.

Such books as I have mentioned can begin to direct thoughts and to focus attention on issues. Yet it is left to credible institutions, especially to places that are fun to visit—aquariums, for example—to create popular interest and advocacy. From their invention in the England of Victoria, and in their European and American counterparts, public aquariums had been primarily places of amusement. In the 1950s, the pioneering aquariums that had opened in the early years of this century were renewing—in Honolulu, Chicago, New York, San Francisco. They would mature into places of learning, recreation and advocacy.

Murray Newman led this reinvention of aquariums. With colleagues and staff, he combined research, education, exploration, marketing, fund raising, political lobbying and enlightened management to build a new kind of institution. The Vancouver Aquarium displays nature for nature's sake.

Honest entertainment might also result, but foremost is the understanding of the world and our place within it. The Vancouver Aquarium reveals the ecosystems of the waters of the world, particularly of Canada, with innovation, accuracy and élan. Today, with marvellous aquariums in almost every major city, and with elegant ones in smaller towns, we may take for granted their quality and influence. Readers of this book need to know that Murray Newman helped make this standard.

With his clear sense of mission and vision, his dedication and perseverance, Murray provides a specific, personal story of an influential and innovative marine researcher and educator—an aquarium director. However, his is also a case study of an increasingly important role in our society—the chief executive of a non-profit corporation. Management scholar and social commentator Peter Drucker has called such organizations the Third Sector of Society. Drucker suggests that they have been among the most influential institutions in our society in the 1980s and 1990s. Although they have strong, often formal relationships with government, business and other third sector groups, such organizations have a distinct ethos, discrete values and specific contributions to make to society. The Vancouver Aquarium, chartered under Murray's leadership, provides a stellar and early example of a carefully managed non-profit, non-business, non-governmental institution that is economically successful while meeting important social needs.

The job of a foreword writer is to provide a social and historical context for the reader. Yet—I yield to the temptation to make this also a personal and professional thank you to Murray Newman for his innovations and his inspiration to those of us who manage aquariums. And, as an admirer of Canada, I have a final word. Thoughtful Canadians, such as Robertson Davies and Margaret Atwood, tell us about our souls and our societies. Others—Farley Mowat and Murray Newman among them—have shown us the living world and our natural place within it. As thoroughly Canadian as Murray Newman now may be, I am proud to remind readers that he was born and grown in the midwestern and Pacific coastal United States. With all that Canada has given its southern neighbours, I am pleased that Murray's life's work has helped with our balance of humanistic trade.

Leighton Taylor
Marine biologist and environmental educator
St. Helena, California

# 1
# The Biologist and the Businessman

Carl Lietze followed a few paces behind me as I walked through the Hobby Mart Building, watching my every move and monitoring each word as it left my lips.

"An excellent rosy barb," I said in what I hoped was a properly judicial tone, stopping in front of a ten-gallon tank. The young entrant in this tropical fish competition smiled nervously and nodded his head to say thanks. Behind me, the tall, white-haired president of the Vancouver Public Aquarium Association cleared his throat loudly in a way I tried desperately to interpret.

Impatience? Disapproval? Had he caught me in an error, or did he just have an itch in his throat? I forced myself not to look back at Lietze's face and tried to keep calm. Damn it, as a Ph.D. candidate in zoology I knew volumes more about fish than he, a middle-aged insurance executive with several (admittedly impressive) tropical fish tanks in his basement. So what if it was transparently obvious that he'd arranged for me to judge this tropical fish competition purely so he could test my knowledge? And so what if he held the key to my future as an aquarist?

I knew I hadn't made an error. That was definitely a rosy barb swimming contentedly in the nicely laid out aquarium—I'd owned dozens of these small South Asian fish myself as a youth in Chicago. The fish and plants looked healthy and there was a nice mix of colour. A worthy effort, all in all. I raised my voice above the hubbub of the competition and told the entrant, "You've made wonderful use of the *Vallisneria*, but you might think about concealing the mechanical equipment more completely." The waving, grasslike *Vallisneria* didn't quite cover the air stones and plastic hoses, and this detracted from the tank's otherwise natural appearance.

The throat behind me cleared again, loudly, and this time I couldn't help turning my head to look at its owner. Far from glowering at me as I'd feared, Carl Lietze was peering intently through his rimless glasses at the previous exhibit in this tropical fish competition. The cause of the throat-clearing was obviously physical rather than any ichthyological misidentification on my part. I turned back to the row of fish tanks I was judging and tried to concentrate on fish rather than on my career prospects with the Vancouver Public Aquarium.

Carl Lietze was the visionary, the most effective promoter and the driving force behind the plan to build a new public aquarium in Vancouver. On that September day in 1955, I was probably the leading candidate to be its first curator, but I wasn't really the type of person he had in mind. Lietze thought the aquarium needed someone as forceful and socially fearless as himself, a showman rather than a diffident zoology student. Fortunately for me, the university academics and government fisheries and wildlife people he'd brought into the association to create the public aquarium were anxious that the curator be someone with a solid knowledge of fish. A biologist, not a businessman.

My major supporter was a distinguished scientist, a man who was in many ways the perfect complement to the overbearing businessman. Dr. Wilbert A. Clemens was as small and quiet as Lietze was tall and domineering. Most oceanography or fisheries students of my generation at the University of British Columbia can conjure up a mental picture of Clemens in his office, seated behind a big desk on which were laid out several neat rows of paper scraps. The tidy, precise Clemens was a highly competent administrator and had organized two institutes at UBC, the Institute of Oceanography and the Institute of Fisheries; those tiny scraps of paper were the way he organized his tasks every morning.

Both men, with their contrasting yet complementary qualities, were necessary for the project's success. It was Lietze more than anyone who got the Vancouver Public Aquarium started, but it was Clemens who got it (and me) through the first years.

Ours was not the first public aquarium this city had ever had. I'd seen pamphlets from the Pacific National Exhibition in the thirties that referred to a zoo/aquarium with fish tanks, birds and flowers. In 1953, when my wife, Kathy, and I first came to Vancouver, there was a small aquarium in the bathhouse at English Bay. The Vancouver Board of Parks and Recreation had leased the property to a Seattle man named Ivar Hagland, who later became famous for his seafood restaurants. You walked down the stairs into the bathhouse basement, the floor of which was usually wet. The water in the tanks was cold and the air in the bathhouse was muggy, so you always had to rub the condensation off the glass with your sleeve to see inside the tanks. Yet I liked the place, and I particularly remember enjoying the little blenny eels, some brown, some green, some even red. All of the exhibits were simple and local, such as sculpins and live-bearing sea perch. A child's admission was five cents, while an adult paid fifteen.

When the Vancouver Public Aquarium opened in 1956, the fish in the bathhouse were released and the damp little aquarium was closed. The sablefish that had been resident there for several years were reported as repeatedly swimming back into shallow water, apparently trying to return to their home in the bathhouse.

A large-scale marine aquarium had been on Carl Lietze's mind since the 1940s. Born in Holland, he'd immigrated to Canada in 1925 and worked his way up to become comptroller at one of the city's major insurance firms, Parsons Brown Ltd. He was an enthusiastic amateur aquarist, with a dozen beautifully lit tanks set into the walls of his basement. But these were freshwater fish, and it seemed to Carl that his adopted city—one of the great harbours of the world—should have an aquarium dedicated in large part to ocean-going wildlife. The fact that there were few marine aquariums in the world at the time made the idea all the more attractive. And he knew exactly where he wanted it: in the verdant peninsula of Pacific rainforest that both protects and defines the western edge of the harbour, Stanley Park.

Lietze became a member of the local home aquarists' society, to whom he talked incessantly about his pet project with little result. One day his frustration boiled over, and at a meeting of the society Lietze rose and angrily complained that nobody was doing anything about establishing a public aquarium. The society dealt with him the way such organizations have always dealt with people who want some form of action: they put him in charge of the project, possibly in hopes that he would shut up. But the formal support was all a dynamo like Carl Lietze needed, and he was off and running.

Aware that the university could be an important ally in his quest, he ran first to the university's Department of Zoology, where he found that Dr. Clemens also had the idea of a marine aquarium on his mind, though a rather more scientific sort of enterprise. Clemens had already given a great deal of thought to establishing a marine biological station as part of the Department of Zoology. Little funding seemed available from the university, so he set his sights on first creating a small laboratory and aquarium on the outlet from Beaver Lake in Stanley Park. That was his way, careful and logical. The brash presence of Carl Lietze might have been a little alarming to Clemens, but it obviously increased the chances of establishing a research aquarium.

Knowing he had an ally in the scientific community, Lietze continued his networking. Groups of aquarium enthusiasts met at the Lietze home, the Clemens home and the home of my professor, Dr. William S. Hoar. Lietze always ran these meetings, at which many of the preliminaries, such as bylaws, were settled. On October 22, 1950, he was able to convoke a meeting in his downtown office—actually, in the boardroom, as he'd managed to interest his boss, Frank Parsons, the head man at the insurance company.

The people who attended that founding meeting of the Vancouver Public Aquarium Association reflected Lietze's three principles in creating the aquarium, principles that to a very great extent have sustained the aquarium throughout the years and that I have always recommended to other aquariums as they started out. The first was to draw in the different elements in the community that had a direct interest in the project. The association bylaws declared that the board must have a certain number of delegates from City Council, Park Board, the federal Department of Fisheries, the provincial Fish and Game Branch, the University of British Columbia and the Vancouver Aquarists Society. Later on, guaranteed representation from different organizations was dropped from the bylaws, but it made a great deal of sense in those first years.

The second principle was to make the association as powerful as possible by enlisting the top man in each sector. In reality, the top man almost always sends his deputy. Norman MacKenzie, president of UBC, sent Dr. Clemens; the superintendent of parks sent his deputy, Stuart Lefeaux, and the head of federal fisheries in western Canada, Joe Whitmore, sent his chief biologist, Rod Hourston. That was fine, not only because they were very able people but because deputies often become top men (and nowadays top women) themselves.

The third principle was to bring in the most powerful members of the business community, whether their business was fish-related or not. At the time, the greatest figure in British Columbia's business world was undoubtedly timber baron H. R. MacMillan; he indicated his support, as did his friend John Buchanan, president of B.C. Packers. Even though they seldom attended meetings, these two men remained loyal to the project over the years, and their support was crucial to its success. In George Cunningham, Lietze hit two birds with one stone: Cunningham was not only the head of a large chain of drugstores but a city alderman. To top it off, he was also chairman of UBC's board of governors.

The meeting decided unanimously on the formation of the Vancouver Public Aquarium Association, and Lietze was elected president at a subsequent meeting in January 1951. At that time, a technical committee was also formed to start planning the new institution.

Forming the association was the easy part. The real challenge was money. The association agreed that the aquarium should be privately operated but built with grants from the three levels of government. The best estimate of the technical committee was that the aquarium building would cost $300,000. Lietze declared his belief that the City of Vancouver, the provincial government and the federal government should each provide $100,000 and proposed making advances to these three bodies. I'm told that no one at that meeting actually believed that any of the three levels of government would provide such money, but they hadn't reckoned with Carl Lietze.

Nor could they fully appreciate the particular times they were living in. It was the early years of the greatest economic growth period North America has ever seen, a time of terrific optimism and will to build things. Canada was beginning to see itself as much more than a nation of hewers of wood and drawers of water, at least potentially. Just as the aquarium association was beginning its campaign, the Royal Commission on National Development in the Arts, Letters and Sciences (known as the Massey Commission after its head, future Governor General Vincent Massey) published its report. This ground-breaking document recognized the need for national support of museums, art galleries, cultural societies and musical organizations across Canada. Largely due to UBC President Norman MacKenzie's participation as a commissioner, aquariums were included in the report.

With the legitimacy lent by the Massey Commission, Lietze and his group started lining up their targets. First they met with Vancouver mayor Fred Hume and made their pitch: if Vancouver would pledge to donate $100,000, they would obtain the other two thirds of the money from the senior levels of government.

The mayor examined the proposition and found the risk to be acceptably low. Well he knew that there was little chance Premier W. A. C. Bennett (known by his opponents as "Wacky" Bennett) would ever commit the province to donating such a sum. These were the early days of British Columbia's period of rapid growth, long before grants became standard government practice, and Premier Bennett was not given to supporting projects outside of the standard highways and hospitals. So Mayor Hume pledged the money, saying, "You get the others and I'll pony up."

Next stop was Victoria to visit Mr. Bennett, who had been elected in 1952. Lietze decided that the best way to handle the premier was to send a delegation, which included Clemens and oceanography professor Dr. Bill Cameron for scientific respectability and Alderman Cunningham for political weight. They found the premier to be, as he himself used to put it, his "ebullient and beaming self." Bennett declared himself to be interested in the project and said, "Sure, I'll go along if you get it from the federal government. But you haven't a hope."

Last on the list was James Sinclair, federal Minister of Fisheries and the

Member of Parliament for the Vancouver riding of Capilano-Howe Sound. The delegation met the minister and told him about their progress to date. Sinclair asked, "Did Bennett promise to give you that much money if I gave you the same amount?" As one man, the delegation nodded. Sinclair grinned. "You've got it."

It was quite a while before any of this money—municipal, provincial or federal—actually appeared, but at least it was promised, and with that promise Lietze was able to authorize architect Ron Nairne to proceed with the working drawings for the building.

The selection of the site for the new aquarium was an important and difficult matter. The first site chosen by the association was adjacent to Lost Lagoon at the foot of Chilco Street. Public opposition to construction at this location resulted in the site being turned down by the Park Board in 1952. A second site was considered on Coal Harbour between the Burrard Yacht Club (now the Rowing Club) and the Royal Vancouver Yacht Club. It was at this point that the scientists proved that they, like the businessmen, had an important role to play. Dr. Hoar and Dr. Cameron helped to design and then construct a small shed on Coal Harbour where regular water samples were analyzed to determine the quality of the water for the proposed aquarium.

Far in advance of public attitudes in those more innocent decades, Cameron and Hoar were concerned about pollution in local waters. The accepted wisdom of the time was that the ocean was an infinite sink into which humans could endlessly pour industrial and human waste. Cameron and Hoar worried that Coal Harbour's water might not be (or remain) pure enough for the aquarium, and they suggested that the water be drawn as deeply as possible from First Narrows, a passage of water where the harbour meets the Strait of Georgia and, beyond it, the Pacific Ocean. The southern shore of the narrows is formed by Stanley Park.

With hindsight, it is clear that they made an excellent selection. First, putting the intake at First Narrows distanced it from major pollutants in the harbour. But just as important, from the point of view of operating the aquarium, the velocity and volume of the currents at First Narrows were later found to prevent the larval stages of mussels, barnacles, sea squirts and other invertebrates from fouling the pipeline.

The search continued for an appropriate site, and in the end it was a future superintendent of parks who clinched the site Carl Lietze had hoped for all along. Stuart Lefeaux was a young engineering graduate from UBC who joined the staff of the Vancouver Park Board in 1945, and he was parks superintendent during many of the years I headed the aquarium. Perhaps more than anyone else, it was Stuart Lefeaux who persuaded the Park Board to accept the aquarium in Stanley Park.

It took some persuading, because the Park Board had reservations about allowing *anything* in Stanley Park. Stu Lefeaux's boss, Superintendent Phil Stroyan, had the traditional philosophy about parks as oases of natural tranquillity where people could seek repose from the hard edges of urban life. He had a strong distaste for large American zoos, which at that time were often blighted by extensive areas of ugly, old cages. As Stroyan saw it, his primary mandate was to maintain a beautiful Stanley Park, nicely landscaped with as few buildings as possible. This philosophy was pursued to such an extent that a number of old huts that had been Indian dwelling places were removed. I have to give Stroyan his due: he was an excellent administrator who managed the city's many parks very well at a low cost. But he was never strongly motivated to sustain the city zoo and for most of his tenure kept it as small as possible. He was, at best, lukewarm about the aquarium.

The Stanley Park Zoo has had many ups and downs as an institution. Unlike the aquarium, the zoo is under the direct control of a local government body. Politics, with its complex interplay of budgets and agendas, is hard to reconcile with dreams, and bureaucrats as well as politicians lacked commitment to zoological facilities.

It was pure luck that the birth of the aquarium coincided with the rebirth of the Stanley Park Zoo. Much of this was due to the arrival of Alan Best, who came to Vancouver from his post as Assistant Curator of Birds at the London Zoo in Regent's Park. He brought ideas from Britain that convinced Phil Stroyan to allow the modernization of the Stanley Park Zoo.

When Alan arrived, the zoo was in one of its worst downs. Where the polar bears were until recently there was a down-at-the-heels exhibit of birds whose cages had been built around 1910. The place also featured a few small animal exhibits, such as raccoons and one or two other mammals, and a monkey house where the rose garden is now. At best, you could say the zoo was inadequate for the animals it housed; at worst, many people said it was a disgrace.

With Alan Best's vision and Stuart Lefeaux's administrative backing, a new monkey house, bird house, river otter slide, penguin exhibit and polar bear exhibit were constructed at their present site in the early fifties. These transformed the zoo into a small but highly interesting collection. Stuart felt a good aquarium would complement the new zoo display. Initially, many Park Board commissioners were opposed; the city was struggling to keep the art gallery going and they did not want any more potential white elephants. With Stuart working from the inside and the association bringing all the pressure they could muster from the outside, the Park Board gave its authorization for the aquarium to locate in Stanley Park.

The Park Board took charge of construction and engaged McCarter,

Nairne to do architectural drawings. Unfortunately, when it came time to obtain the City of Vancouver's contribution, City Council took the money from the Park Board's budget. This was a rude shock and a very sore point for a long time.

As the early 1950s passed and the aquarium association got closer and closer to achieving their goal, meetings with representatives of the Park Board became increasingly difficult. The commissioners thought the hard-working aquarium boosters wanted to take over part of the great Stanley Park, and they became less and less co-operative. The association realized that only public pressure and private influence could provide a counter-weight. On the public front, they started a campaign of letter-writing to the local papers in support of the aquarium. At the same time, Carl Lietze and his fellow association members were tireless in courting support in the business community's favourite hangouts, such as the Terminal City Club. Little by little, public opinion warmed to the project.

And every bit of support was crucial. As predicted, the provincial government was slow to match its pledge. Premier Bennett did not like to write letters or (so political folklore has it) even to sign his name, a problem that cropped up for the aquarium more than once and required help from within the Social Credit Party to solve. A young Member of the Legislature, Leslie Peterson, helped the association to get Bennett's signature in early 1955.

With the final approvals of the city, provincial and federal grants, the basic $300,000 capital was assured, and construction began in the spring of 1955. That left a final task for the association: finding someone to run the aquarium for them.

I'd heard about the aquarium project while I was working on my doctoral research at UBC starting in 1953, and I knew that my professor, Dr. Bill Hoar, was deeply involved with it. I mentioned to him that I wouldn't mind working in the new aquarium, and I said something similar to Dr. Clemens. With their blessing, I attended some of the aquarium meetings in the summer of 1955, and I soon found myself to be a candidate for the job.

I can't say that I really hit it off with Carl Lietze when I first met him in the summer of 1955. He recommended another candidate for the job but, as it turned out, that was one battle Carl Lietze didn't win.

Led by Clemens, the scientists in the association argued that the aquarium would never have the continuity or credibility to take it into the future unless it was based on a solid scientific attitude towards marine studies. There was no showdown—Clemens never worked that way—but by all accounts he was insistent that the person hired first be a good biologist. As Bill Cameron put it, "He believed that the curator had to know his fish before he tried to sell them to the public."

A few weeks after that tropical fish show in the Hobby Mart Building, Carl Lietze, in his role as president of the aquarium association, informed me by letter that the board of governors had ratified my appointment as curator at a salary of $400 per month. The hitch was that my salary would commence only when the finished building was turned over to the association. The letter was dated September 22, 1955. As it turned out, I was a full-time volunteer on the project for another four months.

# 2

# Do You Know Anything about Cash Registers?

The *Vancouver Province* on September 23, 1955, headlined the story, "What more could I ask?" with bold print underneath adding, "New aquarium curator tickled salmon-pink." The article began, "A young American whose fisheries studies have carried him all over North America has found where he wants to settle down—in Vancouver as curator of the new public aquarium."

All of this was true. I was thirty-one, born and raised in Chicago. Like so many men of my generation, I had had my university studies interrupted by the Second World War, much of which I spent with the Marines as a hospital corpsman in the South Pacific. When the fighting finally ended, I remained for a time with the navy and then returned stateside to complete my Bachelor's degree at the University of Chicago and to pursue a Master's degree in zoology from the University of California at Berkeley.

My thesis work investigated the social behaviour of rainbow and brook trout, which I observed in the High Sierras of California and under more controlled conditions in San Francisco's famous Steinhart Aquarium. I was curious about their competitive relationships and spent many hours observing behaviour patterns of wild trout while I lay in a glass box lowered in the stream bed. I learned that the fish were more aggressive immediately after eating, meaning that they fought over territory rather than food, and I learned that the signals, use of body language and fin display were different in each species. With the Master's completed I got a job as a museum zoologist at UCLA, organizing the fish exhibits and assisting with collecting expeditions throughout California and down into Mexico.

It was during that time that I met my future wife, Kathy. Slender, fit and blonde, she'd have stood out even if she hadn't been the only female student in the zoology classes of Dr. Boyd Walker, my boss at the time. During the war, Walker had been a captain in the infantry, and he ran his collecting trips as if they were military operations. He had strong reservations about having women students in his classes—this was, remember, the early 1950s—but Kathy persisted and worked as hard as any of her male classmates on field trips, hauling in the collecting nets and pulling out the fish.

I distinguished myself on our first collecting trip by gallantly offering to look after Kathy's watch and then absent-mindedly smashing it in the glove compartment of the department's four-wheel drive vehicle. A true biologist, Kathy obviously found such an unorthodox mating ritual irresistible, because a few months later she consented to marry me. For our honeymoon we went (where else?) on a fishing trip—in pursuit of golden trout in the headwaters of the Kern River. Shortly afterwards she finished her fish studies, earned her teaching certificate and landed a good job at a high school in Beverly Hills.

I don't know how our life together would have gone if a young Canadian scientist named Casimir Lindsey hadn't dropped in to visit the UCLA fish museum in 1953. Cas was returning from the Galapagos Islands, where he had been collecting fish specimens for the University of British Columbia. An articulate, energetic Torontonian with a Ph.D. from Cambridge, he was full of fascinating tales of cruising among the islands, the ghost of Charles Darwin looking benignly over his shoulder as he observed the differences in the birds and reptiles from island to island. This wonderful trip had been entirely free, thanks to H. R. MacMillan, a towering figure in Canadian industry—equivalent to a Carnegie or a Rockefeller in the United States—who, starting with Cas, established the habit of taking scientists along on his yacht *Marijean* during its yearly cruises to southern waters. I'd never heard of MacMillan before, and I had no way of knowing he would become one of the most important people in the development of the Vancouver Aquarium and in my career.

Cas's flow of stories didn't stop with the Galapagos. If anything, he was even more eloquent about his research on rainbow trout in British Columbia. At Loon Lake in central B.C.'s Cariboo region, Cas was investigating why trout fry in the inlet stream swam *downstream* to reach the lake while trout fry in the outlet did just the opposite, swimming *upstream* to reach the lake (and a good thing too; if they headed downstream, they would flow over a waterfall and be lost to the system). Were these two populations genetically distinct, he wondered? Was this evolution in action?

This is exactly the kind of biological riddle a true "fish guy" loves. If it had been in Cas's mind to angle for a new post-graduate student, he had certainly found the proper bait for his hook. In the Cariboo's hundreds of rivers and streams, he rhapsodized, no less than five different species of salmon migrated to very specific destinations. Some small trout migrated downstream to the ocean, then returned as powerful steelheads. Others remained in streams and ponds as small fish throughout their entire lives. Still others spent their lives in lakes growing into mighty Kamloops trout. Why these differences? We discussed the genetic explanations Cas was partial to at the time and the role that inherent differences in behaviour might play.

As Cas spun his tales about the high plateau country with its trout lakes, vast ranches and rolling pine-covered hills filled with deer, bear and cougars, I grew increasingly certain that British Columbia was the place for me. The trout studies begun for my Master's remained greatly interesting to me; continuing these studies in British Columbia would let me observe several species of Pacific salmon, perhaps even all five, as well as trout and char. Best of all, I might be able to win my Ph.D. at UBC through these investigations. Cas thought it was eminently possible, and he was right: within six months I was offered the first H. R. MacMillan Fellowship in Fisheries at the University of British Columbia. In addition to undertaking doctoral studies under Dr. William Hoar, I would assist Cas with his fish course and also work as curator of UBC's Fisheries Museum.

Despite having to give up a good teaching job, Kathy was game for this new adventure. We arrived in Canada on Labour Day, 1953, and soon took up residence at UBC in one of the old barracks huts that dotted the campus then.

Vancouver seemed very British in those days, a stark contrast to the richly cosmopolitan city it has become. People were more reserved than in California, and I found that suited my personality fine. In fact, almost everything suited me. I admired my professors and enjoyed the great diversity of students at the university. Above all, I was charmed by the sheer physical beauty of my new city. There is nothing in the world like the splendour of Vancouver harbour as you walk along Spanish Banks, with English Bay full of sailboats and the snow-capped mountains of the Coast Range disappearing into the distance.

Like everyone else, Kathy and I fell in love with Stanley Park, but in our own particular way. Joggers running the six miles of seawall remember the smell of cedar and seaweed and the feel of the sea breezes on their skin. People with young children tend to think of picnics on the grassy meadow near Lumberman's Arch. Everyone is impressed by the magnificent Douglas firs, Western red cedars and hemlocks of this temperate rainforest. But for a fish guy like me (and a fish gal like Kathy) it was the shoreline that was most fascinating. Stanley Park is a peninsula jutting out into the harbour, and it is surrounded by a fascinating intertidal area.

The tides around the park are very great and very strange. The daytime tides are extremely low in May, but in the winter the low tides are at night. I got to know both well because Dr. Hoar was very interested in collecting *Eudistylia*, a type of tube worm, for the comparative physiology laboratories on water and salt balance. In the middle of winter, Kathy and I frequently donned our rubber hip waders and accompanied him to Brockton Point for midnight collecting expeditions.

To wander the shore of Stanley Park on a wintry night is very special. The city lights shimmer across the harbour, and even with snow falling it isn't very cold down in the intertidal; the water is much warmer than the winter air and acts as a natural heater. Slithering seaweed wraps around your legs, small fish dart among the flat, olive-coloured kelp, and the sea floor is alive with anemones, starfish of many hues, scuttling crabs and chitons in their segmented shells consisting of eight articulated plates. The smell is rich and pungent, reminiscent of iodine but alive and organic rather than medicinal. And in the back of your mind is the little thrill that comes with being out in the middle of the night.

What a contrast to one of those splendid May afternoons in brilliant sunlight. As you walk out on the shallow tidal flats, little jetting fountains of water announce the presence of clams burrowing in the wet sand. You wander about, turning over rocks and looking at the barnacles and little red and green crabs underneath. There are many places in this world that I love, too many to name (although Koluktoo Bay in the high Arctic, the islands of Palau and the coast of Maine are high on my list) and each is marvellous. But none is as magnificent as Vancouver—even if it does rain a little from time to time.

So I was tickled pink to be offered a wonderful job in a wonderful city, but at the same time the terms of the job were less than ideal. My appointment came with no contract, no guarantees and no immediate salary. Nor was it easy working for a man as bossy as Carl Lietze. And as single-minded: my strongest memory of those days is of watching with amazement and a little embarrassment as Lietze homed in on someone with his pad of aquarium membership forms like some white-haired money-seeking missile. He gave every impression that he thought the aquarium could be financed with the two-dollar memberships, if only he could capture enough of them.

Still, I also remember really good moments with Carl Lietze. One was another winter scene in Stanley Park, when the two of us visited the construction site. There in the basement of the unfinished aquarium, we wished the crew, one of whom was our future chief engineer, Gerry Wanstall, a Merry Christmas and toasted them for their hard work. For in truth, putting together an aquarium is not a simple job. One of the toughest assignments these workers faced was the seawater intake system, the heart of which was a pumphouse built at the harbour's edge almost 1200 feet from the main building. The pumps were at the bottom of a ten-foot well and were fed by a siphon line that went a farther 300 feet out into First Narrows. The water was pumped from the well up to the aquarium, where it moved down through a series of sand filters into reservoirs under the floor.

Although the construction cost had been covered (almost), the money to equip and operate the aquarium was far from assured. Fund raising was a constant concern, and we held an event in January in the Hudson's Bay Department Store in downtown Vancouver. Ernie Brown, the manager of the Bay, was on our board. Volunteers from UBC, the provincial Fish and Game Branch and the Department of Fisheries organized exhibits of both marine and freshwater animals. Since all local specimens required cool water, ice had to be provided. The promotion was a success with the public, but it only worked because we had so many people who helped with the collecting, holding and transporting of animals and ice. The scientists pitched in enthusiastically, including Cas Lindsey, who caused a small traffic jam by accidentally discharging a truckload of ice across a downtown street at rush hour.

With the $12,000 raised, we bought equipment, furniture, supplies and tropical fish. It was an appallingly small amount of money for the job ahead of us, but we were too naive to realize it and were not panicked—yet—by the calculation that another $17,000 would be necessary by our June opening date.

Meanwhile, the aquarium board considered a number of important policy issues. One of the fiercest discussions was about admission fees for children. Some board members thought that children should be allowed to get in free. Others held that if we let them in free, the children wouldn't have any respect for the aquarium—they'd just throw popcorn and gum wrappers all over the floor. The pro-gratis members replied that the children wouldn't throw their popcorn around if they were supervised. And so on. The compromise reached was that children would be charged ten cents normally but would be admitted free if they came in a class accompanied by a teacher. That was the first of many steps over the years to make the aquarium accessible to school groups and an asset to the local education system.

While the board wrestled with policy and fund raising, I began to practice what eventually proved to be my greatest strength: salesmanship. My first target was the daily press, and in particular the most popular columnists of the day, like Jack Scott and Himie Koshevoy. Scott's first article about the aquarium quoted me extensively as I extolled the institution's educational benefits: " 'This is another example of how Vancouver is growing up,' said [Newman]. 'It is particularly needed in a city where fish play such a part in the economy. Considering the value of our salmon catch it's amazing how few Vancouverites can name for you the five species of Pacific salmon.... A surprising number of people don't know the difference between a Kamloops trout and a cut-throat.' 'True,' said I, not knowing the difference."

I dragged in all the important details I could think of about the fish I intended to exhibit. Skates, for instance. Did you know, I asked visiting reporters, that female skates lay eggs called "mermaid purses" that are washed up on shore for hatching? Or that electric eels have muscles that serve as batteries and can generate about two hundred volts? Or that ratfishes, with their weird rabbitlike faces and long tails, are actually distant relatives of the shark and often found locally in the Strait of Georgia? A fish man may not be the most comfortable person to get stuck next to at a party, but I provided good copy for many articles in those early months.

If I sensed that the reporter was more interested in technical details, I spoke of the maze of pipes that would pump thousands of gallons of salt water up from First Narrows for the sea fish tanks and another system to fill the fresh tanks with dechlorinated water. We planned to have twenty-three saltwater tanks, the largest one thirty-five feet in length and holding 12,000 gallons. Another seven tanks would hold local freshwater fish, and still more would feature tropical fish. For those interested in exotic climes, I offered the prospect of alligators basking beside an artificial waterfall at the entrance, and nearby a school of piranhas from the Amazon.

The interviews worked even better when I started inviting the press along on collecting trips. The reporters loved it, and I found them enjoyable to have along. Judging from the articles that got written, I seem to have given the impression of earnest confidence. The columnist Les Rimes noted: "Newman expects to get his Ph.D. from UBC sometime this summer. He doesn't seem worried over the outcome of his exams. What's worrying him is a necessary $17,000 to help pay for fish, gear to catch fish, and wages and expenses for the month's operation."

The truth is, I was worried about *everything*. My doctoral work was in a shambles, and it actually took me another four years to complete it. This was more serious than it might sound, because when they hired me the aquarium association put a price tag on the doctorate: an additional $2,000 on my annual salary. Because of provincial regulations, Kathy was not yet able to teach in British Columbia. I don't know what we would have done if Bill Hoar hadn't taken her on as his research assistant.

Apart from my academic and financial worries, I was increasingly beset by basic management issues as opening day approached. I had no previous management experience to help me face the bewildering challenges of starting up a new institution, organizing a staff and balancing a budget. Despite all the business and scientific brainpower assembled in the association, we were amateurs when it came to operating a public aquarium. The board thought that we could operate with four or five paid employees, and I was inexperienced enough to believe it.

On the positive side, I received lots of advice from many quarters. Dr. Earl Herald of the Steinhart Aquarium, at that time probably the top fish man in the aquarium world, sent me a very candid letter about the realities of operating an aquarium, including confidential information about wages and working arrangements at the Steinhart. That was extremely helpful, although the opulence of his San Francisco institution seemed impossibly grand compared to my unhatched project in Vancouver.

As the opening approached, I began to assemble the paid staff, most of them young and untried. In May I hired Dmitry Stone, who had just received his Bachelor's degree in science from UBC, as the aquarium's first official biologist. Sheila McCormick, newly out of secretarial school, signed on as my secretary, and Mary Cashin became the store manager. I lured a janitor I knew from UBC named Eric Carr to be the live-in caretaker and also hired a local man who said he was knowledgeable about keeping tropical fish. (He wasn't, alas.)

Rounding out the staff was Gerry Wanstall, Carl Lietze's first choice for my job, who signed on as our engineer. An excellent member of the team, Gerry took all the mechanical challenges in stride, nonchalantly telling everyone that there wasn't anything at the aquarium that he didn't do in a ten-gallon tank at home—it was just that the scale was a little bigger. He made it sound easy, but the reality was more precarious. For one thing, the seawater pumping system had no back-up other than a small gas-driven air compressor. In the event of a power failure during those first years, the live-in caretaker had to run down to the basement and start up the compressor manually. Gerry looked after the mechanical system himself for three years, and if something went wrong, no matter what time of the day or night, a call from the caretaker would bring him down to fix it.

There was no budget for an artist, and we had no equipment to print labels for the exhibits. Fortunately, Aubrey Peck, the promotion manager of Hudson's Bay, came to our rescue, lending the store's sign presses to print the names of fish on cardboard cards for us. We had no money for merchandise to sell in our gift shop, either, so the Bay provided us with an attractive array of Indian artifacts and books, all on consignment.

Despite progress on so many fronts, I began to worry that my work with the press had been too successful. The newspapers trumpeted the imminent completion of the aquarium, and with mounting problems I tried to gently reduce their expectations without damping their enthusiasm. The *Sun* reported that "Mr. Newman said some expected exhibits may be missing at first, but there will be local and tropical specimens by the score to enable the aquarium to live up to its advance billing as one of the great aquariums of the continent."

The building was nearing completion but, with four weeks to go, we still didn't have many fish. Thank goodness for our friends in the federal Department of Fisheries and the B.C. Game Commission. The Fisheries Research Board permitted me to use their research trawler *Investigator* for several collecting trips, and the Department of Fisheries kindly constructed a large box on the stern of the patrol boat *Atlin Post*, which they filled with specimens and brought back to me. With their help I soon had a healthy collection of Pacific species like dogfish, rockfish, sablefish and lingcod.

One day a tank truck arrived at the aquarium with a surprise to gladden my heart. The B.C. Game Commission had collected a large assortment of freshwater fishes from the Okanagan region in the province's interior and had authorized a special trip to bring them to me. It was like Christmas! The haul included black bass, suckers, squawfish, yellow perch, chubs, carp and shiners, and some of Cas Lindsey's beloved rainbow trout.

And then—miracle upon miracle—individuals from the greater community began to join in the fish collecting. One of the earliest of these folks was a shrimp boat operator named Kay Tanaka, whom I met one day at the Campbell Avenue fish docks where I had previously obtained local marine specimens for the UBC fish collection. A few days later he came by the aquarium and dropped off some small eel pouts, sea poachers and ronquils that he had netted while fishing in nearby Deep Cove. Finally, he thoughtfully invited me to go out with him on his forty-foot beam trawler, the *Pretty Penny*.

As we rolled gently along the coastline of West Vancouver in bright spring sunlight, Kay explained that his commercial catch was local shrimps of several different kinds. These belonged to the family *Pandalidae* and were firm in texture with an excellent flavour. One of the larger species, known as the coon striped shrimp, was particularly delicious. Although Kay netted a great diversity of fish and invertebrates, he threw the non-commercial ones back into the sea—but this day they were all mine. Since he was dragging along the bottom in fifty to one hundred fathoms, the fish that came up in his nets were radically different from those familiar to us in shallow water. Many of these fish were very soft, with skins of black or dark red; many were structurally strange and interesting. I felt very grateful as I drove slowly and carefully to the aquarium late that afternoon, my car full of tubs carrying baby skates, baby ratfish and rough-spined and spiny-headed sculpins. One of the latter was a slender little fish about eight inches long. With clusters of whiskers under the flattened lower side of its head and thorny scales along its sides, it looked suprisingly like a miniature sturgeon. And indeed, its common name was sturgeon sea poacher, because of its resemblance to its mighty namesake.

In those days, people often fished from the Stanley Park seawall, casting their lines out at high tide. One middle-aged woman began bringing me live fish in a yellow bucket, running breathlessly up the grassy slope from Lumberman's Arch to the aquarium with her latest treasure. I remember giving her a dollar for a beautiful male greenling with bright blue spots decorating his sides. A week later she brought him a mate, a female greenling with contrasting yellow markings. They were a handsome addition to our growing collection.

The local fish exhibits started to look reasonable, and on May 2 I was heartened by the arrival of my first tropical fish: a couple of hungry piranhas. Soon after, five alligators arrived from Florida to take up residence in the newly built pool in the lobby, complete with rocks, tropical plants and a waterfall. They had been sent in narrow, coffin-shaped wooden boxes, one for each alligator. When the excitement of their arrival died down, there was a brief moment of indecision as we asked ourselves whether we would be attacked when we opened the boxes. Dmitry and I gingerly removed the lid of one box and, to our relief, found the reptile was encased in a moistened burlap bag.

We cautiously cut open the bag and found that the alligator's formidable jaws were tied shut with light rope. Even better. We picked the beast up and carried it over to the pool, all too aware of the bright eyes that sized us up. It was safe enough to remove the rope while holding the jaws closed with our hands. The closing muscles of the alligators' jaws are very powerful, but the opening muscles are comparatively weak. Nonetheless, it required some nimbleness to open our hands and leap out of range as the enraged animal snapped and thrashed in its newfound liberty.

Quite by surprise, the stars of the aquarium arrived by air from Honolulu at midnight on June 15, 1956. Spencer Tinker, director of the Waikiki Aquarium, had sent us three magnificent green turtles, which soon swam majestically in one of our largest tanks. Like Earl Herald at the Steinhart, and indeed most people in the field, Tinker was very kind to the new boy on the aquarium block. But the arrival of the turtles was simply the cap to an exhausting, alarming and exhilarating day, for that morning the aquarium had finally opened its doors to the public.

The night before I had taken a last walk around the place with Eric Carr, the tall Norwegian janitor, trying to imagine how the visitors would see it after they had paid their twenty-five cents. The Vancouver Aquarium was a low, one-storey box with sage-green cedar siding, 145 feet long and 99 feet wide. All the colours, inside and out, had been carefully selected by design consultants. They were mainly soft greens and peach colours, which were considered to be very modern. I liked them very much.

Eric and I started at the entrance, inspecting the gift shop counter with its totem poles, Indian wood carvings and books of "Canadiana." At the back of the foyer, philodendrons and palms rose above an alligator pool that we had copied on a small scale from the Steinhart Aquarium's entrance exhibit. From there we entered the main gallery, our footsteps echoing in the empty room as we first looked into the tropical fish tanks. I was particularly proud of one of the three-hundred-gallon saltwater tanks, which was filled with small, intensely coloured tropicals from the Philippines. Bright blue damselfish contrasted with orange-and-white clownfish, while black-and-white-barred humbugs and three-spot damselfish swam among them. I had paid $300 for these fish from a tropical fish store in Oakland, California, and while I was immensely pleased with them I was still shocked at their high cost, an excessive-seeming amount of money to a person reared during the Great Depression.

Next to them were the cool-water exhibits. The largest tank, its front window divided by several concrete posts, was thirty-five feet long, four feet deep and about seven feet wide. Freshly caught dogfish sharks, rockfish and lingcod swam unconcernedly past the glass.

Then we moved into the other half of the aquarium, which few members of the public would see. Out of sight behind all the tanks was a surrounding corridor from which the staff could easily service all the exhibits. We walked its length until we reached the eastern wing, which contained my office, a library-boardroom, a laboratory with running fresh and salt water, and Eric's living quarters. Finally, we went down to the basement, with its mechanical equipment and filters and the three 50,000-gallon reservoirs below. All was shipshape, ready for tomorrow. I drove home and tried to sleep.

Despite steady rainfall, there was a large crowd waiting outside the doors on Saturday morning, with a line-up extending out into the zoo area. Inside, the Honourable Jimmy Sinclair, minister of fisheries, stood kibitzing with Mayor Fred Hume and our friendly provincial MLA Leslie Peterson. Dr. Clemens and Carl Lietze stood quietly by as newspaper photographers milled about smoking, cameras at their sides, waiting for the great moment. Finally all was ready, and the small party of dignitaries moved forward in unison to open the four glass doors. The cameras flashed, the dignitaries stood aside, and the first visitors walked into the world's newest aquarium.

They entered in their hundreds, and then in their thousands, like a human version of the autumn salmon migration. Rivers of nickels, dimes and quarters soon overflowed the cash registers and our capacity to count and record them. Mary Cashin and Sheila McCormick fought valiantly to stay in control but within a couple of hours were clearly being overwhelmed. Just before noon Gerry Wanstall's wife arrived to take Gerry home for lunch. I walked up to her and asked an innocuous question: "Peggy, do you know anything about cash registers?" She did, and I shamelessly put her to work right then and there. I can't remember if Gerry got his lunch that day or not.

The great crowds created dirty floors and messy washrooms, and their breath condensed in great clouds on the windows of the cold water tanks. They gaped at the alligators, pointed at the piranhas, chuckled at the orange-and-white clownfish and asked question after question of anyone who looked like staff. The following day was sunny, and the crowd was even larger. We staff members struggled to keep cool as we desperately tried to keep the public places clean.

It was an exhausting two days. When we finally totalled the receipts, we were flabbergasted to find that a total of 10,000 people had passed through the aquarium. And so it continued. During our first month, over 125,000 people viewed our displays, as many people as had been expected to enter it in a period of a year. The aquarium was so popular we decided to keep it open from 10:00 A.M. to 9:00 P.M. every day of the week. That of course led to hiring more staff, including a total of five cashiers.

By this time I was almost hysterical with the demands set upon me by high expectations. Lack of staff meant volunteers were essential for everything from feeding the animals to cleaning the floors. We brought in anybody and everybody to help make it work, including the relatives of board members and friends. One of these was David Hoar, the son of my professor. David is now a geneticist with a Ph.D. after his name, but his father likes to say that David got his start in science wielding a broom at the Vancouver Aquarium. Another high school student, Josef Bauer, made himself so useful that the board awarded him a life membership. Who could know that eight years later he would play a major part in capturing a killer whale, the first orca to be exhibited live by an aquarium?

The research program began when Dr. Hoar started working in the aquarium's research lab. He also brought my wife, Kathy, into the aquarium, for she was still assisting him in his salmon research. I'm afraid that she too was pressed into service; her training as a teacher made her the perfect person to deal with the crowds of schoolchildren who visited us, and she became the first volunteer docent. Other volunteers materialized in the following months, mainly university students from the UBC science faculty but also teachers, high school students, and a totally unexpected group: Vancouver's scuba diving enthusiasts. In those days we didn't think of them as "volunteers"; the concept hadn't yet struck us in any organized fashion. We simply invited enthusiastic people we liked to participate with us in our activities.

Although glowing write-ups in the newspapers and *Time* didn't hurt, sunny weather and word of mouth were the main drivers of our attendance. However, the hot weather also seriously elevated the temperature of the aquarium's seawater tanks, with the result that many fish didn't survive very long. The loss of specimens was very frustrating after our hard work to collect and transport them. The starfish, anemones and octopus were especially sensitive to the high temperatures and low salinities. They and the other invertebrates were the first to go, and they were followed by the more delicate of the deep-water fish that we had collected on our expeditions with the *Investigator* and Kay Tanaka.

The problem was that the original arrangement of pipes and pumps made it impossible to simultaneously pump from the sea and recirculate water within the building. While water was being pumped from First Narrows, all circulation within the aquarium ceased, with the result that the water warmed up and became deficient in oxygen. Clearly, a bypass system was necessary to permit both of these activities to take place at the same time. Even more important was the extension of the pipeline intake to deeper water, for the seawater being drawn into the aquarium was not only too warm but too dilute and too dirty. We estimated that an extension of five hundred feet would lower the mouth of the intake ten feet and make the water colder, saltier and cleaner.

The loss of specimens made it very difficult to maintain an adequate number of fish on display, and several of the tanks remained empty for long periods. That highlighted yet another problem: the aquarium needed much better collecting equipment even to maintain mediocre exhibits. We had no boats or nets of our own, and any collecting required us to borrow equipment from other agencies. We didn't even have a vehicle of our own to transport the specimens that we caught.

Extending the pipeline and obtaining collecting equipment would clearly take a lot of money, and money issues were already getting me into trouble with the board—and with the extremely frugal Carl Lietze. We had seven full-time employees already and I had been forced to hire extra cashiers to keep up with the workload. Carl denounced me at one memorable board meeting as "getting too big for my britches."

What probably saved my job was the fact that Dr. Clemens had replaced

Lietze as president just before the aquarium opened. With his organizing skills and quiet logic, Clemens was the right man at the right time. Among his most important actions was the formation of board committees, including a finance committee and one responsible for liaison with the Park Board. That spread the work around and put it in the hands of the people best able to do it. It also diffused some of Lietze's personal influence and took some of the direct heat off me. Instead of the previous system of ad hoc meetings, it was decided under Clemens's presidency that the board would meet once a month and be preceded by a finance committee meeting. This sensible arrangement has been followed ever since.

By the end of the summer, several things seemed clear. First, we had been spectacularly successful. Within a month of opening, the aquarium had established itself as a top Vancouver attraction for both local people and tourists. Second, even with our unexpectedly high attendance, the low admittance fees were inadequate to pay our mounting bills. We were forced to go to the Park Board and ask for an increase from twenty-five cents to thirty-five cents. The increase was approved, but only after some fierce lobbying and closed-door sessions at City Hall.

The last thing was clear to me, if not to anyone else. Despite its successful start-up, the aquarium was a stark, unfinished and unembellished facility that needed massive improvement and enlargement. Unexpected construction costs had forced cutbacks to our original plans. Where handsome terrazzo floors had been envisaged, red-painted concrete floors had materialized. Cut granite stonework was in the design for the entrance but green-coloured concrete had been substituted to reduce costs. There was still no budget for labels or graphics, and as an educator I felt this lack keenly. Of course, none of this discouraged me from telling everyone that ours was one of the great aquariums of the world.

And a mere fifteen years later, it truly was.

# 3
# Fish, Funds and Plumbing

If you walk into the aquarium's Arctic Gallery today, down the stairs from the frolicking sea otters and past the eight-foot-high acrylic windows looking into the beluga pool, you'll come to an interactive exhibit with a video playing on television screens. Sometimes when I pause in front of one of these high-tech displays, I think back to the first year of the aquarium's existence and try to run it through my mind as if it were a video program. The impression is of a mad, Keystone Cops scramble to operate the machinery, satisfy the public, and collect the fish and find the right people to look after them. And always the desperate search for funds.

With the help of age-yellowed newspaper cuttings and the reports and newsletters I wrote nearly four decades ago, the blur comes into focus. Billy Wong appears, not as the relaxed senior he is today but as the shy nineteen-year-old who saved our tropical fish collection. Gladys Clawson clatters in to resume her design work, fresh from some adventure in South America or Japan. And the World-Famous Mystery Fish again swims close to the rippled surface of my memory, looking for some choice tidbit to pull from my fingers. I'll get to all three in due course, but first let us fast-forward to the end of the year, when my report on our first twelve months of business was presented to the board.

Those early meetings of the board always made me feel as though I were a student in a classroom. I'd look around the table, watching the reactions to my reports as nervously as if they'd been essays submitted to a very demanding group of teachers. The most demanding of all was Carl Lietze, who was never anything but formal and serious, and who always wanted more—more information, more explanation, more results. Mercifully, at the other end of the table sat the benign figure of Dr. Clemens, who gently but firmly kept the agenda moving. The board system was a good one, I finally decided, but it took some getting used to.

Watching the reactions at that meeting in July 1957, however, was like receiving an exam back with a big A+ on it. There were smiles all around, even from Carl Lietze, when I repeated what everyone already knew: despite the municipal government's fears that we'd turn out to be a white elephant, the aquarium had proved that it could pull its financial weight. We had not only paid for our operating costs during the first year without tax support but had made enough to buy some new equipment and pay for a major improvement: the extension of our seawater intake pipe.

If an army can be said to march on its stomach, it is equally apt to say that an aquarium lives or dies on the quality of its plumbing. You'd swear, if you overheard some of the discussions at an aquarium conference, that you were eavesdropping on a plumber's jamboree. The quality of the water, its temperature and its steady supply are all essential, and to a great extent the pipes, machinery, filters and plumbing make possible the high water quality.

It had become clear in the first weeks that the asbestos-concrete intake pipe for our sea water simply did not extend far enough out into the harbour. The Fraser, one of the continent's longest rivers, floods each year in the spring and summer, and its waters spread unhurriedly from the delta south of Vancouver out into the Strait of Georgia and around to the harbour that bisects the city. The fresh water stays near the harbour's surface, warming up in the sunlight; before long it combines with river silt and run-off pollution into an unappetizing "soup." The soup overwhelmed our filter system—and killed some of our fish. We needed a longer pipe to reach below the thermocline farther out in the harbour so that cooler, salty water could be pulled in even at low tide.

Despite our already uneasy territorial relationship with the Park Board, Deputy Superintendent Stuart Lefeaux took charge of the project and in the middle of that first winter led a gang of hip-wader-clad workers out into the intertidal area below Lumberman's Arch to extend the pipe. In order to take advantage of the few hours of low tide that occurred each twenty-four hours, the construction work had to be done in the middle of the night—not the most pleasant of working conditions. Nowadays you would just unroll a length of heavy plastic pipe and anchor it down, but Stuart had to deal with pre-cast concrete, and that required everything to be precisely prepared beforehand to take absolute advantage of time. Once the week-long job was finished, the better-quality seawater had an immediate effect on the life expectancy of our animals. The grateful aquarium association made Stuart a life member for these labours.

In the first twelve months since the aquarium had opened, a total of 342,870 people had passed through its turnstiles. The population of Vancouver was only 344,833 at that time. This fact allowed us to suggest somewhat cheekily in our publicity that "if you are one of those 1,963 unlucky Vancouverites who did not get around to see the fish in 1957, perhaps you will be able to make it in 1958."

The attendance patterns begun during that year have repeated themselves ever since. Peak months for admissions had been July and August, with a sharp drop in attendance following Labour Day. It had continued to fall through December, then begun slowly rising in January. April was unexpectedly high because of the Easter Holidays. The lesson was that the burden of paying for the aquarium's operation fell most heavily on July and August.

In any month, strong attendance was related to three factors, the first two being good weather and public holidays. On sunny days people flocked to Stanley Park, and many strolled into the aquarium. But a rainy public holiday brought more people to the aquarium than a sunny work day. Sunday was the biggest day of the week, but school holidays were also important. The latter were when we often saw adults who don't have traditional job schedules—everyone from loggers to flight attendants, and of course stay-at-home parents, babysitters and grandparents—bring children.

The third factor, and the only one over which we had any control, was specific interest in the aquarium. That interest could only be created by maintaining high-quality displays and by publicizing ourselves in whatever way we could. In that first year I worked very hard to get free publicity. An early media favourite was our World-Famous Mystery Fish.

"Mr. E.," as he was punningly baptized by Kathy, was a chunky little fish about one foot long with handsome black and white markings like those of a Holstein cow. He'd been scooped from the ocean surface by the crew of weather ship *Papa*. Stationed about six hundred miles off the coast of British Columbia, *Papa* used to keep us informed about Pacific weather changes in the days before satellites took over the role. (To my way of thinking, this is not progress: for all their high-tech capabilities, satellites can't collect fish for you.)

Like many celebrities, Mr. E. wasn't really that unusual, but he had a hard-working press agent: me. I called him the World-Famous Mystery Fish so many times that eventually he became exactly that. No one at the aquarium had ever seen anything like Mr. E., and I told some of my reporter friends about this mystery before we had made a real effort to identify him.

Mr. E. played his role splendidly. Among his other qualities, he was something of a performer and very responsive to humans. When you went around to the back of his tank he would always rise to the surface to see if you'd brought him something to eat, and he quickly got used to being fed by hand. One of the early photo opportunities in his career was a photo that got picked up and distributed worldwide by the wire services. It showed aquarist Bill Duncan with one end of a fish fillet in his teeth and the plucky Mystery Fish pulling determinedly at the other end. Eventually one of the staff found him in Dr. Clemens's book *Fishes of the Pacific Coast of Canada*; Mr. E. was actually an immature skilfish (*Erilepis zonifer*), relatively common in the open ocean but rarely seen nearer to land.

Celebrity fishes are great for free publicity, and it is an unwise aquarist who forgets or disdains the fact that one of the first aquarium directors was P. T. Barnum. But the public aquariums of this world are much more than mere attractions; the better ones are very important biological science institutions. From the Vancouver Aquarium's earliest days we recognized our primary educational nature and put a great deal of effort into providing special service to schools.

During the first months of the school year we circulated a letter inviting school classes from all over the Lower Mainland, and we were gratified at the response. Hundreds of children of every age group passed through our doors each week, and the tours were so popular that Kathy wrote a small guidebook that we mimeographed for their use. Each class got a tour lasting about forty minutes, in which they were told about the basic relationships of animals, the difference between plants and animals, and the names of the region's common fish and marine plants. Kathy and our biologist Dmitry Stone did yeoman's service, taking the first groups of kids on the tour and answering their questions, and I did my share of it too.

Nor did we neglect adult education. We started up a public lecture series at the aquarium with local and visiting experts. Dmitry and I spoke often to service groups, clubs and anyone else who asked. We also held evening open houses, when we invited members and the general public to see behind the scenes. The visitors loved it, and I enjoyed watching them get pulled into the world that so fascinated me. Many of our animals had become tame due to the loving care they received from our staff and volunteers, and like Mr. E. would respond to human movement above their tank by surfacing for a look. I was usually exhausted by the time evenings rolled around, but it was always a pick-me-up to see serious adult faces transformed by childlike delight as a sea turtle or octopus rose noiselessly to the surface before their eyes. The staff, of course, watched closely and somewhat nervously; while we worried that a turtle might decide to snack on the fingers of anyone who tried to touch him, we were far more worried about protecting our animals from the people.

My main concern was to create life support systems within the aquarium in which we could maintain healthy aquatic animals, not only the local fresh- and saltwater species but also the tropical ones. In the first months of the aquarium's life, we had problems with the health of our fish, particularly the small but precious collection of tropicals.

The problem was simple: they were getting sick and dying at an alarming rate. The man I'd hired as our first tropical aquarist claimed to know a lot about these fish, but I soon had my doubts. Some of the tropicals started getting ichthyophthiriasis (ich for short) or white-spot disease, and then tail-rot and furunculosis. Fish have to be quarantined when they first come to an aquarium to prevent this sort of thing and treated if necessary. It seemed that this fellow wasn't doing it correctly. The problem couldn't be blamed on the seawater intake, either, because most of our tropicals were freshwater fish from rivers like the Amazon. Something had to be done, and as curator it was my responsibility to do it.

The most unpleasant job in the aquarium world is not washing the water filters, or cleaning tanks, or even scrubbing the toilets after a busy Sunday crowd has done its collective worst. The lousiest job, which I would gladly exchange for a month of janitorial work, is firing someone. Having to do so was one of the gloomier clouds on my horizon during those first months, but it came along with one of the biggest silver linings the aquarium ever had: a nineteen-year-old tropical fish expert named Billy Wong.

Billy's father was a tropical fish dealer who had come to Canada from southern China when Billy was in his early teens. I'd already heard about Mr. Wong from Carl Lietze and other amateur aquarists, and the word was that Billy was almost as knowledgeable about fish as his father. But having been too casual about hiring once, I was determined to be very careful and professional this time. As I recall, the store was somewhere on the downtown eastside, and in accordance with my Chicago birthright I casually wandered by one morning to "case the joint." From the outside it looked promising: neatly tended shrubs framed the shop window, and the large tanks of tropical fish behind them looked clean and nicely arranged. Thus encouraged, I made an appointment for Billy to visit the aquarium for an interview.

I had a little trouble understanding him at the beginning—in those days he had a choppy, occasionally mystifying accent and spoke very fast—but it didn't take long for me to decide to hire him. A few questions revealed that Billy did indeed know quite a bit about keeping tropical fish alive. For instance, one of the secrets is aging the water. Water often contains small amounts of chlorine and other toxic chemicals when it comes out of your tap, and frequently it is supersaturated with air. Billy knew that the water had to stand for a few days for the gases to disperse into the air and the toxicity to diminish. Once hired, Billy wasted no time; he installed himself in the aquarium the following day and stayed with us for thirty-five years.

Billy quickly showed what he could do when he took charge of one of the sixty-gallon tanks. In it, he tended a beautiful assortment of tetras, those sparkling little characins from South America with such pleasant names: neons, glowlights, dawns, head and tail lights, rosy fins, lemon tetras, pretty tetras and jewel tetras. Characins belong to a large family of toothed fish that includes the fierce piranhas. However, unlike their chunky and ferocious cousins, the tetras are delicate and characterized by their brilliant metallic colours. Most of what you see of these colours is created by the passage of light *through* their skin rather than the reflection of light from colour pigments. So far as we understand them, the conspicuous colour patterns enable each species to recognize members of its own kind and also communicate the basic emotions such as fear, hunger and courtship excitement.

Under their new aquarist's care, the tetras positively sparkled. Billy's trademarks were simple: his tanks were kept spotlessly clean and the fish in his care were always fatter and healthier than you'd think possible. He put in long hours, often coming in on weekends or during the evenings, and he even brought his fish treats. Sometimes, after Christmas or Thanksgiving, I'd find Billy feeding scraps of turkey to some of his charges. That's not a practice that would be approved by current aquarists, but it certainly proved how much he cared about his animals.

With the tropical fish in Billy's capable hands, I could stop worrying about that end of the aquarium. And that suited me fine, because my great joy in the early days of the aquarium was learning about the extraordinary marine life along the coast of the Pacific Northwest.

It is now fairly common for aquariums to emphasize special regions, often their own, in their exhibits. However, when I began my professional life most existing aquariums were regional not by design but out of necessity. Small aquariums exhibited local fish because that was what was available; only richly endowed institutions like the Shedd in Chicago or the Steinhart in San Francisco could try to be encyclopedic in their holdings, with representation from all over the world. Nonetheless, most aquariums made efforts to devote at least some space to the colourful fish of the tropics.

There was a strong constituency for tropicals within the aquarium association, since Carl Lietze and the other members from the amateur aquarists society saw the brightly coloured coral reef fish as the most desirable specimens anyone could hope to exhibit. I was interested in these fish, too, from studies in Hawaii and from my experiences with the Marines in the South Pacific during the war. At New Caledonia, Guadalcanal and Peleliu I had gazed into shallow pools and admired scintillating little fish that quickly dashed into hiding places. But the North Pacific was a new world to me. This region has fish quite different from those found in any other ocean. I've already mentioned my collecting expeditions on the Stanley Park intertidal with its sheets of red, green and brown kelps, purple starfish and red sea cucumbers. Beyond the intertidal lived fish species that I had never seen alive before; until then I knew most of them only as colourless dead specimens in the fish collection at UBC.

One of my early goals was to find an exhibit balance between four water systems: warm salt water, warm fresh water, cold salt water and cold fresh water. Each supported its own forms of life, and each had its champions on the board. In a way, we had a sort of microcosm of Canadian federalism right in our own aquarium: balancing the tropical enthusiasts, who were mostly local, were the representatives of the federal Department of Fisheries and the provincial Fish and Game people. In Canada, saltwater and migratory salmonid fish are a federal responsibility, so that is what the Fisheries representatives promoted; fresh water in British Columbia is provincial, so that is where we got our support for the cool freshwater specimens. Of course, our board's local/provincial/federal microcosm differed from the original in one outstanding way: instead of wasting time in debate or fighting each other for scarce resources, each group made efforts to bring in or fund the types of fish that interested them.

Some of our most faithful sources of specimens were the amateur diving clubs like the Vancouver Aquaholics and the Kelp Kutters of nearby New Westminster. I was particularly grateful to them for their revelation of the wonderful invertebrates that exist in our local waters, among the most impressive of which are the starfish. There are almost ninety different species of starfish in the North Pacific, brilliantly coloured and highly varied in size and shape.

I remember going out to Whytecliff Park on a chilly November morning with a couple of young men who worked for the local telephone company and had formed their own diving club. Gil Saunier and Ken O'Neil conformed to the diver's archetype of robust good looks and nonchalance about their somewhat risky hobby. The two of them intended to dive about sixty feet down along a steep submarine cliff, where they said a profusion of starfish, sea urchins, sea cucumbers and other colourful invertebrates could be found clinging to the rocks. The water temperature was about 45° F and both divers wore neoprene wet suits, which had only recently been invented.

After a time the divers returned to the surface and handed over their collecting bags. The starfish were the best specimens I had yet seen, and I couldn't help thinking gleefully of how jealous senior colleagues like Earl Herald or Chris Coates would have been at this haul. Pushing such unworthy thoughts from my mind, I busied myself transferring the starfish into galvanized metal tubs that were covered with a red-coloured, fish-oil-based paint that was non-toxic to the specimens. As I worked I began planning in my mind the labels for the aquarium tanks: sunflower stars (*Pycnopodia*), sun stars (*Solaster*), long rayed stars (*Orthasterias*), leather stars (*Dermasterias*), blood stars (*Henricia*), slender stars (*Evasterias*), pink stars (*Pisaster brevispinus*), slime stars (*Pteraster*) and vermillion stars (*Mediaster*).

Just as the scuba crowd was an important source of invertebrates, the fishing community was a godsend in bringing us local fish. One early benefactor was a wiry Estonian immigrant named Peter Lipsberg, who operated a small fish boat along the rocky shores of West Vancouver. Peter made a living from the fish he sold to the local markets, and much of his livelihood came from running a setline at Garrow Bay, where the water drops to great depths quite close to the shore. His setlines measured up to one hundred yards long, with a profusion of five- or six-foot lines running off the main line, each with a baited hook at the end. Peter would set the line in the afternoon, leave it overnight anchored down at both ends and in the morning pull it up by the float line to see what he'd caught.

Peter gave us several longnose skates (*Raja rhina*), ratfish (*Hydrolagus colliei*) and—the most difficult to keep alive—the yelloweye rockfish (*Sebastes ruberrimus*). Also known as red snapper, the yelloweye rockfish is common between 30 and 150 fathoms but is rarely found in shallow water. Bright red in colour, it has a swim bladder filled with gas that enables it to achieve a weightless equilibrium in its medium, like a hot air balloon floating in the sky. At 100 fathoms the fish is exposed to a pressure of about 250 pounds per square inch, and the gas inside the swim bladder must have an equivalent pressure to maintain inflation. Unlike salmon, yelloweye rockfish have no passage between the bladder and the esophagus, so the only way for the gas to escape is through the slow process of transport by blood. It is very distressing to see what happens when this poor fish is brought to the surface in a trawler's net or a fisherman's hook—it swells and swells until its bladder forces its way out through its mouth and its eyes pop out.

The yelloweye rockfish Peter brought us were caught in only 20 fathoms (120 feet) and thus the gas pressure inside them was not as great as usual. Peter had it all figured out: when he brought the fish to the surface he removed the hooks, then quickly placed the fish in a wire cage and lowered them back down to ten fathoms. On the following day he brought them up to six fathoms. By slowly decompressing them, he enabled the fish to adjust to the small amount of pressure in shallow water. Most of the ones he caught died before completing the process, but some went on to live happy, well-fed lives in the aquarium.

Decompression remains one of the great challenges of local collecting. Over the years we and other aquariums have worked out various systems for collecting specific types of fish, but there are some species we've never managed to exhibit. Aside from the problem of air bladders, deep-water fish usually do not have the vitality in captivity seen in shallow-water species. The spiny-headed sculpins, black eel pouts and various sea poachers obtained from shrimp trawlers are hard to keep alive, despite the tender ministrations of our aquarists. They usually have softer and more easily injured bodies, and their skin appears to be more delicate than that of other species.

I enjoyed getting out on the water whenever I could, particularly since it got me away from that modern slavemaster, the telephone. It was a particular joy to go out on the research boat *Investigator No. 1*, which was based at the Nanaimo Biological Station. The wide-beamed 58-footer was a major source of specimens for the aquarium before we opened and, happily, the Fisheries Research Board continued to allow us to use it. Even in the winter months, the *Investigator* was a comfortable place to be: the coffee pot was always on in the galley if you wanted to step in from the weather, and even a cold day wasn't bad when you were protected by a slicker and several layers of sweater and jacket.

It was during one of those early expeditions that the crew of the *Investigator* and I came to an understanding about collecting that greatly increased the survival rate of the specimens they caught for us. The trip began in Nanaimo, a pulp and paper town on the sheltered east coast of Vancouver Island. There I joined Captain Claire Watson and his crew just before they cast off from the dock.

The day had turned windy and rainy, and there were whitecaps whipping up as we sailed southeast out of Departure Bay. As we neared Porlier Pass and looked out across the strait, we could see a dark line on the horizon made by heavy seas. Nothing daunted, we made several drags of the otter board trawl net on the lee side of Galiano Island. At fifty to sixty fathoms the net brought us a hundred beautiful red and white plumose anemones (*Metridium*), several species of crabs, several kinds of starfish, prickly skates and a number of kinds of flatfishes. Late in the afternoon we sailed through the pass towards Vancouver and bucked a heavy sea for three hours. The fish were badly tumbled about as the water in their tanks sloshed back and forth. Most of the specimens had already suffered considerable bruising from their time in the net.

Something had to be done, and the captain and I talked it over. The *Investigator* used a big trawl, which was logical for its normal business but not at all good for my purposes. We decided to shorten the time the net stayed down. It meant smaller catches with fewer specimens, but the fish had a far higher rate of survival.

During the next three days we fished between Point Grey and Point Atkinson at the mouth of Vancouver harbour and down to the light ship off the Fraser. These collections brought us small octopuses and squids, sea mice (*Aphrodita*), spider crabs (*Chionoecetes*), longnose skates, big skates and brilliant red thornheads (*Sebastolobus*). A wonderful haul.

Even with the short trawls, many residents of the lower depths were so fragile that they could not be collected in good condition. These included herring, smelts, walleye pollock (*Theragra*), hake (*Merluccius*), long-jaw flounder (*Atheresthes*) and greenstriped rockfish (*Sebastes elongatus*).

All good collectors know that you have to be sympathetic to the delicate nature of the animals you want to bring home in good condition. Aquariums *have* to learn about the requirements of each species, and their work over the years has contributed greatly to our understanding of the natural world.

But collecting fish is only the front end of aquarium work. You also have to exhibit them in ways that will not only interest but educate the visitors. And for that reason, even though not directly concerned with the animals' survival, an artist is as important to an aquarium as anyone else on the staff.

In the first months we were dependent on the Hudson's Bay Company and their department store press to produce labels for our exhibits, but that arrangement obviously couldn't go on for ever. Nor did I want it to; the labels contained only the name of the fish in black ink on a white card. I had no budget for artwork, nor did any of us have a concept of the importance of it. I was increasingly frustrated with this aspect of the aquarium. It wasn't the size of the budget in itself that bothered me, because I still didn't really understand budgeting. All I knew was that everything seemed to cost a frightening amount of money, right down to the metal frames needed to hold the labels on the wall. And it all seemed to take a great deal of time to figure out all the details about even so mundane an item: what kind of metal, how should the edges be done, what kind of screws to hold it to the wall. . . .

I was drowning in details and dabbling in areas I knew nothing about. What felt worst of all was that nothing I designed seemed to come out the way I'd pictured it. The work was crude, the colours were wrong, and the illustrations were often childish. The long and short of it was that we needed an artist on staff if we were going to fulfill our educational mission in a way I thought appropriate for a great public aquarium. Some members of the board thought otherwise, and no money seemed forthcoming for such "extras" when it was all we could do to feed the fish and meet our monthly payroll.

Once again, the gods who look after earnest young aquarium directors must have been watching, because one day Gladys Clawson appeared at the aquarium with her portfolio under one arm and a box of drawing supplies under the other. Gladys had been recommended to me by Professor George Spencer, an entomology professor at UBC. Like Billy Wong, she immediately made herself indispensable. Rotund and voluble, with an astonishing fund of knowledge about arcane subjects like military history, she was fun to have around the place. She also worked for nothing in the first months, simply because she enjoyed it; after a while I managed to add her to the payroll part-time, and finally full-time when the value of her work was so visible that the board could not avoid authorizing her salary.

Gladys's first job was to produce proper labels for each tank. That done, we started expanding with graphic panels showing fish evolution through the geological periods, complete with jaw and gill arch changes, changing positions of the fins and other structural developments. Graphics on the families of fishes and their worldwide distribution soon appeared on the previously bare walls, and these were joined by drawings of the anatomical structure of marine invertebrates. My impoverished orphan of an aquarium was beginning to look like a schoolhouse.

We moved on to producing booklets and posters, and in October 1957 we launched the first edition of the *Aquarium Newsletter*. Its simple, mimeographed format made it relatively easy to produce, but I needed volunteers to help with its assembly. The newsletter was important to the growth of the aquarium as a way of keeping in touch with people who had expressed an interest—and of making everyone that Carl Lietze had intimidated into buying a membership feel that they were getting something extra for their two dollars.

Gladys had been a widow for many years when she first came to the aquarium, and she had got into the habit of taking off on exotic holidays to places that most people would never have thought of going, at least in the 1950s, such as the altiplano of Peru. Relatively few North Americans went to Japan at that time, but Gladys did and in doing so made something of a mark. In the summer of 1993, when I visited the wonderful Port of Nagoya Public Aquarium, Director Itaru Uchida surprised me by telling me that he possessed a complete collection of Vancouver Aquarium newsletters. He and Gladys had crossed paths in Japan when he was just starting out as a young aquarium biologist in the Enoshima Aquarium under the great Ikusaku Amemiya, and she had made sure he got on the mailing list.

Perhaps Gladys's most spectacular efforts were in exhibit production. Anxious to celebrate the marine habitat around Vancouver, I asked her to redesign our biggest tank, which until then had been pretty stark. So the background had to fit with a collection of marine life found in the Strait of Georgia. Gladys rose to the challenge, painting a wonderful mural on the back and side wall with rocky topography, dock pilings, brilliant starfish and a kelp forest. Paints for this type of work had to be non-poisonous to fish and extremely resistant to water, and it took some experimentation for Gladys to get the effects she wanted.

Rocks and various types of sea plants and creatures were found and placed according to Gladys's design. By the time we were finished, four tons of rock had been placed in the tank, and most of the staff had been involved in one way or another. And not only staff but also volunteers, for we made an arrangement with some of our faithful local scuba divers to bring us as many sea anemones and starfish as possible, producing a colourful underwater garden effect. When it was completed and filled with a selection of rockfish, lingcod and dogfish, the tank proved to be very popular with visitors. The crowning touch came when a large octopus, the gift of a diver from Washington State, took up residence in the tank.

Of all the biological phenomena I wished to display, the spawning of adult Pacific salmon was most compelling to me. When I first came to British Columbia I was fascinated by the large and beautifully marked salmon that fought, spawned and died in the coastal streams. I spent many hours watching them at Jones Creek, near Hope, and at Sweltzer Creek at Cultus Lake. Now I wanted to properly show this great spectacle in the aquarium.

The Northwest Pacific salmon run is one of the great migratory events of the animal world, comparable to the great waterfowl migrations on the Pacific flight path or the massive caribou treks in northern Canada. When the leaves on the trees begin to turn colour and the British Columbia skies darken with autumn rains, hordes of salmon swim silently up the rivers to their spawning grounds—the places where they themselves were hatched. Some rivers literally change colour, so full are they of fish fighting their way upstream. As many times as I've observed it in the past forty years, it is a spectacle that never fails to excite and move me.

For the species of Pacific salmon that wander far out into the ocean, this last long journey may involve swimming thousands of miles. The Fraser River sockeye (*Oncorhynchus nerka*), for instance, may return to river tributaries 650 miles from the sea, while the chinook (*Oncorhynchus tshawytscha*) swims over 2000 miles up the Yukon River to its headwaters in northern British Columbia. By contrast, the humpbacked pink salmon (*Oncorhynchus gorbuscha*) usually does not go very far to reach its spawning location in streams near the coast.

My goal was to exhibit these fish in their different life stages and to reveal what magnificent animals they truly are. Wanting something that would catch the public imagination, I decided we would do our first special exhibition on the Pacific salmon. Most organizations concerned with salmon in British Columbia contributed to it, including the fishermen's union and the big fish companies, and there was much co-operation. John Buchanan, with whom I travelled on the *Marijean,* was the president of B.C. Packers and Homer Stevens, an avowed member of the Communist Party, was the head of the Fishermen's Union. Natural enemies in other circumstances, both of these men were good supporters of the aquarium.

Half of the display would be devoted to the significance of the salmon to humans, from the prehistoric peoples of the region to our modern industrial society. The other half would depict the biology of the salmon in all its stages of development: what it is, how it develops, where it migrates and how it returns to spawn and die.

The project hinged on the co-operation of the International Salmon Commission biologists, who were collecting and tagging fish along the

Fraser River. They supplied us with nine mature pink salmon that obligingly spawned, leaving eggs buried beneath the gravel of the tank bottom, some even doing so along the edge of the glass where the public could see them. The fertilized eggs were taken from the stream tank and nurtured in a special hatching tank with fresh water percolating up through the gravel in order to bathe the eggs in life-giving oxygen. The emerging alevins, the fingerlings, the smolts, the jacks and salmon in the final adult stage were all displayed.

The exhibit was something of a breakthrough, because migrating fish usually died before spawning when they were placed in an aquarium tank. We discovered that only when salmon were taken directly from their natural spawning grounds did they readily spawn in the aquarium. In fact, they would fight, mate and exhibit most normal behaviours within the exhibition tank. Following this, they would decline steadily in condition and die a few days later. All five species of Pacific salmon die after spawning, both females and males, in nature as well as in the aquarium. As the pinks died, we replaced them with other species of salmon in the natural sequence of their spawning in coastal streams. People are always saddened by death, but they are fascinated by the life and death struggle of the salmon.

The exhibition was a solid success with the public and made me feel that we'd somehow arrived. Certainly, I had taken pride in the aquarium's successful start-up and its survival through the first year. But surviving was the bare minimum of my goals and dreams. The salmon exhibition was something new, and it put us on the aquarium map as an institution that was doing original work.

# 4

# Manta Rays in the Icebox

The phone rang. I picked it up and heard a deep voice rasp, "Murray, can you come with me to Mexico tomorrow?"

"Yes, that will be great, H.R.," I replied, greatly relieved but trying not to let it show in my voice. At least this time there would be no panic-stricken rush to collect gear and clothes. In anticipation of the invitation, I had been down to the *Marijean* a month before to discuss the trip with Captain Scott Steen and to put books, nets, formaldehyde and other equipment on board.

It was my favourite phone call, one I received each year (except one) between 1954 and 1967. The call always came at the last minute, and always in the dead of winter, but I was never absolutely sure that it would come. (One year I was apparently too bold in loading my gear onto the ship, and the invitation never materialized. I learned my lesson and was more circumspect in the packing thereafter.)

Even though I was studying at UBC under a fellowship bearing his name, I got to know H. R. MacMillan accidentally, the way we often meet people who become important to us. One day in late January of 1954 I was trudging through the snow by the UBC Biology Building when Dr. Hoar leaned out the window and asked me if I would like to go to Mexico.

"Yes," I said.

"Tomorrow?" he continued.

I took a deep breath and repeated myself.

"Fine, come in and I'll tell you about it," said my professor, pulling his head back into his office.

The snow in Vancouver was deep that year. Kathy and I were still camping in sleeping bags on the floor of our hut in UBC's Wesbrook Camp, gradually accumulating household necessities through shrewd purchases in used furniture stores.

"I'm going to Mexico tomorrow," I announced proudly when I came home for lunch. The reply is lost in the dim corridors of time but can readily be imagined. Nonetheless, that afternoon I went down to the old MacMillan Bloedel Building on Hastings Street. Outside his office door, H. R. MacMillan's loyal secretary, Miss Dorothy Dee, fiercely guarded against intruders. I gave my name and she escorted me into a room with the biggest desk I had ever seen.

Behind the desk was a great bear of a man in his late sixties, with bushy eyebrows and twinkling blue eyes: H. R. MacMillan himself, one of the most powerful businessmen in western Canada and a figure of almost mythic status in British Columbia. Smiling warmly, he offered me a chair, and I sat down while he explained that we would fly to Mexico City and then to Acapulco, where we would board his yacht for a cruise along the Pacific coast of Mexico. I would be the ship's naturalist.

"What will you need for the trip?" he asked. Having been briefed by Dr. Hoar, I was ready with my answer. "Twenty five-gallon cans, a barrel of formaldehyde, some nets, various chemicals and some books," I replied. Out of the corner of my eye I saw Miss Dee registering discreet shock at the extent of my requests, but I pressed on. "And a raincoat," I added; coming from California, I didn't have one and, being a student, I was too poor to buy one.

H.R. said to Miss Dee, "Get the details and then contact Urtiaga in

Mexico City. Have him arrange to get the equipment and put it aboard the *Marijean* in Acapulco."

The following day at midnight, H.R. and I took off in a four-engine, propeller-driven DC-7 on the eleven-hour flight to Mexico City. We were seated in the first-class section of the plane, a new experience for me. H.R. was asleep, I thought, as the stewardess rolled the liquor cart down the aisle. "Make mine a double Manhattan," I declared eagerly, at which my new friend and patron opened an eye and wryly said, "I didn't know zoologists drank."

In Mexico City, we were met by H.R.'s agent, Urtiaga, a Basque gentleman who quickly moved us through the formalities of customs. After lunch at Urtiaga's beautiful hacienda-style home, H.R. and I flew to steamy Acapulco, where we found the *Marijean* anchored alongside the president of Mexico's elegant yacht. The latter was truly splendid but the *Marijean* was a tough, seagoing vessel, not just a pretty ship.

The evening was beautiful as only tropical nights can be. The sea was calm and reflected the lights of the harbourside hotels; the air was warm but with a gentle breath of coolness. Our anchorage was ringed by the lights of the town and the dark silhouettes of mountains against a sky full of stars. Across the water could be heard the laughter and music of Acapulco.

Despite the beauty of the scene and the exalted nature of the company, I was very conscious of my mission: to collect Mexican fish specimens and bring them back preserved and labelled for UBC's research fish museum, of which I was curator. I felt lucky but also well-qualified for the job, as I already had considerable experience with Mexican fish from my two previous years as curator of the fish museum in UCLA.

At the height of his power when I met him in 1954, Harvey Reginald MacMillan was born poor in Newmarket, Ontario. His father died when he was two and his mother had to work as a housekeeper while the young boy was raised by his grandparents. As a youth, MacMillan enrolled in the Ontario Agricultural College at Guelph because it was the cheapest college to attend; to support himself he worked in the school's experimental forestry section. After Guelph he put himself through Yale University, winning a Master of Forestry degree that led to work in the logging industry in Georgia. One summer while visiting the Rocky Mountains near Waterton National Park he fell ill and was discovered to have advanced tuberculosis. He then spent two and a half years in a TB sanatorium in Quebec where he almost died. It was there, he told me, that he developed his profound appreciation of reading.

In 1912, he became the first chief forester of British Columbia. The government sent him around the world to find markets for B.C.'s seemingly inexhaustible stands of great trees. Arriving in Britain, according to a story I heard on the *Marijean,* he met businessman Montague L. Meyer, who backed him with $5000 for the establishment of the H. R. MacMillan Export Company, which he created with his friend and adviser W. J. Van Dusen. Meyer's trust in the brash young Canadian was well-founded: the company became a strong force in the lumber industry. During World War II, MacMillan worked in Ottawa in a variety of high-profile assignments under the legendary C. D. Howe, ending up as president of Wartime Shipping Limited, a Crown company supervising the building of merchant ships in Canada. After the war, he returned to B.C. to continue building his company, which soon after merged with Bloedel, Stewart & Welsh Limited to become MacMillan Bloedel Limited.

According to his daughter Jean, the only recreation in H.R.'s humble boyhood had been the occasional escape to a stream where he could spend an afternoon fishing with string and a homemade hook. Years later, he made up for this by purchasing the Duke of Sutherland's big game rods and reels and going after some of the world's most impressive sports fish.

H.R.'s qualifications as a fish guy went well beyond recreation, however, for he was a major figure in B.C.'s fishing industry. His involvement started during the Great Depression, when Alan Williamson, the B.C. western manager of Wood Gundy, asked MacMillan to take over the bankrupt firm B.C. Packers. The largest fish products company on the coast had too many plants, too many canneries, too many fishing boats, too much of everything. MacMillan stripped it down to the bare essentials and started it back on the way to financial health. He was paid with shares in the company and ended up owning most of them.

Through this connection with B.C. Packers, he took on a strong interest in fishing and fisheries along the west coast of the Americas, from B.C. to Peru. H.R. always wanted to see things for himself, and soon after the Second World War he and some friends launched several fishing trips to the Pacific coast of Mexico. They brought back freezer-loads of specimens, including big game fish such as marlin, sailfish and wahoo, small game fish such as sierras, roosterfish and jacks, and exotic forms they knew nothing about, among them parrotfish, triggerfish, wrasses and needlefish. All of them ended up in the freezer vault of the Imperial Cannery of B.C. Packers in Steveston, where MacMillan invited B.C. scientists to take a look at them.

MacMillan bought the 137-foot *Marijean* in 1948. Wooden-hulled, it was originally built in Tacoma as a U.S. Navy minesweeper. During the war, it had a crew of thirty-five, but after its refitting as a luxury yacht it needed only six: two on deck, two in the engine room and two in the galley. I remember H.R. telling two American guests, "This ship cost the American taxpayer two million dollars, but I got it as war surplus for $20,000." He had a crusty sense of humour. I once asked him about the cost of operating such a large ship, and he replied, "Doesn't cost me a cent—it's all at the expense of my heirs."

When it was first relaunched as a yacht, the *Marijean* had a sedate black and white hull, and then an all-white one that was soon changed to a daring turquoise and white combination.

Spotlessly maintained, with an engine room kept so clean you could have eaten off the floor, the *Marijean* was an excellent seagoing ship. Mac-Millan cruised it on the B.C. coast in the summertime and then for three months in Mexico every winter. The crew took it south right after New Year's with his family's suitcases on board, and the family followed by plane once the yacht had reached Mexico. With family and friends he cruised down the coast as far as Guyaquil and the Galapagos, travelling at least once to Hawaii and through the Panama Canal to Jamaica. The *Marijean* was fitted with a huge freezer on the afterdeck; as the food and supplies taken on for the southern trip were consumed, H.R. replaced them with rare fish for transportation back to Vancouver.

The first winters aboard the *Marijean* were spent travelling to southern regions in a quest for sailfish and marlin, a fairly typical pursuit for someone of MacMillan's wealth and sense of adventure. But H.R. was far from typical; he had a genuine curiosity about nature and had made a point of getting to know some famous naturalists in his day. Beginning in 1953 with Cas Lindsey, he invited scientists along on virtually every trip.

On that first evening in Acapulco, I was eager to collect specimens and pleased to find some good ones right on my doorstep. Some fish are like moths on a summer night and cluster about lights. When they do so, you can often catch them by dipping with a small net. The boatswain of the *Marijean* rigged a brilliant light over the side to see what could be attracted by it.

I stood on the landing platform at the base of the ship's ladder. The platform rode about a foot above the surface of the water and immediately in front of me was the light concentrated by its circular reflector. As I peered into the water, a cloud of pink crustacean larvae appeared in the light, each about one sixteenth of an inch in length. The cloud looked like a puff of smoke moving up from deep water and then spreading out over the surface. Soon little fish moved in schools among the crab larvae, many of them larvae themselves. They were transparent and thin, little ghosts with bright eyes. Like the crab larvae, they were drawn to the light as if hypnotized.

Beneath these little organisms there suddenly appeared schools of silvery scad, each about five inches long, darting and swimming after the juicy morsels that were exposed by the light. Soon there were hundreds of scad swimming rapidly and erratically back and forth in the region of the light. A few minutes later a school of moonfish joined the activity and fed upon the first arrivals. The moonfish were silvery, deep-bodied fish, wafer thin and between ten and twelve inches long. From above they presented only thin lines with great curved pectoral fins in front to guide them.

Sea water is very clear in the tropics. One of the reasons for this is that water becomes thinner when it is warmed and particles settle out faster. As I stood on the boat landing, staring down into the water with net in hand, I could see dim forms moving about far below. Suddenly a group of jacks, perhaps two feet in length, rushed through the circle of light, and the scad and the moonfish disappeared. In a few moments the small fish returned, feeding as before, and again they were attacked by the larger jacks.

It would have been easy to see the carnage beneath the ship's light through the imagination rather than through the observing eye. One could imagine the large new fish representing a kind of justice that punished the predators for slaughtering the innocent worshippers of light. But nature knows no justice. Justice is a human concept. What was taking place was an exchange of energy from one form of life to another. I put a few specimens in some tubs to keep till morning and went to bed.

The next morning, Acapulco harbour revealed a surprising host of marine species as the mate and I crossed the harbour in a small outboard motor boat searching for new specimens. Around noon we saw seven or eight little *Mobula* rays jumping and splashing at the surface. They disappeared as we approached. Towards the centre of the harbour, we suddenly struck bottom with a mighty bump. The mate and I stared at each other in disbelief; we'd looked at the charts and we knew there was no reef at this location. Then a huge fin rose quietly out of the water, and beneath us the form of a gigantic shark took shape. Almost twice as long as our twelve-foot boat, the shark swam slowly at the surface beside us.

My heart nearly stopped, but my eyes kept taking in information and my mind kept processing it. The huge dark body had bands of light-coloured spots circling it, and the shark's broad head was spotted—that meant something to me, and slowly I started to breathe again as I realized it was a harmless whale shark (*Rhincodon typus*). Though they can grow to be forty or more feet long, these placid giants eat nothing bigger than plankton and small fish. Scarcely believing what I was doing, I reached out and held on to its dorsal fin.

It must have looked like a surrealist painting: two men, a small boat and a twenty-foot shark moving slowly in brilliant midday sun across Acapulco harbour. Ahead of us was a large new resort hotel with hundreds of people on the beach. Between us and the beach was a diving raft where some people lay absorbing the rays of the sun. A few people noticed us, then more and more as we approached. About seventy-five feet away from the raft, the shark submerged and quietly swam under the raft before finally disappearing. Well, I thought to myself, another fish story to tell Kathy. . . .

After the Vancouver Aquarium opened in 1956, I continued to collect and preserve specimens on the winter Mexican cruises for the UBC Fish Museum, but I became more and more interested in obtaining live specimens for the aquarium. Collecting live fish and successfully transporting them to Vancouver proved to be extremely difficult. The rolling of the ship damaged the fish as they swam in the large container erected for them on the boat deck of the *Marijean*. Because of this, I restricted live fish collecting to the last few days of each trip. We packed the specimens in plastic bags with sea water and oxygen, then packed them again in insulated cardboard cartons for me to bring back with my luggage. Jean Southam and some of the guests helped by taking plastic bags of tropical fish with them when they flew home from Mexico. Ultimately we collected enough live Mexican fish to make a good exhibit, but not without the occasional misadventure.

One day, when the *Marijean* was anchored in Acapulco harbour, I organized a collecting trip along the concrete embarcadero waterfront. With me were Captain Scott Steen, the cook, Ed McConnell, and steward Dave Lea. Our objective was to capture alive the brightly coloured but extremely elusive small fishes that were abundant there.

When Ed and I hopped up on the landing we saw a scattering of local people sitting around in the shade of coconut palms, oleanders and hibiscus shrubs. A few looked us over and one ambled closer to examine our net, which was similar to the beach seines used by shore fishermen along the coast of Mexico but had a much smaller mesh size and a larger bag in the middle. Ed and I held a line attached to one end of the net while the captain whirled the boat's wheel neatly, turning at right angles from his previous line of movement. Dave then payed out the net.

Looking down along the concrete wall, I could see layer upon layer of small fish, with the bright-coloured ones clustered against the wall and the silvery ones swimming in and out of the picture from farther out in the water. There were round little surgeonfish with yellow tails and spotted bodies, striped sergeant-majors, and brilliant blue devils swimming near the extremely long spines of a cluster of sea urchins. Below them were small damselfish, the upper parts of their bodies bright blue, the lower parts orange. Schools of flashing scads swam by, with thin darts of barracuda or needlefish in pursuit.

The quick, efficient movements of our net-setting caught the interest of more and more of the people on the shore. They eagerly approached to learn about this new system of fishing. I explained as well as I could in my meagre Spanish that we were after small specimens for the aquarium, pointing at the little fish swimming in small schools below us.

The captain brought in the other line attached to the net, and we began pulling this large scoop towards the wall. A growing crowd assembled from all sides to witness the catch. Closer and closer came the net, stretching ten feet below the surface and one hundred feet from side to side. Fish glittered and sparkled as they sought escape from its inexorable approach.

As if to herald this new type of fishing to Mexico, a brass band went marching past. We four northerners eagerly pulled the dripping net up along the wall and out of the water. By this time it seemed that half the town was panting down our necks. Captain Steen and Ed were pulling at one end of the net while Dave and I manned the other, so that the bag at the centre was the last part to be removed from the sea. As foot after dripping foot of the web emerged empty, quiet smiles developed on the faces of our audience. We set our teeth in grim determination and continued pulling. A small brown boy came dancing by singing "*nada, nada*" while he shook his finger at us. I felt a puckering of perspiration break out on my forehead as the last bit of net was hauled out of the water. One extremely small, striped fish flopped about in the pouch of the net.

Chuckling, the people of the waterfront returned to their shady places while we returned to our yacht, considerably chastened by our international mission. Acapulco returned to normal. I decided that this was one fish story Kathy didn't need to hear about.

The years passed, and with each new trip on the *Marijean,* my appreciation of H. R. MacMillan grew. His strength of personality was such that his mood usually prevailed over the rest of us. As we sat in the lounge of the *Marijean,* his quiet moods would drive his friends and family into their books, while his conversational moods would lead to rich and wonderful discussions. Most of all, I remember him as a sort of traditional father figure. He was always challenging the people around him to face up to the moment, show spirit and accomplish something, however small, each day of their lives. We wanted to impress him with our purposefulness. As a man of action, he stimulated action in those around him.

I watched him do this in February 1962, when the *Marijean* was anchored off the village of Zihuatanejo. Nowadays you would say "near the resort centre of Ixtapa," but at that time the resort had not even been planned and the place was a quaint, forgotten pocket of the Pacific Coast. Early one evening, two members of the crew and I set a gill net just off the shore from a small hotel. When we returned at 10:00 P.M. we noticed the floats of the gill net had been pulled quite close together and wondered why. One of my companions seized a float and began pulling the net into the boat. Suddenly, something powerful in the net began pulling the line away from him.

Several feet away, something began to thrash about as we cinched the line around a cleat and started pulling the entire net into deeper water. The beam of our flashlight on the water revealed the net-entangled shape of a huge creature near the surface. The first impression was of green luminescent eyes set far apart and a huge fin: a gigantic shark? Finally, it rose to the surface and revealed itself to be a manta ray (*Manta birostris*). Our launch was pointed towards the *Marijean* and its engine was roaring, but the steady pull of the beast propelled us backward for a while. It took a half hour more to pull the ray to the ship.

The crew and guests came out on deck to stare at the fish as it floated alongside, entangled in the net under the glare of the mercury vapour lamp, too heavy to pull up onto the *Marijean*. H.R. paced back and forth on the deck as I told him that the schoolchildren of Vancouver would love to see this fascinating fish mounted in the aquarium. As I spoke I could see the captain grimace as he thought of the mess this slimy beast would make of the deck and railings of his immaculate ship. I looked around for allies; finding none, my face fell. A tremendous specimen like this, I thought, slipping through my fingers. Everyone shook their heads, shrugged their shoulders and said it would be impossible to keep. Behind me I heard that deep voice rasp quietly, "I wouldn't presume to tell you how to perform your job, Captain, but I am sure you can find a way to do it."

And the captain did. After some thought, he finally conceived the idea of putting a cargo net around the manta and lifting it aboard with the heavy boat davit. That was one job done, but the ray still had to be moved to the stern where the icebox was. Again the captain's expression was full of doubt and again H.R. spoke up, saying in a stage whisper to the rest of us, "This is a matter of pride for the captain now." After more thought, a block and tackle was rigged and the crew swung the ray onto the stern deck.

There, under the lights, I had my first chance to examine the ray close up. On its head were the curving cephalic lobes, which bent downward under the fish. The black body, as it lay belly down on the deck, was covered with sharp, heavy sandpaper-like shagreen (sharp, tooth-like scales), making it uncomfortable to touch. Black mucus came off on my fingers as I started measuring the body, which was 12½ feet from the tip of one pectoral fin to the other. The body was 54 inches long, and the long slender tail measured an additional 58 inches. The ray weighed just over a thousand pounds.

Next morning, we were still faced with the problem of lifting the manta ray into the freezer box on deck. The captain went over to visit the captain of a nearby tuna clipper, taking some bottles of Canadian Club whiskey.

Shortly after, the tuna clipper sailed over alongside the *Marijean* to give assistance. In very short order, the icebox was opened, the food removed, and the ray deposited by the tuna boat's derrick into the icebox. The food was replaced on top of the ray, and that was that.

Our manta ray arrived in Vancouver with the *Marijean* a month or two later. Soon after, a team of Smithsonian Institution technicians came to town. They prepared a fibreglass replica that can be seen today suspended from the ceiling of the H. R. MacMillan Tropical Gallery in the aquarium. An identical replica is on view in the National Museum of Natural History in Washington, D.C.

When the *Marijean* was sold on August 6, 1968, to a contractor from Portland, Oregon, it was the end of an era. Those twelve years of travels with H. R. MacMillan and his family and guests were important to the Vancouver Aquarium for a variety of reasons. There were all the specimens we collected from the *Marijean*, both in southern waters and locally during the months the ship docked in Vancouver. There was the considerable capital the MacMillan family ultimately gave to the aquarium association. A more subtle benefit was the tremendous support the aquarium received from the business community when it became known that H.R. and his family were seriously involved. His son-in-law John Lecky joined the board in 1962 and worked hard on the building and finance committees. An incalculable boost to the aquarium board was the arrival of Ralph M. Shaw in 1965 when he retired as president and vice-chairman of MacMillan Bloedel; Shaw presided over our greatest period of expansion in the late sixties and early seventies.

The MacMillan legacy continues even now through H.R.'s daughter, Jean Southam, who joined the board of governors in 1976. She rapidly became a significant factor in the major developments that followed and always supported me when difficult decisions had to be made.

# 5

# My Brothers, the Ichs and Herps

Friday evenings are a time when hard-working aquarium curators should be putting their feet up in their living rooms and reading a book. And that's exactly what I was doing on the evening of March 21, 1958, when Dmitry Stone called to say that a pane of glass in our largest tank had shattered.

I drove across the Lion's Gate Bridge from my home in North Vancouver as fast as I could and hurried into the main gallery. There was Dmitry with his friend Marcia and Eric the janitor, all three equipped with hip waders and dip nets, chasing the couple of dozen fish that were swimming around the floor in their newfound liberty. Ten inches of water is not very much, but it's quite enough for a small dogfish shark to think he's back in the open ocean and decide to get some exercise. Murderous-looking shards of glass were only semi-visible in the water, which was slowly running out through the drain holes in the floor. I spent the next few hours with Dmitry and the others recapturing the fish and putting them in the reserve tanks behind the public exhibits.

Over 12,000 gallons of seawater had escaped through the glass. Most of the fish were saved, and there was no significant damage other than the loss of some very expensive glass. Despite our efforts to figure out what had happened, the cause of the break remained a mystery. There was no evidence that the one-inch-thick glass was defective, that the public had damaged it, or even that the building had settled and somehow put extra strain on it.

I wrote to several other aquarium directors and got a number of opinions and some useful advice. Earl Herald wrote me a long and informative letter from the Steinhart in San Francisco, discussing various options such as laminated glass. He also added an interesting piece of information. "With regard to salaries," he wrote, "you have the distinction of being the lowest paid curator in the country, based on the size of an operating unit like the Vancouver Aquarium." Some distinction, I thought, but I turned my mind back to repairing the tank.

After replacing the glass, we refilled the tank to forty-two inches instead of the previous forty-eight. Those six inches of water reduced the pressure on the glass considerably. Bit by bit, as the money became available, we replaced the one-inch glass in all the large tanks with one-and-a-half-inch plate. This was, of course, prior to the age of that marvellous substance, acrylic. Acrylic can be cast in any reasonable size and thickness. It also has better transparency, produces less distortion of the view, and is stronger and safer than glass. Today, with the exception of seal or turtle habitats, where scratching is a problem, we use large acrylic panels in all of our larger exhibits.

Being able to consult with the network of aquarium curators and directors across the United States and Canada made my life as the new boy on the aquarium block very much easier. Of course, the world of fish studies wasn't anywhere near as big in the 1950s as it is now. The senior fish experts were people I knew as teachers or mentors, while many of the younger ones had been fellow students during my years in academia. The aquarium community was even smaller.

When I began my job in Vancouver, Earl Herald of the Steinhart was the doyen of North American aquarists, and his aquarium had only the Shedd Aquarium in Chicago as competition in the first ranks of such institutions. Some might say that Walter Chute, the remarkable first director of the Shedd Aquarium, was the greatest leader in our field. I would contend that Earl Herald was both a pioneer and a model for present-day aquarium directors. If you wanted to list most of the qualities needed to make an aquarium a success, you had only to look at Earl.

First, he was a builder: in the years following his appointment in 1948 he gutted and renovated the Steinhart, and he stayed on top of technical developments in life support and exhibits. He invented an ultraviolet system of water purification and was usually the first to try new systems out. Second, he was a media-smart showman. Earl may have been the first person to see the possibilities of television for boosting awareness of his aquarium, and in the early 1950s he had a television show called "Science in Action" that popularized the work that went on at the California Academy of Sciences. Third, he was a serious fish man and a respected scientist. In 1961 he published *Living Fishes of the World,* still one of the best popular books on the subject. Among other projects, he had worked on the biological study of the Marshall Islands following the Bikini atomic bomb experiments. Finally, he was adventurous and was prepared to go anywhere for interesting specimens. I remember being very impressed when he mounted a trip to Pakistan in 1968 or '69 to bring back freshwater dolphins, an expedition I knew had terrific logistical challenges. It was tragic, but in a strange way fitting, that Earl died during a diving expedition at Cabo San Lucas in Baja California. He was fifty-eight years old.

A builder, a showman, a scientist and an adventurer: that was the public Earl. The private Earl was all of those things but also a very demanding boss, quick to criticize and slow to praise. I found this out during my graduate studies at the University of California at Berkeley in 1950–51, when I was in and out of the Steinhart quite frequently. Nonetheless, I learned to get along with him quite well. Many of the top people in the profession today worked for Earl at one time or another, including Lou Garibaldi of the New York Aquarium and Dave Powell, director of animal exhibits at Monterey Bay. All agree that Earl was not an easy person to work for: we used to say that anyone who'd been fired by Earl was clearly an excellent man. Yet he was extremely helpful to me when I was starting at the Vancouver Aquarium.

Another of the senior fish guys at the beginning of my career was Christopher Coates, director of the New York Aquarium. Like Earl, he was always very helpful to younger colleagues, but he was much more easygoing. In my exchanges with Chris, the Vancouver and New York aquariums began a long tradition of co-operation that has continued to this day (you might say that the most recent gift sent to Vancouver by the New York Aquarium is my successor, John Nightingale). It was through Chris's urging that I made the effort to attend the 1957 annual meeting of the American Society for Ichthyology and Herpetology, and thus met or reacquainted myself with the generation of men—almost all of us were men—who reshaped the aquarium world. Chris's letter said:

> I wonder, would it be possible for you to come to the Annual Meeting of the Ichs and Herps? I think that this meeting is very important for all us aquarium people for there is to be at least one whole period devoted to aquarium matters only, with Bill Gray, of the Seaquarium, Miami, for instance, and Ken Norris of the Pacific Marineland to discuss collecting techniques, and Lawrence Curtis of Ft. Worth, and Craig Phillips, talking about feeding problems, and Finneran is coming from Detroit to talk about something, I forget what, and Earl Herald is coming from San Francisco. Woody of Marineland, St. Augustine, is the Program Chairman.

You bet I wanted to go: all of the important people in my profession were going to be there. *And* it was in that wonderful city, New Orleans. Finally, having known a lot of these fellows personally, I expected it was going to be a lot of fun. But first, I had to get the money and the permission to go.

When I asked to have my attendence at the conference funded by the aquarium, I got some resistance from Carl Lietze and some of the amateur aquarists on the board. Most of them had grown up in or been strongly shaped by the Depression, and they were not in the habit of spending money on what they saw as frivolous get-togethers. Fortunately, I was supported once again by Dr. Clemens and the other scientists, who understood the value of conferences as places to trade information. The compromise agreed to was that the aquarium would fund my attendance at one conference per year. After that, I was on my own.

The conference in New Orleans was both enjoyable and very useful to me, but I remember even more vividly the next one, held in 1959 in La Jolla, California. Sam Hinton, curator of Scripps Institution's nearby T. Wayland Vaughan Aquarium, was our genial host. A nationally known folk singer, Sam was also an artist who did his own drawings for labels and graphics and published a column on marine life in the local paper.

You couldn't have asked for a more stimulating conference. Everybody seemed to be involved in something fascinating, and all aspects of the business were discussed—fish, funds and plumbing—sometimes heatedly. On the one hand, you had men of action like the tall, nautical-looking Captain Bill Gray. A former sportfishing captain who had developed his own techniques for catching bluefin tuna off the coast of New Jersey, Gray had put the Miami Seaquarium together and was probably the best collector of Atlantic marine life at the time. He gave a fascinating talk about a new collecting boat he was designing to capture live dolphins along the coast of the Carolinas. Gray was not highly educated, but his demonstrated expertise and natural presence made everyone think of him as "the Captain."

On the other end of the spectrum you had Dr. James Atz, Chris Coates's scholarly sidekick from New York, who loved researching subjects in libraries. Intense but friendly, Atz was focussing his considerable brainpower on aquarium filters at the time, and he was the first person I heard talk about the concept of "biological filtration." From him we learned that most gravity-fed, gravel filters removed wastes through the biological (rather than mechanical) action of bacterial slime living on the particles of sand and gravel. Most of us had such filters, but we didn't understand why they worked as well as they did.

Somewhere in the middle you had Ken Norris, whom I'd got to know while he was a UCLA graduate student. He had started out as an ecologist; I carry this mental image of him chasing reptiles in the Mojave Desert, thermometer in hand, taking their temperatures in order to understand how they survived the desert's climactic extremes. Ken's Ph.D., however, was earned at the Scripps Institution of Oceanography and his thesis was on the life cycle of the opaleye fish, *Girella nigricans*. He arrived at the Ichs and Herps conference having been curator at Marineland of the Pacific for several years.

Marineland of the Pacific was one of the largest and most spectacular aquariums in the world—in fact, it was an oceanarium, a relatively new development in aquarium design at the time, with three half-million-gallon tanks as well as a number of smaller ones. One tank featured California fish, from small orange Garibaldis to large sharks, stingrays and sea bass, while trained porpoises and pilot whales leapt from the water and did tricks in other tanks. In his efforts to keep such an operation stocked, Ken had quickly developed a reputation as a determined and innovative collector. But he was (and remains) as much a man of thought as a man of action, and after he left Marineland in 1960 he metamorphosed into one of the world's foremost marine mammal scientists. Over the years at Marineland, Ken hired and trained several great aquarium professionals, including John Prescott, Dave Powell and Jerry Goldsmith. John later became director of the

New England Aquarium, Dave went to the Monterey Bay Aquarium and Jerry went to Sea World.

Every profession has its "bad boys," and the 1959 conference featured not one but three of them, each of whom has had a positive effect on the development of the aquariums of the future. One was Craig Phillips, curator of Miami Seaquarium. Craig was a sensitive man with a self-mocking sense of humour and a considerable artistic talent as shown by the drawings with which he illustrated his book, *The Captive Sea.*

The second bad boy was William Kelley, a brash, argumentative man with a shock of black hair that stood straight up from his head. He constantly interrupted everyone else and hijacked conversations into areas people didn't want to talk about at the time. "But you're forgetting the water chemistry!" he'd break into some discussion. "Why doesn't anyone see how important it is?" Or tank construction techniques, or the physics of lighting, or filtration, or any of a number of topics that he was working on. As fish enthusiasts most of us were more interested in the biology of marine life than the intricacies of aquarium technology. An inventor as well as a theorist, Kelley was the head of the small Cleveland Aquarium, where he put a lot of his ideas into practice. He later built the Mystic Aquarium in Connecticut and another in Niagara Falls. He also got into the business of manufacturing sea water when he created a company called Instant Ocean, Inc.

The strangest, most charismatic and probably most far-seeing of all these people was Lee Finneran. He had a dark presence, almost an aura, that hinted at a daring lifestyle; if any of us had taken our mothers to the Ichs conference, they would probably have said that Finneran was a "bad influence" and we should stay away from him. Yet, like the other bad boys, he was extremely influential and stimulating to be around. More than anyone else, Finneran had a vision of where aquariums as institutions were headed. "It's far, far more than just another animal facility in a zoo," he'd say, and plunge into a stirring call for dramatic exhibits with strong interpretative and educational values. In the following decade he conceptualized many of the exhibits that went into the New England Aquarium, and he became its first curator.

Finneran, Phillips and Kelley together in one room were unpredictable, exasperating and exhilarating at the same time. Even without them, the discussions were lively. Should design of the aquarium be architect-driven or exhibit-driven? Could artificial sea water be used satisfactorily in inland aquariums like Shedd or should natural sea water be tanked in? Should the water come down by gravity from an overhead tank or should it be pumped directly from the basement to an exhibit tank? If the latter, how would you prevent the supersaturated water causing bubble problems in the fish? These weren't exactly earth-shattering questions to most of the world, but they were important in the evolution of the modern aquarium.

I sometimes think of that conference as a stone cast into a pond, its ripples far-reaching in time and space. Each of us took away many lessons, but of course we applied them differently, depending on our circumstances and our individual visions. I remember visiting the Steinhart in 1963 shortly after Earl Herald had completed his renovations. I was impressed with what he had done but realized that his vision was much different from my own. He believed that the function of the public aquarium was to present a display of living fish, not thematic exhibits. He advocated well-conceived water systems, simple tanks and intense lighting so viewers could easily see the fish. Each tank should be crowded with fish to enhance viewing by the spectator. This was a very practical approach, but as I toured his newly rebuilt aquarium I noted some beautifully arranged tropical tanks, particularly one containing a school of piranhas. The fact that it differed from Earl's approach made me suspect that some of the newer members of his staff had some good ideas about backgrounds as well as fish. (I only found out recently that my suspicions were correct. The "culprit" was Dave Powell; while I was researching this book he wrote to say, "I had to do some of the tank decorating when Earl was out of town. . . . He put me in charge of the Steinhart tank decorating during the renovation but gave strict instructions that no rockwork should protrude more than three inches from the concrete tank wall! He was furious when he came back—I'd taken up some of the fish space with habitat.")

At the same time, there was no denying that the Steinhart Aquarium was greatly improved and had once again taken the lead in many aspects of aquariology. This was particularly evident in some new tank shapes, in which the sides angled away from the viewer so they were not visible. This simple improvement had been advocated by Bill Kelley at the 1959 conference and developed by Jean Garnaud at the 1960 Monaco Aquarium Congress; typically, Earl Herald was the first to put it into practice. I was particularly interested in a special tank designed for a live coelacanth Earl hoped to catch some day in the Indian Ocean. For the time being the tank contained California specimens. Actually, there were always many rare species on display at the Steinhart because Earl was a taxonomist and had a good eye for unusual fish. Behind the scenes it was equally impressive. For one thing, the Steinhart boasted all-new plastic piping, a major improvement over the lead pipes installed in older aquariums such as Chicago's Shedd Aquarium. It had a walk-in freezer to contain food for the live aquatic animals, a stainless steel kitchen, a warm room for reptiles and a staff library. In retrospect, these all seem obvious necessities for an aquarium, but it was at conferences like La Jolla that many of these ideas became widely known.

As with most good conferences, a lot happened outside of the formal sessions. Most of us were lodged at a motel next to the Scripps Institution, and it was interesting to watch the different ways people presented themselves. As befitted his age and rank, Earl Herald kept himself a bit apart from the younger and more exuberant members. Captain Gray was friendlier, though held in great respect by the rest of us. The "bad boys" did what what bad boys always do, from partying late and loudly in their motel rooms to initiating free-for-alls at poolside that ended with a lot of wet ichthyologists.

For visual impact, however, Lawrence Curtis easily beat out everyone else. He was head of the zoo and aquarium in Fort Worth, and he played up his Texan image for all it was worth. Lawrence wore a Stetson, spoke in a slow drawl and smoked long black cigars like an oil millionaire or a cattle baron. Yet the colourful camouflage couldn't hide the fact that he had a formidable intellect, and he was one of the most influential zoo men of his time. I once drove with him from Fort Worth to New Orleans on the way to a conference, and I hold the fond memory of a midnight collecting trip we made along the way, wading with our nets in a swamp full of water moccasins. In 1968 Curtis published *Zoological Park Fundamentals* for the American Association of Zoological Parks and Aquariums (AAZPA). The book became the bible for anyone establishing a new zoo.

It was a wonderful conference, and after three years of running the Vancouver Aquarium, I found I had a lot to contribute to the discussions. All of us left energized and with our network of help and advice greatly strengthened.

One of the best aspects of the network was the opportunity to visit other aquariums. Soon after Chris Coates completed the new aquarium at Coney Island for the New York Zoological Society, I managed to travel to New York to see it and to have some heart-to-hearts with him about aquarium economics. Chris, a man of great style who drove a Cadillac and dressed like a banker, was furious with the more academic members of his staff at the time; at one point in our discussions he took me outside where no one could hear us.

"These damn Ph.D.s!" he stormed. "They don't know we make more money from the parking lot than we do from all the rest of the aquarium put together!" I don't know if he was talking about his assistant curator at the time, Dr. James Atz, or about his other assistant curator, Dr. Carlton Ray, but I remember Chris's amusement later that day when we found Atz in a tight spot, cornered by an amorous walrus he was trying to give medication to. A half-ton walrus is an awesome thing close up, and the situation was as dangerous as it was funny. Once Atz had been rescued and we'd left the gallery, Chris resumed his diatribe about academics. I permitted myself to agree with him about Ph.D.s—after all, I still didn't have mine, and sometimes my workload at the aquarium made me fear I never would.

Not everyone came into the aquarium community through the fish side of things. While at the New York Aquarium that year I met a young aquarist named Bill Flynn who was just starting out in his career. A versatile and extremely practical man, Bill was actually an electrician who had worked on the construction of the new aquarium and got himself a job as a tank man when the construction finished. I would cross paths with him many times and in many places over the years before he reached the top as president of the new Tennessee Aquarium in Chattanooga.

Most aquarium directors have strong academic qualifications these days, often in management as well as the biological sciences. But back in the 1950s many of the smaller aquariums were run by people with no credentials at all. This was true of most of the aquariums down the coast in Washington and Oregon, many of which were family businesses. Yet they were valuable members of the aquarium community, and those days were marked by remarkably close and friendly co-operation.

One of my earliest and strongest bonds was with the late Cecil Brosseau of the Point Defiance Deep Sea Aquarium in Tacoma, one of the finest collectors of live marine specimens I have ever known. Cecil had a soft spot for the Vancouver Aquarium because of his Canadian ancestry, and I felt an affinity for him because we had both served in the South Pacific with the United States Navy. He had little education, but he was good with boats and had an extraordinary sensitivity to the small fish and invertebrates he collected. He was as kind and generous a person as I've known.

Cecil's aquarium in the late 1950s was an old wooden building supported by pilings on the waterfront of Point Defiance Park. Like Vancouver's Stanley Park, Point Defiance is a peninsula. It was an excellent place for a marine aquarium because of its unlimited access to clean, cold, ocean water, which was high in salinity and full of nourishing plankton.

Like us, Cecil had no funds; what he did have was great energy, a sixteen-foot outboard motor boat, empty garbage cans, and a knowledge of how to catch live fish and invertebrates. He was a one-man collecting operation, equally adept at using nets, hook and line, or traps that he just dropped over the side of his building into the sea below. Cecil's tanks always contained an excellent representation of the local marine flora and fauna, and I enjoyed seeing many species there that were rare in Vancouver. One of my favourites was the gruntfish, a funny little orange and beige sculpin with a tiny snout and a big head.

Our relationship with the Pacific Northwest aquariums was very informal, with a great deal of trading that generally worked out to everyone's satisfaction. I remember one evening, while I was working late, the caretaker knocked on my office door to say, "Some lady just telephoned from Everett in Washington, Murray. She says she'll be here at ten tonight and you should wait up for her."

I called my wife to say I'd be home late and waited, not knowing what to expect. A little after ten, Mrs. Ferguson of the Depoe Bay Aquarium drove up to our entrance with two yard-long wolf eels in a large, watertight box. I was touched to find that she had driven frantically all the way from Oregon with these specimens so that she could repay us for a small sea turtle we had given her the previous year.

The network permitted us to make expeditions that we could never have financed alone. For instance, in the early 1960s, Billy Wong and I ventured to California with a 150-foot beach seine that had been lent to us by the Canadian Department of Fisheries. We planned to set this net and several long lines in Tomales Bay, just north of San Francisco. Even with the loan of the net, this operation would have been far beyond our means if Earl Herald hadn't consented to give us a base at the Steinhart Aquarium and to let us hold specimens as we caught them in the Steinhart's reserve tanks. By this time we had outfitted the aquarium's truck with a 320-gallon carrying tank and a water pump that rapidly recirculated the tank's sea water through a filter.

I was most interested in getting some bat stingrays (*Myliobatis californicus*) and leopard sharks (*Triakis semifasciata*), neither of which are found along the coast of B.C. The bat stingray is black above and white below. Large winglike fins spread out on each side; the tail is whiplike and surmounted by one or more long jagged spines used for defence. Large stingrays are known to be four feet across and weigh over 150 pounds. Their powerful teeth are flat, crushing structures used for breaking open oysters and other bivalves. The leopard shark is a handsomely marked bottom fish found from Oregon south to Lower California. It bears its young alive and reaches a maximum length of about five feet. An added quality, from an aquarist's point of view, is that it is hardy and active in captivity.

We drove southward with tanks, nets, fishing gear, wading boots and camping equipment and spent the first night at the Point Defiance Deep Sea Aquarium in Tacoma. Cecil Brosseau very kindly gave us some gruntfish and sailorfish for bartering at the Steinhart Aquarium.

On arriving in San Francisco we went directly to the Steinhart in Golden Gate Park. Those were the days before the present façade of the California Academy of Sciences had obscured the entrance of the aquarium, which was flanked by the African and California Halls. Golden Gate Park was as beautiful as ever, its air perfumed by the eucalyptus trees. Donald Simpson, the assistant curator, greeted us and told us we could sleep in the lab if we wished. Wonderful, I thought: not only did it reduce our costs but it enabled me to "window shop" through the Steinhart's exhibits every night after the staff went home and to make a wish list of specimens we hoped to take with us on the homeward trek. Earl Herald joked that he would have been worried if our truck had been any larger.

Billy Wong was less enthusiastic than I was about sleeping in the lab, especially since the only place for his sleeping bag was alongside a cage housing an enormous boa constrictor. Worse yet, next to this cage were several others containing anacondas, pythons and other reptiles. Billy was definitely a fish man (an Ich), not a snake man (a Herp), and as soon as possible he moved into the chief engineer's office.

Each morning we rose early, filled our transporting tank with water and drove across the Golden Gate Bridge to Marin County and Tomales Bay. The chill wind blew fog up along the shoreward hills and into the mouth of the bay, but the hot California sun made itself felt as soon as we drove inland from the coast.

It was a glorious time of year. The green, grass-covered hills around Tomales Bay were sprinkled with orange poppies and blue lupin. Here and there could be seen the occasional ranch, its white-washed buildings protected from the incessant wind by rows of pines that had been blown into all sorts of interesting shapes.

Tomales Bay is an elongated, shallow bay opening northward and running northwest and southeast. Being for the most part less than thirty feet deep, with black heat-absorbing ooze on the bottom, it warms up quickly in the springtime and contrasts markedly with the cold clear water off the open coast. It is a nursery for oysters and also for sharks and stingrays, which seek out the warmer waters in which to bear their young. When we talked to local people we heard about leopard sharks, smoothhound sharks, angel sharks and even great white sharks, one or two of which had been captured there in 1959. A skindiver we chatted with told us he had been severely bitten in the foot by one of the great white sharks and showed us the scars to prove it.

On our first day out on the water, Billy and I were pulling a setline into our rented fourteen-foot boat when on the first hook appeared a seven-gill shark (*Notorynchus cepedianus*) over six feet in length. This was wonderful luck, but it was also a problem. I looked at the two washtubs that we had brought with us to hold the specimens until we reached shore, then at the shark. It was obvious that a larger container would be needed, so I suggested bailing water into the boat—just enough to float the fish without sinking the boat. This would allow the fish to swim around in comfort. "After all," I argued, "it's not as if it's a really nasty shark like a great white or something." Billy was unconvinced by this idea, but he manfully agreed to let me try it.

"By the way," he added, "I can't swim."

Unfortunately the shark was weakened by its struggle on the line and died quite soon after we took it aboard. When we returned to Steinhart that night, Earl Herald listened to our story with interest.

"Did you know, Murray," he asked in his pedagogical way (he tended to treat most people as students, even fellow aquarium directors), "that there's a significant behavioural difference between a seven-gill shark and a six-gill shark?"

I didn't.

"There is. The seven-gill shark is vicious and generally attempts to bite anything that gets near it."

Billy shot a look at me. I looked elsewhere.

During the next few days we captured a number of surf perch, a few small brown smoothhound sharks and a couple of leopard sharks. Our major success was with stingrays. As I liked to tell people later on, the Vancouver Aquarium captured one of the best collections of stingrays Steinhart Aquarium ever had—we'd got so many that we had to leave most of them behind. As a parting gesture, Earl presented us with some marvelous specimens from Tahiti. There were six fabulously marked triggerfish (*Balistapus undulatus*), one little triggerfish known as "Humuhumu nuku-nuku apua'a" (*Rhinecanthus aculeatus*) and two very ornate wrasse (*Halichoeres ornatissimus*) with orange, blue and green stripes. We packed these in two 20-gallon wooden tanks and the California specimens in a 320-gallon tank.

After saying our good-byes we drove north through the heat of the Sacramento valley, past snow-capped Mount Shasta, into Oregon along Klamath Lake and, towards evening, entered the Willamette National Forest. It became very cold, and I was surprised to find snow among the tall Douglas firs in this forest. The temperature of the tropical fish tanks fell from 75° F to 68° F and, concerned for the survival of the specimens, we stopped at a drugstore and bought two hot water bottles. The young salesgirl was somewhat startled when I asked her to fill them on the spot. We found that by changing the water in the bottles every half hour or so we could maintain a temperature of 70° F in the tanks, but it was a bit embarrassing taking our hot water bottles into so many cafés.

We reached Vancouver the next day after twenty-eight hours of driving. Casualties were minor and the result was several very fine new exhibits.

With all the collecting going on, the Vancouver Aquarium was growing up and holding its own in comparison with other North American institutions. I was curious, however, about what was going on in Europe and got my chance to find out late in 1960 when I attended the first International Congress of Aquariology in Monaco. Again, some board members looked askance at my request to go to the congress, and later that year they expressed their disapproval of my high-flying ways (as they saw it) by turning down a request to go to the Amazon. Still, the congress was clearly an important event, and once again the scientists on the board rallied to my support.

I planned my trip expressly to be able to visit some of the finest aquariums, zoological gardens and museums in the world, beginning with the London Aquarium in the Zoological Gardens at Regent's Park. The aquarium itself was fairly minor, since exhibition was less of a priority at the time than research. Nonetheless, the curator, Dr. Gwynne Vevers, showed me some exceptionally fine exhibits. The most fascinating for me was the strange, beautifully ugly manatee. The manatee is a sea mammal that for centuries has been the source of sailors' mermaid stories. The London Aquarium's specimen from South America resided in a large circular tank located in one corner of the building. Its staple food, of all things, was cabbage.

What impressed me most in London was the British Museum of Natural History in Kensington with its animal models. The main gallery of this splendid old building was dominated by huge elephants. The gallery of fish featured a mounted whale shark, and the gallery of whales had a range of whale species from small to large. It set me thinking: why couldn't we exhibit models of large sea creatures in the Vancouver Aquarium?

My aquarist's heart was captured by the Danmarks Akvarium just outside Copenhagen, at Charlottenlund. It simply had to be the prettiest aquarium in Europe. The building itself was relatively small and simply decorated outside, but the light colours and carefully chosen materials throughout showed excellent taste. And more to the ichthyological point, each tank was a work of art. The Akvarium was experimenting with realistic habitat displays and doing so with considerable flair. Underwater scenes were simulated by a combination of beautiful rockwork and coloured panels that suggested distant vistas through the water. In the freshwater tanks, the verdant lushness of a stream bank was achieved by growing terrestrial plants so that roots and branches dipped into the water. I felt I had found kindred spirits.

Many of the European aquariums were buildings within zoological gardens, subsidiaries of the zoos rather than independent institutions. I was anxious to study how they fit with their organizational parents, and I started my observations in Hamburg, where the Carl Hagenbeck Zoo was one of the first ever built to display animals outdoors in naturalistic habitats without bars or cages. Many American zoos had learned from the Hagenbeck's use of natural-looking concrete stone. Carl Hagenbeck, the grandson of the founder, showed me through the entire building. We spent a good deal of time in the Troparium, a new building housing various tropical creatures such as monitor lizards, alligators, ring tail lemurs, coral reef fish and tropical freshwater fish.

Bright and modern in its presentation, the Hagenbeck Zoo showed no evidence that it had been bombed during the war. However, there was no escaping the oppressive reminders of war outside its gates. War damage and flak towers were still very visible in 1960 as I travelled eastwards towards Berlin. It was the year the Berlin Wall was built to separate the east from the west.

The comprehensive Berlin Aquarium was a grand institution, built on the scale of the Shedd and Steinhart aquariums back in the United States. Where it surpassed its American counterparts was in its diversity of specimens. A zoo aquarium, it contained not only fish, aquatic invertebrates, reptiles and amphibians but insects and their arthropod relatives—in fact, the entire third floor was devoted to glass cases containing live locusts, ants, bees, walking sticks, moths, butterflies, spiders, centipedes and scorpions. The bees were not restricted: from their beehives, narrow passages led outside so they could fly out to gather nectar and pollen from nearby trees and flowers.

The tropical freshwater fish were particularly well represented and many rare types were exhibited. One tank contained over ten species of the loach genus *Botia*. There were a number of species of African polypterids, as well as several kinds of lungfishes. The most outstanding display was an enormous tropical pool for crocodiles and alligators containing twenty species. Since there are only twenty-one species in the whole world, the maintenance of twenty in a single exhibit was a remarkable achievement.

The greatest treat of my visit to the Berlin Aquarium was the opportunity to meet its director, Werner Schroeder. White-haired and in his sixties, he was very proud of his building and its collections, which had been badly damaged in the war. A bomb had actually dropped through several floors before exploding in the crocodile display. At the time of my visit, the restoration had been completed only recently. Mr. Schroeder lived in an apartment in the aquarium building. He took me up there, and we played several games of violent ping-pong before returning to the animal collections. Because of the war he had not been able to complete his zoological studies, and he never received his doctorate.

At Frankfurt am Main I visited the Exotarium with Dr. Dieter Backhaus, its curator, and the famous director of the Frankfurt Zoo, Professor Bernhard Grzimek. If the Danmarks Akvarium was the most charming of my tour, this was the most imaginative and unusual. The Exotarium avoided the traditional, monotonous succession of uniform tanks by creating landscapes in exhibits of varying shapes.

After entering the building I found myself in a darkened room. On one side was a polar seascape with penguins swimming around cakes of ice. On the other side was the bank of a tropical river in which fish, reptiles, birds and plants formed a natural tropical community. As I walked through the aquarium I found seals, sea turtles, coral reef fish, trout and other creatures, most of them displayed in special settings suggesting their natural environments. On the second floor, the reptiles resided in glass cases; between these cases, masses of tropical vegetation grew up and arched over the hall. It was like walking through a jungle.

I left the country impressed with the Germans' achievements in my field, and I have continued to be so ever since. They were very advanced in breaking down the artificial barrier between zoo and aquarium, something that has interested me all through my career. I got my chance to do such border-crossing when the Vancouver Aquarium built its Amazon Gallery in the late 1970s; a more recent example is the Biodome in Montreal, a wonderful mix of terrestrial and aquatic.

Finally it came time for the congress, the original objective of my trip to Europe. The meetings were held in the splendid hall of Monaco's Museum of Oceanography, a stately institution created in 1910 by the grandfather of Prince Rainier. The congress was organized in honour of this anniversary under the patronage of the prince and his movie-star wife, the former Grace Kelly. The involvement of these people was a bit of thrill, but as much of a thrill was the fact that the congress was chaired by Captain Jacques Cousteau. Even in those days, long before he became so famous on television, he was internationally known as an underwater explorer, coinventor of the aqualung and author of the influential book *The Silent World*.

There were over one hundred people in attendance, representing some thirty countries. The lectures were wide-ranging affairs reflecting the state of the rapidly advancing art, and there was something for everyone, a giant aquariological smorgasbord. For those most interested in the animals themselves, there were seminars on selection criteria or the treatment of diseases; the technically minded could talk to their hearts' content about pumps, filters and refrigerators; those contemplating new facilities discussed architecture, tank construction, glass decoration and exhibit labelling. Some of the most interesting talks had to do with the behaviour and physiology of confined specimens, a field in which Heini Hediger and his Swiss colleagues were very advanced.

It was exciting to talk to people from aquariums I'd only vaguely heard of and to find out that they were doing all kinds of interesting work. I spent a great deal of time talking with a curator from the aquarium in Bergen, Norway, which was engaged in a fascinating project: presenting habitats not from different geographic regions but from different depths. Part of the technical challenge was to draw the aquarium water system through intakes at various depths.

The Vancouver Aquarium caused its own little stir of interest when I delivered a paper about Japanese aquariums. There were no Japanese representatives at the congress, and no one in Western aquariums knew much about the interesting work being done there—no one except the Vancouver Aquarium's globe-trotting artist Gladys Clawson, who had gone there a little over a year before. Gladys had written a paper based on her visit, and that was what I read at the congress. The paper was the first intimation many people in Europe and North America received of the major contribution the Japanese would make to the field of aquariology.

Despite the intellectual treats offered by the congress, it would have taken a high degree of tunnel vision to ignore the charms of Monaco. The tiny city-state occupies a mere 370 acres, about one-third the area of Stanley Park, and many of its buildings, including the palace, are perched on a high rocky peninsula that forms the west side of a yacht-filled harbour. Above all of them stands the noble architecture of the museum. One of the high points was to be invited to lunch by Captain and Madame Cousteau. Proficient in English, Cousteau had a presence that was both proud and gracious. He was already exploring the use of film to popularize marine science, and during the congress he showed his latest production. In contrast to his scientific documentaries, this was an allegory about a young boy and his pet goldfish. The film had an odd effect on the congress participants: on the one hand, it was not specifically relevant to aquariology; on the other, it was very moving in its evocation of how important a fish—a living creature in a different medium—could be to a small boy growing up in a big city. Only Cousteau could have pulled something like this off, and he continued in the following decades to surprise us with his understanding of how various media could be used.

Before the conference ended, a number of us were invited to the palace to meet the prince and princess of Monaco. My fellow Ichs included Sam

Hinton, Spencer Tinker and Earl Herald; the group also included my recent hosts Gwynne Vevers from London and Werner Schroeder from Berlin. For the North Americans this royal visit was like going back in time. After passing the palace gates, which were flanked by two enormous guards whose chests were covered with medals, we were ushered into a spacious cobbled courtyard, then up a set of stairs to an open colonnaded corridor whose arched ceiling was covered with painted figures. At every door we were met by meticulously uniformed guards who passed us farther along. Finally we came into a heavily draped, high-ceilinged room with great gilded pictures of the ancestors of the prince on the walls.

The prince and princess were in the adjoining room, and we walked in one by one to be introduced to them. The princess was slender, beautiful and very regal. In the polite small talk that all royalty have to make, she said she had never been to British Columbia. I realized I had been given a cue, and I was just getting my mouth in gear to invite her to Vancouver when someone with reflexes honed by years of directorhood intervened. Earl Herald, who had already been introduced to the royal couple, had somehow returned.

"When you come back to North America, Your Majesty," said Earl, "you must come and visit us at the Steinhart."

"That would be wonderful," said the princess of Monaco. "I shall plan on it."

I couldn't think of anything smooth to say, and Spencer Tinker was being ushered in, so I bowed and left the room. I guess it takes an Earl to know how to talk to royalty.

# 6
# Octopus by Air Freight

Stuart Lefeaux's garbage can stood in front of me at the Horseshoe Bay ferry dock, flanked by two husky young men from the Royal City Diving Club. It wasn't Stuart's everyday garbage can; it was the one from his cottage on the Sechelt Peninsula, up the coast from Vancouver. Why had the new superintendent of parks (Phil Stroyan had retired shortly before) sent me his summer garbage can? Because it contained a large octopus, and Stuart had kindly lent his property for the animal's safe transport to the Vancouver Aquarium. The gesture was especially kind given the fact that relations between the Park Board and the aquarium were somewhat cool at the time. Poor Stuart: it seemed that even on his weekends off he couldn't escape us. He had phoned the evening before to tell us that the two divers, Ron Innes and Lloyd Sutton, had captured an octopus while spearfishing near his cottage. Did we want it? I suppressed my usual impulse, which was to say yes to everything. The chances of keeping the animal alive overnight and transporting it all the way to Vancouver seemed poor. But I wanted it very much, and I gave Stuart some instructions for the divers.

First, they were to lower the octopus, in a sack, thirty feet into the ocean, the depth at which they'd caught it. Second, they were to keep it there until they were ready to come to Vancouver. Third, they were to transfer it to a container of seawater of the same temperature as that of the thirty-foot level. Stuart patiently took the instructions and signed off.

The next afternoon Ron and Lloyd arrived at Horseshoe Bay in a borrowed car; in it, Stuart's garbage can bulged with seawater, icebags and octopus. A female weighing about forty pounds, it survived the trip in good shape and flourished in the aquarium.

Nineteen sixty-one was a good year for octopuses; a total of five had been captured and successfully transferred to our tanks. When Elmer Taylor, curator of the Calgary Aquarium, arrived in late September and requested an octopus, we decided that Stuart Lefeaux's specimen, this veteran of hazardous travel, stood the best chance of adapting to jet flight. We sent it by DC-8 to Calgary, and it became the biggest attraction at the Calgary Aquarium.

The octopus has always fascinated humans. Part of the attraction is that strange symmetry that is suggested by the name of the animal group, *Cephalopoda*, or "head-foot." It has eight arms, each of which is equipped with double rows of independently controlled suckers. High intelligence, good eyesight, a sturdy parrotlike beak, great strength and an astonishing fluidity of motion make the octopus perfectly adapted to its predatory existence. It feeds mainly on crabs but will eat other crustaceans and also fish. The octopus behaves in a way that we associate with intelligent "higher" animals. It has large eyes that watch you, and it learns to come to you to be fed or to flee from you if you treat it badly. It is quick and reactive.

Octopuses are very aggressive and do not tolerate each other in the same vicinity. For this reason, we seldom put them together in the aquarium, although once when we obtained two small ones (six inches in diameter) from Tacoma, we kept them together in a jar for several weeks. After they had a severe battle in which both lost patches of skin, we decided to separate them.

I can watch an octopus for hours, and to judge from the visitors to the aquarium, so can most people. One reason is their colouring: octopuses are capable of rapid colour and skin texture changes, apparently associated with changes in mood. I have seen one go from a pale, cream colour with smooth skin to a dark red, roughly wrinkled surface in just a few minutes. Lacking a skeleton, an octopus can assume all sorts of strange shapes, and it is capable of squeezing through very narrow spaces, sometimes making it difficult to confine. A voracious appetite causes it to grow quickly, but it matures in three years and then dies after breeding.

We had octopuses in the aquarium from the very beginning, and they were among the animals most affected by our problems with water temperature and salinity. The first extension of the seawater intake in late 1956 made them more comfortable, but in the early 1960s we still had problems during the sunny month of May, when very low tides occurred at midday. At low tide it was difficult to pump water into the aquarium as often as we wanted to, and with the heat of the sun the temperatures in our tanks rose to the high fifties. That was too much for many of our local fish and marine invertebrates, and it very visibly affected George, our largest octopus. George was named after George Cunningham, our president in 1958 and one of my all-time favourite governors.

As temperatures rose in May, George the octopus lost his healthy, dark-red hue and moped about his tank like a dirty grey ghost. Outside of his colour, one of the clearest signs of his distress was the way he sloughed off the skin of the round outer margins of his suckers, making the water of his tank appear very untidy. This was a far cry from his usual performance, which often included graceful jet-propelled glides across the tank.

Once again, I called upon the aquarium's support network, and this time my call for help was answered by Fisheries Research Board staff at the board's technological station. Two of their engineers, Stuart Roach and George Baker, designed and constructed a remarkable heat exchanger to be used with our one-horsepower, electrically driven refrigerator compressor.

The heat exchanger looked like a classic Rube Goldberg contraption. It consisted of a series of stainless steel pipes, each of which was contained in a larger copper pipe, which in turn was insulated by a thick layer of fiberglass. Liquid refrigerant flowed in the space between the two pipes and cooled a stream of seawater that flowed through the core stainless steel pipe. Since copper and stainless steel have different rates of expansion and contraction, the two types of pipes could not be welded and were therefore joined by a specially made accordionlike fixture that yielded but did not leak. The unit worked nicely, and the octopus appeared more comfortable at a pleasant 53° F while the rest of the aquarium denizens sweltered at 60°. Unfortunately, it was a very small unit and would not cool a large volume of seawater.

In the early days, some of our octopus-collecting methods were rudimentary, to say the least, so it was probably a good thing that the largest ones we ran into were no more than fifty pounds, with tentacle lengths of six or seven feet. Most were collected by our local scuba friends, whose primary method was to swim over rocky crevices on the ocean bottom where an octopus was most likely to live. If the diver was seized by a long slithery arm covered with powerful suckers, he waited until the octopus had a good grip, then gathered the animal in his arms and swam to the surface. As time went on, our collection methods advanced considerably, particularly when we discovered a new tool: itching powder in plastic squirt bottles (the best were mustard bottles, which somehow fit most easily into the divers' gloved hands). By squirting the itching powder into a cave, we could easily drive the octopus out into the open, where we could catch it.

When Don Wilkie became assistant curator in May 1961, he greatly increased our knowledge of the Pacific octopus. Don was a biologist by education and a superb diver who brought many friends to the aquarium as volunteer collectors. He was also a good showman, and he frequently took a small octopus with him to appear on a local television show for children called "Uncle Bob and Shandy."

Don and his volunteers became so proficient at capturing the wily cephalopod that we were able to send specimens to other aquariums, usually by jet plane to keep travel time to a minimum. One of our earliest air-freight octopuses went to the New York Aquarium in March of 1962. We were delighted a few days later to see a photo in the *New York Times* showing Director Chris Coates admiring his newly arrived Pacific octopus. Word started to get around, and we got more and more inquiries.

Around this time, my old friends from UCLA, Ken Norris and Bill McFarland, were providing creative consultation for the development of a private, for-profit, oceanarium in Philadelphia. Known as the Philadelphia Aquarama (alas, no longer in existence), the $3.5 million aquarium featured an indoor porpoise display and a huge freshwater tank representing a lake. Its large tanks exhibiting multitudes of fish were built on the Marineland principle but indoors, to protect the specimens against the cold winter climate.

I had a number of telephone conversations with Aquarama's manager, Frank Powell, about an exchange of animals, and eventually we sent them a large octopus by air, along with a shipment of anemones, sea urchins, sea cucumbers and other local fish. Unfortunately, the octopus died soon after arrival because of a delay in changing planes in New York. That led to more calls from Frank, and these led to a plan: since the New York Aquarium also wanted more specimens from the Pacific Northwest, Don Wilkie would deliver the animals personally to the New York Aquarium and the Philadelphia Aquarama. Nor would Don be returning empty-handed, since Frank promised us several good-sized nurse sharks in exchange. It seemed like a good deal; I had no idea that the trip would allow Frank to do a little poaching on my territory.

On January 31, Don left for New York with four octopuses ranging in weight from thirty to sixty pounds. The trip was sponsored by Trans-Canada Airlines (now Air Canada) because of their interest in the development of handling techniques for the transportation of large aquatic animals. This is more involved than it might sound. The amount of water must be kept to a minimum to facilitate handling and reduce costs, but the extent to which this can be done depends on the distance and time involved as well as the kind of animal. The four travelling octopuses were cooled to near-freezing temperatures, then placed in triple plastic bags containing water. The air in the bags was replaced with pure oxygen prior to sealing them shut. Finally, the shipping boxes were well insulated to keep the temperature down.

The flight from Vancouver to New York took just under nine hours, including a brief stopover in Toronto. It was met at Idlewild Airport by staff of both aquariums. Frank Powell himself had come to claim his boxes, which he opened immediately in the airport. Much to everyone's relief, the two octopuses were found to be alive and in excellent condition. Frank whisked them away, and during the three-hour truck ride to Philadelphia the specimens were aerated and warmed up gradually to 45° F, the temperature in which they would live.

Meanwhile, Don accompanied the remaining two octopuses to the New York Aquarium, and on arriving, he found that they too were in first-class shape after their fourteen hours of confinement. They were dark red and healthy looking as they slowly stretched out their tentacles to explore their new surroundings. Both octopuses fed on lobster during the evening—as did Don, except that his was in a fancy restaurant as the guest of Carleton Ray, New York's famous associate curator.

Don studied the New York Aquarium's facilities and techniques for three days. The high point was when he went diving in their large whale tank and fed the gentle and intelligent belugas that were a major attraction at the aquarium. When Don told me about this, it put the idea in my head that someday we should consider having belugas and possibly other cetaceans in the Vancouver Aquarium.

After his stay in New York Don caught the train to Philadelphia. There to greet him at Aquarama was Isaac Levy, president of the board, along with Frank Powell and a number of other officials. If I'd known any of this, I might have told Don to come home immediately; I know a head-hunting committee when I see one.

Don set out for Vancouver with two nurse sharks, the larger of which was five and a half feet long. In preparation for the long journey, the specimens were tranquillized with tricaine anesthetic (MS 222), and the water was aerated with oxygen all the way. The airline did everything possible to ensure the sharks' safe arrival in Vancouver. In fact, instead of waiting for a connecting flight in Calgary, the plane was rushed straight through for the sake of the fish.

The sharks arrived safe and well. Don, however, had been hooked and landed by Frank Powell: so impressed were they with his performance that they had offered him the position of curator.

When Don told me the news I was torn between my happiness for him and my frustration at losing such a good man. But that's the aquarium biz for you. Don moved on from Philadelphia after a few years to La Jolla, California, where he became Director of the T. Wayland Vaughan Aquarium and wrote the excellent book *Aquarium Fish*. Ultimately he organized a splendid new aquarium on the bluff above the Scripps Institute of Oceanography. Opened in September 1992, it was named the Stephen Birch Aquarium-Museum.

About a year after Don left, the Vancouver Aquarium geared up for a very special collecting trip. For several years we had heard stories of giant octopus specimens being captured along the coast of northern British Columbia, but we had never obtained one over seventy pounds in weight for exhibition in the aquarium. I brought the subject up with the board of governors several times, and we started thinking about an expedition. Things really jelled when John Lecky told his father-in-law H. R. MacMillan of our interest and obtained the *Marijean* for the adventure.

About the same time we heard about a Prince Rupert diver whose prowess in hunting these animals had earned him the sobriquet "King of the Octopuses." The diver's name was John "Jock" MacLean. Through the Department of Fisheries we got in touch with Jock, and the department arranged to have him flown to Port Hardy in time to join the *Marijean* expedition. Another Port Hardy diver named Joe Akerman (who happened to be a MacMillan Bloedel employee) joined the group, which was rounded out by our new assistant curator Vincent Penfold and underwater photographer Bob Blackmore.

The very words "giant octopus" are enough to excite most people's interest, and as I put the word out about our impending expedition I started to get inquiries from all over the continent. First to call was the Smithsonian Institution in Washington, D.C., which asked if a specimen could be reserved for their new hall of sea life. Then *Life* magazine called, asking if a large octopus could be photographed underwater so that they might publish the picture.

The stage was set for a dramatic event, and as usual that left me of two minds about the whole affair. On the one hand, the publicity for the aquarium was terrific. But what if there were no such thing as a giant octopus? And if it existed, what if we didn't catch one? As an avid angler since boyhood, I knew all too well the feeling you get when you come back from a fishing trip empty-handed—especially when you've told everyone you're going after the "big one."

The expedition began on July 2 at 6:00 A.M. when Captain Scott Steen backed the *Marijean* out of her berth in Coal Harbour. On the stern was a new seawater tank six feet square and four feet high, custom-made for the prospective octopus. That day we cruised northwest up the Strait of Georgia, passing into Seymour Narrows and finally reaching Port Harvey, where we anchored for the night. Next day we continued northward and reached our destination, Port Hardy, about 11:00 A.M. It was a glorious day with golden sunshine, clear cool air and light winds.

At noon Joe Akerman put his gear on board, and a little while later a float plane descended from the sky with the King of Octopuses, Jock MacLean. Jock proved to be a veritable porpoise of a man, six feet two inches tall, over 250 pounds in weight, and thirty-six years old. As the *Marijean* rolled majestically seaward, I asked Jock where he'd come from and how he'd got into the octopus business. He had been born in Saskatchewan, he told me, but had moved west and become a hard hat diver. He started to scuba dive for "devilfish" (another nickname for octopus) at the village of Sointula in 1955 without knowing anything about their habits. The only information he could find in books consisted of hair-raising stories of bloody battles with ferocious cephalopods. As he continued his pursuit of local octopuses he discovered that they were not only harmless but a source of good income when sold to halibut fishermen as bait.

Jock operated a thirty-eight-foot fishing boat with an eleven-foot beam, and on it he and his partner carried an air compressor to fill his scuba tanks. Each January he began his search for octopuses at Comox and proceeded northward until he finished the season in May at Port Hardy. The average weight of the specimens he caught was about forty pounds, and he received thirty-three cents per pound for the flesh. The biggest order he'd ever filled was 13,000 pounds.

"Say I get an order for a thousand pounds of devilfish," he said. "I can go out and catch that many in an afternoon. Why, end of April in '58, I went out for two hours before breakfast and came back with sixteen of 'em. Eleven hundred and twenty pounds, total!" I looked at the big man and wondered if I was hearing a West Coast tall tale. Well, we would see. I asked some more about the animals from which he made his living.

They lived in colonies, or "beds" as he called them, usually where rocks rise out of mud rather than clean sand. However, the individual octopuses lived in dens excavated beneath rocks. These could usually be recognized by the excavated material in the "front yard," which was also cluttered with empty crab shells and brightly coloured objects such as empty tin cans, shiny shells or a lone anemone. "They're trash collectors, like crows," said Jock. He added that the largest octopuses did not usually stay in dens but lurked on the bottom in the neighbourhood of smaller specimens, which they often captured and ate. Lacking smaller octopuses, they would eat crabs, shrimp, clams, moon snails and the occasional rockfish.

All of that squared with what we already knew about our local species. So I finally asked Jock just how big the animals were that he'd seen or hunted.

Well, said the King of the Octopuses, you can tell about how large an octopus is by how far the eyes are apart when you are nose to nose with it on the bottom. In March 1956, he'd happened upon a large octopus in a cave. Its eyes were very far apart, but as he measured it in his mind a huge shadow passed over him. He looked up in fright to see a gigantic octopus above him with its arms fully extended. He breathed hard through his scuba regulator, and as he swam beneath the octopus he filled its umbrella-like skirting with air from his breathing equipment. This caused the animal to rise to the surface, where Jock's shipmate gaffed it and the two men dragged it on board the boat.

How big? "Twenty-eight feet across from the tip of one arm to the tip of the opposite one. Four hundred and thirty-seven pounds she was, and completely filled a forty-five-gallon barrel. But that wasn't the biggest I've seen."

No?

"No, sir. Next year in the same place, I saw one, maybe thirty-two feet across and six hundred pounds. Didn't go for her, though, no place to keep her!"

By the time I'd finished my interrogation, we arrived at the edge of an island near Port Hardy where Jock said he'd had good results in the past. The four divers entered the water from one of the *Marijean*'s small boats. Later, Vince told me that our Octopus King had proved to be a powerful diver. Jock had swum rapidly away from the others, coursing back and forth as he searched the kelp layers that concealed so much of the bottom. Jock examined every hole and rock, and he put his head right into every likely cavity, regardless of the spiky sea urchins and the possible presence of a giant octopus.

The team discovered several dens but no octopuses at home. Since the heavy growth of kelp made it difficult to hunt, Jock suggested we go south to the Alert Bay area, where one of his best locations was found. It was late in the afternoon when we arrived, but the summer sun was still high in the sky and would not set until ten that evening. So the divers promptly went back into the water and the ship's engineer, Burt Lenz, and I followed in a small skiff with a tub of water.

A moment later Jock rose to the surface with a thirty-pound octopus covering his head like a fantastic red hat. Burt and I netted it and rushed it to the *Marijean,* placing it in one of the barrels. Octopuses were suddenly being caught on all sides, and Burt and I were very busy shuttling them to the ship. Of the five we kept, the biggest was a fifty-four-pound female that was captured in only ten feet of water. All of our captives squirted ink up to three times apiece, and the water turned a rich dark brown colour in the sunlight.

Back on the *Marijean,* Jock showed me how he killed and dressed octopuses for his bait business. His method of killing them absolutely astounded me; he simply forced his strong fingers through the skin around the outside of the beak and pulled out the entire buccal mass, thus damaging the central nervous ganglia situated behind it. After he did it the first time, I mentioned that some species of octopus are known to be venomous and I'd even heard of a person in Australia dying suddenly after being bitten by a small one. Jock just snorted and moved to the tub that held a second specimen.

"You can't make one of these here devilfish bite," he declared. "Look," he said, tapping the octopus's mouth area. The animal made no attempt to snap with its powerful beak. Jock said no more, and again his powerful fingers made short work of the specimen. After he'd finished, Vince and Joe measured the second octopus, finding it had a span of exactly ten feet. Vince counted the number of suckers on one arm. There were 280, of which fully half were minute in size and located on the delicate last six inches of the arm.

After more hunting the next day, Jock and Joe were flown to their respective homes in small float planes, and the *Marijean* headed back to Vancouver. We brought with us the three largest octopuses, which weighed fifty-four, forty-six and thirty-four pounds respectively. On arriving at the aquarium I received some bad news: after prolonged sunny weather, the seawater being pumped from the intake at First Narrows had so declined in quality that the temperature was a warm 60° F and the salinity a low seventeen parts per thousand. This was far from the cool 50° and salty thirty parts per thousand where the animals were caught.

Next day all three animals had faded to a pale pink colour and were dead. I was devastated, particularly after all the effort that went into their capture. It made me even more determined to have the once-and-for-all extension of our seawater intake and redevelopment of our cool saltwater system we so needed, and this was urgently requested of the board of governors. Nonetheless, we had learned a lot in our expedition with the King of the Octopuses, and our divers were able to keep us well-stocked with these fascinating creatures. I never saw Jock MacLean again nor have I ever seen an octopus weighing more than a hundred pounds. However, I was impressed by Jock's stories and have often wondered about the possible existence of gargantuan Pacific octopus specimens.

As we gained more experience with octopuses, we learned to manage their domestic lives, a job that occasionally made us feel like marriage counsellors. Octopuses are so territorial in nature that we normally kept only one per aquarium tank, except during their breeding season when pairs were brought together. We had to watch them very closely during this period, for their marital bliss is short-lived. Once mating has been completed, the female may turn on the male—who is generally larger than she is—and kill or severely injure him. We usually managed to separate the animals before this happened.

In the early 1970s a young woman named Susan Gabe Hoffer joined the aquarium as a research assistant. As we discussed possible projects, I told her that we had various special animals in the aquarium that could be studied and suggested that she concentrate on observing the octopus. Susan focussed on their parental behaviour and egg and larval development. She worked long hours in the research area of the aquarium, which members of the public rarely see, and in the spring of 1973 was able to record a whole cycle of procreation and hatching involving a mature male and a mature female and their eggs and larvae.

The life cycle of the octopus, like that of most marine animals, is incompletely understood, but over the years the gaps in our understanding are gradually being filled. Researchers at the Seattle Aquarium were successful in breeding a pair of octopuses, then rearing a few of the young, an experiment that revealed the length of time required to go from one stage to the next. Sunshine City Aquarium in Tokyo has been very successful in exhibiting the North Pacific octopus. They have kept several of them for their entire three-year life cycles, feeding them live krill (small, shrimplike crustaceans) and maintaining them in chilled seawater.

As yet, however, the mystery of the truly gigantic Pacific octopus has not been solved and, if these giant octopuses truly exist, they have never been exhibited in aquariums. I often think of Jock MacLean and his adventures and wonder whether we may just have missed the big ones. Perhaps if we organized one more diving expedition to the cool, dark waters off the northeast coast of Vancouver Island, we would find them.

# 7

# Shark Hunting and Politics, and How to Tell the Difference

The year was 1961, and as I walked through the aquarium each day I could see that it was bursting at the seams with activity—and with visitors, for the annual attendance was over 300,000 in a building designed for a third of that. It was time for us to expand. The bold green and yellow with which we had repainted the exterior the year before expressed a new confidence; we were no longer a mere "fish house" trying to blend diffidently into the forest of Stanley Park. Healthy specimens filled our tanks, and behind the scenes a dozen or so research projects were fighting for space. It was not a question of letting out the seams a little but of adding a new suit to the original wardrobe.

I felt ready to do it, for much in my life had come together around that time. In the five years since we had opened I had learned a lot about management, and in my travels through the U.S. and Europe I had seen the best the aquarium world had to offer. My Ph.D. was finally finished, to the great relief of both Dr. Hoar and my wife. Most important, I had learned something about myself in those years: as an aquarium director, I had my own style and strengths and my own vision of what an aquarium—our aquarium—should be. I was not a heroic autocrat like Earl Herald, nor a clever technical innovator like Bill Kelley, nor the guardian of a glorious tradition like the London Aquarium's Gwynne Vevers. Where Earl Herald would point the way and give the marching orders, I had a talent for explaining where I wanted to go and finding people who would help me get there; where Bill Kelley would design some complicated new filter system and build it himself, I could clearly describe the result or effect I wanted and give people with more expertise than I the freedom to make it happen. And as to tradition, we were creating our own particular way of approaching things, one of commitment to education and science and love of adventure.

Nineteen sixty-one was also a good time for tackling something new because in March the aquarium association had just elected a new president, Robert McLaren. Bob was chief biologist of the federal Fisheries department's Fish Culture Development Branch at the time and had behind him a wide network of people and vessels that were immensely helpful to the aquarium. He was frequently able to get us several days' collecting time on one of the department's patrol vessels or the loan of fishing equipment. He helped get us a special fishing licence allowing us to fish "anywhere, any-time" on the coast, just as our friends in the provincial Fish and Wildlife Branch had given us a collecting permit for the province's rivers and lakes.

But connections are only a small part of Bob's contribution over the years, for he has been with the aquarium in one capacity or another almost as long as I have. It was always great comfort to have that compact, im-perturbable figure at the boardroom table. As a biologist, he knew his fish; as a bureaucrat, he knew how organizations worked and was a skilled negotia-tor; as a friend, he was a loyal and forthright sounding-board. The expansion project was a challenge Bob cheerfully accepted, and he put his organizing skills and strength of personality behind it.

One of the first people to get "organized" was my long-suffering profes-sor, Bill Hoar; still dazed (I thought) from the relief of seeing me finish my thesis, he permitted himself to be appointed head of the building committee. In concert with the aquarium staff, the committee worked steadily with architects McCarter, Nairne, who had designed the original building, and with the engineering company D. W. Thomson. The committee had a lot of good people on it, including Aubrey Peck, the Hudson's Bay Company man who, with the store manager Ernie Brown, had been so helpful in the start-up of the aquarium.

The aquarium community in North America was just beginning to translate the forward-looking discussions of the Ichs and Herps into new buildings. The majority of the world's public aquariums were still boxlike buildings with long halls, usually dark and rather drab, containing series of rectangular tanks fronted by a few parsimoniously worded labels. (I'm leav-ing out the oceanariums, obviously, but they were mainly interested in sensational animal presentations to draw crowds and generate profits.) I wanted to combine the good features of the traditional aquarium with the grandeur of the natural history museum and the excitement of the oceanar-ium to create a new kind of public aquarium.

Our plan was an almost complete departure from conventional aquari-ums of the time. Its most important element was a new wing containing the B.C. Hall of Fishes, and in planning for that we brought together the newest ideas in the aquarium community plus some original thinking of our own. We intended to be guided by environmental logic, presenting the province's aquatic habitats in their natural succession: from the open ocean through the straits to the shores of Vancouver and finally up the Fraser River to the trout and salmon headwater streams in the interior of the province.

The interior of the new wing would be contoured and decorated to resemble living aquatic environments. There would be various sizes of tanks with angled side walls that, like those advocated by Bill Kelley of the Cleveland Aquarium, would give the illusion of disappearing into the distance. I was also influenced by the new natural history exhibits in the great museums of New York, Washington, London and Chicago. If I got my way, the Vancouver Aquarium was going to be one of the strongest educational aquariums ever. My vision was for it to be a living museum of natural history, telling its story in a thematic way.

Behind the scenes we planned for additional research rooms with independent water systems for scientific work. There would also be a laboratory for high school science classes and a lecture hall for visiting schoolchildren. There would be improved service areas with an overhead monorail for transporting large specimens from the service entrance to our largest tank; no longer would Billy Wong and other staff have to struggle to carry large creatures and equipment to and from the displays. Finally, a new temperate freshwater system and (once and for all, we hoped) an efficient pipeline for bringing cool seawater in during the summer.

The most striking feature of the plan was a high-ceilinged, glass-sided entrance hall. Some of my favourite natural history institutions, like the Field Museum in Chicago, presented mounted elephants in their entrances. A similar effect was created by the Hall of Whales in London's Museum of Natural History. I wanted to produce the same awe-inspiring effect by suspending life-size models of large marine animals from the ceiling of our new entrance.

The plan would make the existing building fifty feet wider and forty feet longer. Projecting from the side of the building would be a porpoise pool fifty feet in length. As the overall project gradually came into focus, the architect estimated that it might cost $750,000. Thinking back to the beginnings of the aquarium, the board of governors decided to repeat the original strategy and ask the three governments to contribute $250,000 each.

On October 10, 1961, Bob McLaren submitted identical briefs to the federal, provincial and civic governments. And then we organized as much support as we could. Board members, friends and associates all were enlisted to contact the press and as many influential people as they could rally to our cause.

In the meantime, I decided to start work on the models for the planned entrance. It seemed logical to start with a species close to hand, so we settled on capturing a basking shark (*Cetorhinus maximus*), the largest shark of temperate seas and fairly common in the North Pacific. Known to reach forty feet in length, these sharks get their name from the fact that they frequently rest at the surface with the tips of their dorsal fins jutting into the air. Basking sharks have huge mouths but very small teeth. They feed by straining krill from the water through their highly developed gill rakers.

I mentioned our plan in the *Aquarium Newsletter* and in short order received a letter from Dr. Leonard Schultz, curator of fishes at the Smithsonian Institution in Washington, D.C. We had taken care to put the most important fish and aquarium experts on our complimentary mailing list, and we were gratified when they responded to specific articles. If we captured a basking shark, Schultz offered, technicians from his institution could be sent to British Columbia to prepare a mould of the shark from which two replicas would be cast—one for the Smithsonian and one for the Vancouver Public Aquarium.

Bob McLaren passed the word on to the fisheries patrol fleet to notify us if they sighted any sharks, and on April 3 we got word that a number of them had appeared at the mouth of Barkley Sound on the west coast of Vancouver Island. The next day we took the ferry across the Strait of Georgia to Nanaimo and then drove across Vancouver Island to Port Alberni. There we boarded the *Comox Post,* a stout fifty-nine-foot patrol boat whose five-man crew already had a lot of experience with basking sharks. The huge beasts had become a problem for the fishing industry along the west coast of Vancouver Island, frequently getting tangled in expensive nets. Responding to the fishermen's requests for help, the Department of Fisheries equipped the bow of the *Comox Post* with a sharp blade. When the sharks appeared in an area where fishermen were operating, the patrol boat ran them down and cut them to pieces. That was the last thing I wanted on this trip, of course; our collecting was going to be done with a harpoon.

You may think this sounds like a bloodthirsty piece of business—but of course that is the advantage of hindsight from the present era of heightened sensitivity towards animals. Animal rights did not become a major media issue until the 1970s, although humane societies were actively concerned about the treatment of domestic animals. I had collected specimens for years as a student and as a scientist. That usually involved killing the animals and preserving them in formaldehyde and afterwards dissecting them. These activities were never considered a problem by humane societies. Our work attracted the attention of the public to unusual species of animals and we wanted the public to know about them. My goal was understanding the nature of the specimens and educating other people about them, and collecting a basking shark seemed the only way to get the anatomy as correct and realistic as possible at that time. Nowadays, we work from underwater photos, the results of which are considerably different from even the best efforts using dead specimens. Unlike air, water counters the effects of gravity and allows an aquatic animal to keep its shape and work its muscles naturally.

We got underway immediately, cruising thirty-two miles down Alberni

Canal and Barkley Sound to the little fishing village of Bamfield. The village is tucked into a small cove on the outside of which is the open Pacific Ocean. Along this outer coast, great seas pound the rocks and reefs. It is the graveyard of many ships. Islands, overgrown with great conifers from which bald eagles survey the horizon, protect the mouth of Bamfield's cove. It is a beautiful area. The old cable station (now reincarnated as the Bamfield Marine Station) stands on a bluff above Bamfield, marking the point where the submarine cable first connected Canada to other British Commonwealth countries in the Pacific.

We soon received word by radio that some huge sharks were at the surface near the shrimp fleet at Swiss Boy Island. When we arrived there in the early afternoon, Captain Don Brooks immediately sighted several sharks. Standing on the flying bridge of the *Comox Post,* he shut off the engines and steered the boat quietly alongside a twenty-foot shark wallowing at the surface, its dark fin out of the water. A muscular crewman named Barney Ririe took position at the bow, holding the shaft of the harpoon in his right hand. The harpoon consisted of a ten-foot steel rod with a sharpened, barbed head fastened to a stainless steel cable and seventy-five fathoms of three-quarter-inch manila line.

As the *Comox Post* drifted up to the great shark, Barney threw the harpoon at precisely the right moment and hit his target just behind the head. The shark sounded with a great splash, heading for the bottom far below. Barney quickly secured the end of the heavy line, a loop was thrown around the winch, and we started the slow pulling of the struggling fish towards the surface. So mighty was the shark, however, that halfway to the surface, the stainless steel cable parted and we lost both the shark and the harpoon head. Night was falling so we tied up in Bamfield. There a new harpoon head was forged out of steel and we feasted royally on fresh shrimp presented to us by a local fisherman.

Next morning, north of Folger Island, we sighted a shark slowly cutting the surface with its fin. Once again, Barney sank the harpoon deep into the back of the beast and it rushed to the bottom. It took an hour to pull it back to the surface, where the captain finally killed it with a rifle shot through the brain. The crew lashed the great beast to the side of the boat and we transported it up Uchucklesit Inlet to the B.C. Packers plant at Kildonan.

"Big fish, that one," the plant manager said laconically when the boat arrived. We watched him scratch his head as he figured out how to handle it. The plant's dock had a boom attached to a winch for lifting heavy loads, but so big was our shark that the boom had to be reinforced with additional supporting cables. When the shark was hauled onto the dock, we discovered it measured twenty feet, six inches in length, and estimated its weight to be about two tons. We then wheeled it into the enormous B.C. Packers freezer. Once the shark was frozen, a large truck took it to the B.C. Packers Imperial Cannery in Steveston, south of Vancouver, where it arrived to great fanfare.

As good as his word, Leonard Schultz of the Smithsonian Institution arrived from Washington, D.C., at the end of April. With him was his chief technician, John Widener, who was also eager to model the Mexican manta ray and sawfish I had collected during one of my trips on the *Marijean*. John had developed a totally new technique for creating plastic mouldings of specimens, so I was very interested in seeing him at work.

A large coffinlike box had been constructed in one of the Imperial Cannery's large buildings. We half-filled the box with sand, then hoisted the shark up and placed it inside the box to let it thaw, which took almost two days. Once the fish thawed, John was able to adjust it to a life-like shape, which he did with the help of one of the aquarium's old friends, Joe Bauer. Joe had to cut the fins off the shark when it proved impossible to pass the specimen back though the door of the freezing room with its fins naturally positioned.

When the shark became rigidly frozen again, it was brought out, placed on a truck and driven to the Industrial Coatings plant in Vancouver. John consulted with their team of plastics specialists and the moulds were prepared. John decided that the head would present particular difficulties because of its complicated gill structure and that it would be advisable to mould only the body in Vancouver, sending the frozen head back to Washington, D.C.

Shark fishing is one thing; fishing for funds is quite another. For a number of months in 1962 I angled for the support of Rufus "Rufe" Gibbs, an elderly bachelor who had built up a successful company that manufactured fishing tackle. His star product was the celebrated Gibbs Spoon, one of the best salmon lures ever invented, which his company produced in its small foundry near Vancouver's False Creek. As an important figure in B.C.'s fishing industry, at least the recreational end of it, Rufe was a natural for us to contact when we were looking for financial support. His reponse to that first contact was cautious: he might be interested in sponsoring an exhibit of British Columbia sport fishes, particularly if it could be made interesting for children. My job was clearly to turn "might" into "would," and that's why most Friday afternoons found me in Rufe's cramped little office drinking Buchan's Whiskey and talking about the prospective Rufe Gibbs Hall of Sport Fishes. This I did in company with another financial angler: Bob Smith, a local social worker who was also a radio personality on CBC's weekly "Hot Air" jazz program.

I'm not much of a drinker by nature, but fund raising sometimes makes extraordinary demands on you. Bob and I drank a lot of Buchan's as we courted Rufe for our respective causes, and the old man seemed to enjoy the courting as much as the whiskey. As befits a jazz aficionado, Bob Smith had a certain visual presence I couldn't match, particularly in his choice of colourful jackets and his fondness for black cigars. He seemed to be having more success than I was, for he soon persuaded Rufe to make a large donation for a children's arthritis ward. By contrast, my ichthyological erudition alone wasn't doing the job.

I had been keeping my board informed all along. The ever-changing board had some new faces, among them AEneas Bell-Irving, an alderman and a member of one of Vancouver's most illustrious families. AEneas was a shrewd judge of character: he suggested that what might please Rufe more than my fish talk was some pomp and circumstance, and he undertook to recruit Mayor Bill Rathie to help us.

And so it was that one Friday afternoon a huge limousine pulled up outside Rufe's office. Out stepped His Worship the Mayor, preceded by his uniformed Sergeant-at-Arms bearing the official city mace. Rufe loved it. With the mayor, sergeant-at-arms, Alderman Bell-Irving, cigar-smoking Bob Smith and me jostling each other in the small office, Rufe finally handed me a cheque for $50,000—a down payment, as it turned out.

I have to confess that I also sought support among Vancouver's children, and in this I was aided by a spirited, red-haired businesswoman who joined the board in 1960. This was Grace McCarthy, now a political legend in the province as an organizer, cabinet minister and new leader of the Social Credit party, but back then a young florist and a neophyte politician who had just been elected to the Park Board. In that capacity she frequently went with Bob McLaren and me to appear before City Council to speak in favour of the city's financial contribution to the expansion. Grace was also interested from the beginning in the aquarium's educational efforts, the reorganization of which was one of Bob's priorities as chairman.

Like every good biologist, Bob was trained to look for patterns, and he was concerned with the patterns of attendance by schoolchildren. The aquarium had always been popular with schools, but their visits mainly came in April, May and June, when general attendance was already on the rise after the winter doldrums. The board discussed ways to spread school visits over the whole year, and we worked out a deal with the School Board. In 1961 we offered a program of free visits, two classes per day from January to March. Lacking staff to deal with such a flowthrough, we went to the Vancouver Natural History Society and won their participation as docents, volunteers who were part guide, part teacher. Our training program for docents was one of the first established in a public aquarium. By the end of March, some 4000 kids had visited the aquarium through this program.

Grace McCarthy was supportive of the organized school visits and the docents, but she felt that 4000 students was still thinking far too small. Typically, she waited until she had a concrete idea, which she revealed at a board meeting that summer. The subject on the table was general attendance figures and how to increase them. Grace bided her time and then spoke up. "If we want to bring more people, the best way is to reach the children." A few glances were exchanged between some of the board members around the table at this seemingly obvious opinion. Grace was the first woman on the board and in many eyes had yet to prove herself. She carried on.

"If we could get a ticket to the aquarium into each child's hands," she continued, "that child will make his parents miserable until they use that ticket. And the ticket can't be used unless someone else accompanies the child, right?" More glances shot around the table, but this time they were accompanied by nods and chuckles. The idea was brilliant in its simplicity and its understanding of human nature; most of the board members were parents or grandparents and could easily picture the scenario Grace painted for us. It also struck a chord in me that suggested a refinement of the idea. As a kid in Chicago I'd grown up collecting and trading the illustrated baseball cards that used to come with bubble gum. What if, instead of baseball players, we featured aquatic animals on our tickets? There would be a tear-off section for the turnstiles, but the kids would keep—and, I hoped, collect—the fish cards.

The idea was accepted, and out of it came four cards, each featuring a different animal: a sunflower starfish, a Pacific octopus, a copper rockfish and a lingcod. Our artist, Gladys Clawson, painted the illustrations, which were accompanied by the animal's common name, its scientific name and a life history sketch. The cost of printing was kept low by running the cards with a four-colour printing of cereal boxes, thanks to the public-spirited generosity of both the printer and the cereal manufacturer, and we ended up with just over 400,000 of the cards, enough for every schoolchild in the province. All we had to do then was distribute them, and regarding this Grace talked with the aquarium's old friend Leslie Peterson, who was by now minister of education.

When report cards came out the following spring, children across the province received with them—pass or fail—a free ticket to the aquarium. Within days, we were hit by a tidal wave as youngsters dragged in their parents, older sisters and brothers, aunts and uncles, in short *anyone* who would help them use their free ticket. Receipts went up dramatically as attendance jumped by tens of thousands over the previous year. It couldn't have come at a better time, for City Council was about to throw us a curve ball that could have wrecked our expansion plans.

On October 2, 1962, Council side-stepped the issue of contributing to the aquarium by voting to hold a plebiscite on December 12. The plebiscite would decide whether the city would authorize a grant of $250,000—providing, of course, that matching grants were received from the federal and provincial governments. It was not exactly a setback, but it made our job more difficult. Such a plebiscite required the assent of a 60 per-cent majority of taxpayers (i.e., homeowners) in order to pass. The issue was further complicated because the plebiscite was a three-part affair: as well as the aquarium expansion, voters were being asked to approve the Park Board's purchase of two golf courses at a cost of $3.8 million and $2.25 million respectively.

This was before the days of taxpayer revolts, but Vancouver homeowners were being asked to swallow a lot. As never before, we needed the help of all aquarium members and friends if we were to survive. As usual, we had no money to do things by traditional means such as advertising. Jack Long, the photographer of the shark hunt, prevailed upon a printer friend of his to produce a brochure for us at little charge. We distributed thousands of them, especially in doctors' waiting rooms. The two Vancouver newspapers gave the aquarium's development project strong approval, partly I think as a result of the good relations I had tried to cultivate with them over the years.

Despite all the support, I was very worried about the plebiscite. I leaned a great deal on Bob McLaren, who exhibited nothing but optimism in public and then kidded me mercilessly in private. If we lost, he suggested wickedly, a fellow with my qualifications could easily get another job. . . gutting fish in a cannery.

The night of the plebiscite found the McLarens and the Newmans sitting nervously in the McLarens' living room following the tallies on television. The night was long and the vote was exceedingly close: 40,415 ballots in favour and 25,689 against, with 1316 reject ballots. If the reject ballots were counted in the total vote, the bylaw would only have a 59.945 per-cent majority, a heartbreaking fraction short of the 60 per cent we needed. However, City Clerk Ron Thompson magnanimously threw out the reject ballots and declared the plebiscite carried by 61.14 per cent. We had won!

As president of the aquarium, a euphoric Bob McLaren immediately issued a statement that he expected construction of the extension to start in the winter of 1963, following the finalization of architectural plans and project budgeting. It seemed perfectly achievable. The federal government had already started the wheels in motion to set aside for funds for us in the next budget: all that was needed was a written commitment from the provincial government and we could start work. More than a little anxiously, we wrote to the provincial government, reminding them of the verbal commitment we had received. And then we waited. . . .

Of course, we waited busily. An early necessity was to find a new assistant curator, since Donald Wilkie had been lured away to Philadelphia. After a short search we hired Vincent Penfold, an excellent scuba diver and former Canadian Navy officer. Vince was completing his training as a science teacher at UBC.

In June 1963 we heard from the federal government: the minister of fisheries wrote that Treasury Board had approved Ottawa's contribution of $250,000—on the condition, of course, that the provincial government and the City of Vancouver made their matching contributions. We wrote again to the provincial government. And we waited. . . .

I dealt with the mounting frustration by going out on the water whenever I could. The never-ending administrative work made it difficult to get out into the field, and the energy of the collecting staff under our new assistant curator made it something of a luxury; the tanks were simply teeming with new specimens. Still, rank has its privileges, and I occasionally managed to get out on the aquarium's none-too-stable collecting boat, the *Aquarius*.

From the beginning months of our existence, we had recognized the necessity of a collecting boat. However, our chronic funding problems limited us to purchasing a used fishing boat. With the help of a fisheries captain I had selected an old thirty-foot cod boat in December 1959 and sailed it from Campbell River around Cape Mudge and across the Strait of Georgia. This first voyage was not terribly propitious: a powerful storm blew up, and as the boat was skittish in even moderate weather we decided it might be best to visit some friends on one of the islands up the coast. We had no radio, and we were out of communication for several days. Kathy, having decided that on balance I was still a "keeper," soon contacted the Coast Guard, and a search team was sent out to rescue us. They found us happily sitting around the fireplace in a cozy cottage on Nelson Island.

The *Aquarius* was double-ended, a live-cod boat similar to a coastal gill netter but deeper and narrower. Her hull was perforated amidships and had two supposedly watertight bulkheads (I stress the supposedly), creating a live-tank for captured fish. We converted the boat for collecting by adding equipment to keep the seawater in the tank aerated and filtered. New decks were put in place and the whole hull was renovated. We also placed a winch on the afterdeck and a boom over the stern to enable an otter-board trawl to be dragged over the ocean bottom.

We collected a lot of fish with the *Aquarius,* but we also had to collect the boat itself fairly frequently—from the bottom of its mooring in False Creek. The bulkheads on either side of the live-tank were only nominally watertight. If you left the *Aquarius* at night with the live-tank full you often returned in the morning to find the boat hanging at a crazy angle from the dock by its line, with half of the boat totally immersed.

In December, the federal minister of fisheries publicly warned that Ottawa's offer would be retracted if the provincial government didn't cough up a written commitment to provide the promised money. Fortunately that brought the press back into the debate. The influential columnist Jack Wasserman called down fire and brimstone on the recalcitrant premier, charging that

> [Vancouver's] chances for a magnificent public aquarium are going to dribble down the drain while the senior governments play a game of musical chairs with our money. . . .
>
> This is all part of Premier Bennett's perpetual hassle with the Feds and I'm not about to argue with the general principle involved. If we miss out on the coliseum and the new First Narrows crossing [two other issues at the time] because of the premier's fight that's too bad. But if we lose Murray Newman it will be a tragedy of the first magnitude. Even greater than if we lost the premier.
>
> Dr. Newman combines the best qualities of Louis Pasteur and P. T. Barnum. He is a unique public servant in that he has the complete respect and recognition of his professional colleagues all over North America and at the same time has managed to appeal to the public fancy.

I paid the price for Wasserman's effusiveness the next day, when I had to meet with Bob McLaren. "So, how's Louis Pasteur?" asked the aquarium's president solicitously. "Or are we P. T. Barnum today?" I let it go with as much dignity as I could muster; when you are more important than the premier, you can afford to be gracious.

I was never entirely sure if Wasserman's analysis of federal-provincial gamesmanship was actually correct. We had had the same trouble with Premier Bennett ten years before, and my understanding was that he just didn't like signing documents. On the other hand, Bennett had pledged to make B.C. debt free and went to great lengths to reduce expenditures and apply any surplus on payment of debt.

Whatever its cause, the failure of the government to respond to our requests for payment led us to believe that the provincial funding for the aquarium was at risk. We once again called for help from Grace McCarthy, now the MLA for Vancouver–Little Mountain, and from Leslie Peterson, now the minister of education. Each met with the premier individually and successfully argued our case. Bennett directed the minister of finance (himself) to pay the money forthwith.

It all taught me a great lesson that anyone running a large public institution eventually learns: you simply can't ignore politics. You are best off not to get involved yourself, but you must find allies who can defend your institution's interests. Your allies should be people with savvy who understand the game and have connections. It's a hassle, but it's reality.

Personally, I'd rather be fishing.

# 8

# The First
# Killer Whale in Captivity

Of all the requests I've ever had to make on behalf of the aquarium, by far the most audacious was one made by radio from a small fishing boat anchored off Vancouver Island. It was a Thursday evening in the summer of 1964 when David Wallace, general manager of Burrard Drydock, picked up his phone and heard my static-distorted voice say, "It's Murray Newman from the Vancouver Aquarium. We've just captured this killer whale, and I was wondering if we could keep it in your drydock for a few days."

I hate making phone calls to ask people for their help, especially when I've never spoken to them before. I didn't know if Wallace had heard of me, and if so what he'd heard. A few years earlier I had participated in a practical joke played on his father, former Lieutenant Governor Clarence Wallace. It was during one of the *Marijean* cruises in Mexico. Clarence Wallace was on another yacht anchored nearby in Mazatlan harbour when H. R. MacMillan's guests decided to send over a shark's head dressed up like a roast pig, complete with an apple in its mouth. It crossed my mind that with a historical connection like that, the younger Wallace might not be inclined to take my request seriously.

And I definitely needed his help. Not a hundred yards away from the fishing boat swam a fifteen-foot killer whale with a harpoon through the blubber in front of its dorsal fin. As I waited for Wallace to reply, I still hadn't decided if this killer whale project was going terribly right or terribly wrong. We never expected actually to capture a live member of this species, which was generally viewed as the marine world's Public Enemy Number One. Now we had one, surprisingly docile and relatively uninjured despite the harpoon, and we didn't have anywhere to keep it. Or any money to pay for its room and board.

David Wallace asked a couple of questions and then made his decision. "Okay," he agreed, "you can put it in one of our drydocks. But only till Monday. We're kind of busy at the moment." I thanked him profusely and put down the radio's microphone. So what if I had no idea what to do after Monday? The point was that the aquarium now had the first and only killer whale in captivity, soon to be known by millions as Moby Doll.

"Captivity" and "killer whale" have an ugly sound to many ears in the 1990s, but in 1964 putting these words together was pretty much unthinkable. The killer whale, *Orcinus orca*, is the largest and fiercest predator on earth. A world traveller but especially common along the coast of British Columbia, it is a magnificent animal with sharply contrasting black and white body colours and a swordlike dorsal fin. Fittingly, the Haida people of the Queen Charlotte Islands have traditionally revered it as a supernatural being, calling it *S'qana*, or Chief of the World Beneath the Sea.

In the first half of the twentieth century, however, most fisherfolk regarded killer whales as little more than salmon thieves and competitors. In 1959 complaints from fisherman on the Pacific Coast caused the Canadian government to mount a heavy machine gun at Seymour Narrows, where killer whales were frequently seen. The plan was that the gun crew would slaughter as many whales as came into range. Luckily for the whales, however, it was hot and dry that summer. The forests were closed by the government and the machine gun was never used for fear of causing a forest fire. In any case, fishermen did not see many killer whales that year and did not complain so much. In the end the gun was never used.

At the time I made my phone call to David Wallace, no killer whales had yet been exhibited in aquariums. However, a number of other small cetaceans (the biologist's name for marine mammals like whales and dolphins) had been successfully maintained, and professional aquarists were becoming increasingly skilled in their husbandry techniques. The great American showman P. T. Barnum had exhibited belugas as early as 1861, but they only lived a short time.

The first successful cetacean exhibition was created not by aquarists but by the film industry. In the 1930s a group of movie producers constructed a large tank just outside of St. Augustine, Florida, filled it with marine life and named it Marine Studios. Their objective was to use it as a safe, convenient set for undersea adventure movies. However, the place excited so much local interest that they soon realized more money could be made by charging admission to their exhibit. In a quick change of strategy, they renamed the huge tank Marineland of Florida and presented the world with its first oceanarium. Marineland's undisputed stars in those days were a colony of bottlenose dolphins (*Tursiops truncatus*) maintained and observed by curator Arthur McBride and his successor, F. G. Wood. These animals were extremely social, apparently intelligent and could be bred in captivity. Public interest was excited far beyond Florida, especially after a dolphin adventure film called "Flipper" was produced and distributed worldwide.

Marineland of the Pacific, the world's second oceanarium, took the display of cetaceans several steps further under the leadership of the young UCLA scientist Kenneth Norris and his manager Bill Monahan. When Marineland opened in 1954 near Los Angeles on the Palos Verdes peninsula, Ken was its first curator. He and his collectors, Captain Frank Brocato and "Boots" Calandrino, became very adept at collecting live marine mammals (Ken tells this story in his thoughtful and immensely readable book *Porpoise Watcher*). They successfully captured most of the small species, such as common dolphins, bottlenose dolphins and Pacific white-sided dolphins, and were the first to catch and exhibit the larger pilot whales. Ken and Frank observed killer whales along the coast of southern California and for many years considered the possibility of exhibiting them, but they shared the general apprehension about the dangers the whales posed to both staff and visitors.

That apprehension was well-founded, as shown in both anecdote and scientific observation. I still have a scientific paper that Ken and John Prescott wrote in 1960 in which they describe sighting a pod of killer whales near Santa Barbara Island. One of the whales seized a sea lion in its jaws and played with its unfortunate victim, throwing it high into the air and causing the water to become red with blood. The same paper quotes a 1937 anecdote from British Columbia in which an Alsatian dog standing on the shore was almost seized by a large killer whale.

Accordingly, Marineland of the Pacific made little effort during its first years to capture killer whales. Then an old specimen was captured and held for eighteen hours before it died off Newport, California, in December 1961. That started the ball rolling, and the following summer Frank and Boots arrived in Vancouver from California with their thirty-nine-foot collecting boat, the *Geronimo*. When it emerged that Marineland intended to catch a killer whale alive, there was a great deal of scoffing, especially when the papers reported that *Geronimo*'s bow sported "a 28-foot boom with a pulpit at the end from which the whale could be lassoed after it was netted." A local fisherman summed it up for the Vancouver *Province*: "Catch a 2000 or 3000 pound killer whale with a net and lasso? It can't be done."

The wily Brocato thought otherwise, and he announced he planned to catch the whale in American waters off Point Roberts just south of Vancouver. Still, he was cautious, telling the papers that he hoped to catch a baby whale but was concerned that the mother might attack the boat. "That is why we have a high-powered cannon," he told the papers.

High-powered cannon! His concern turned into reality a few weeks later when his crew actually managed to lasso a killer whale. The whale, understandably alarmed by the situation, tangled the line around the boat's propeller in its efforts to get away; the equally alarmed hunters responded to the apparent attack on the boat with a blast from the cannon, killing the hapless killer whale. Its sorry death signalled the end of the expedition, and the *Geronimo* sailed for home.

Although I had great respect for Brocato, I must admit that I too had my doubts. Like everyone else I considered the idea of exhibiting live killer whales in an aquarium potentially dangerous. In any case, while interested in *Orcinus orca*, I had a broader concern about the whole range of marine mammals on the Pacific Coast. Seals and sea lions had been hunted in the early days for profit, then killed for government bounties when the fishing community became concerned about their consumption of salmon. Sea otters, first described by the German scientist Georg Steller on the Bering Expedition to Alaska in 1741, were totally exterminated in Oregon, Washington and British Columbia. Large whales were killed for oil and meat. Species by species, it seemed, marine mammals were either being slaughtered for business or killed as pests.

As a biologist, this seemed wasteful and backward to me. Why couldn't our society appreciate and protect these animals? Obviously, part of the answer was that people knew so little about these fascinating creatures they had no respect for their lives. And that brought me back to our mission of presenting animals to the public so that people would know and care about them and generally develop more sensitivity towards living things.

Since we were sure the aquarium would never exhibit live killer whales, we decided to create a life-like sculpted replica. Planning for the great aquarium expansion of the mid-sixties was already underway, and we envisaged the killer whale sculpture as a symbol of the marine life in the waters of British Columbia. Suspended from the ceiling of the new foyer, it would join the model of the basking shark and perhaps other oceanic species too large to exhibit alive. Creating an accurate model would involve capturing a specimen in order to photograph, measure and take moulds of particular features of its body.

This approach was firmly in the tradition of the great natural history museums, and when I presented the project to the board I spoke nostalgically of the Field Museum in Chicago and the British Museum of Natural History in London with their mighty mounted elephants. The board pledged several thousand dollars and the Leon and Thea Koerner Foundation contributed a grant towards the project.

With some financial resources behind me, I started assembling the human resources. First, I checked with local scientists about the likeliest places to catch a killer whale and found that orcas frequently swim close to East Point on Saturna Island, where the water drops to almost one hundred fathoms close to the shore. A shore-mounted harpoon gun might be all that was necessary for the job. Once again, our excellent relations with the Department of Fisheries helped to clear away many of the obstacles we might otherwise have faced. Robert McLaren found us an experienced harpoonist named Ronald Sparrow, a native gill-net fisherman who had the respect of all the fishery officers. Ronald agreed to help us and volunteered to bring his own harpoon gun. Fisheries also assigned us their sixty-five-foot patrol vessel, the *Chilco Post*, and its five crew members to assist with the capture.

The next job was to find a sculptor. For that I visited the Vancouver School of Art, where the principal, Fred Amess, introduced me to Sam Burich. Born in Yugoslavia, Sam was a stocky, bearded man of thirty-eight who was not only a highly regarded artist (he'd studied at St. Martin's School of Art in London, among other places) but turned out to be a commercial fisherman as well. I was impressed by his stoic calm and even more by his large, capable-looking hands. The expedition obviously appealed to him, for Sam not only agreed to sculpt the whale but signed on as assistant harpoonist.

The project clearly had great scientific potential as well, and in this regard we had the enthusiastic support of Dr. Patrick McGeer, professor of neurochemistry at UBC's School of Medicine and at that time a Liberal member of the provincial legislature. An amiable but ferociously bright man whom a local columnist dubbed "the man in the grey matter suit," McGeer eventually became the province's minister of education. At the time, however, he was deeply into brain research and looked forward to examining a killer whale's brain, about which nothing was known. A number of other scientists also expressed interest in the project.

The hunt began on May 22, with Ronald and Sam manning the gun by the shore and a team of watchers stationed on the sandstone bluffs above East Point. An isolated and beautiful spot, the Tumbo Channel is about a quarter mile across at that location. The current runs fast, and the water is deep and clear. The whales appeared as predicted: Vince Penfold sighted a pod of them approaching the gun early the first morning. Unfortunately, they passed by before the harpoon could be mounted and readied for firing. And so began a long, frustrating wait.

From May 22 to July 16 a number of pods were sighted but only one whale came close enough to warrant a shot. The harpoon passed just over its back and the whale was so startled it jumped out of the water before disappearing into the channel.

Gunnery practice was held from time to time with the *Chilco Post* towing a small raft near the shore as the target. Our harpoonists took aim and fired their harpoons. In most cases, they missed. An easy target appeared in the form of a slow-moving minke whale who for a few weeks became a regular visitor to the channel and often came up close to the shore. The harpoonists named her Minnie and left her alone. To kill time, Sam spent hours carving whales all over the sandstone cliffs. They must look like proper archaeological artifacts by now.

As time dragged on, the team got smaller and smaller. The *Chilco Post* had to go back on patrol; luckily, a local fishing company donated the thirty-five-foot *Corsair*. Ron Sparrow left to go halibut fishing in the Bering Sea and was replaced by our old friend Joe Bauer. The scientists went back to their jobs at the provincial museum, the university or the fisheries biological station. Finally, only Sam Burich and Joe Bauer remained at East Point.

Then came July 16. I was in my office at the aquarium when a radio-telegram arrived in the late morning saying the two men were struggling with a whale and desperately needed help.

Bob McLaren put a Department of Fisheries seaplane at my disposal and flew with me out of Vancouver harbour late in the afternoon. As we descended towards the Tumbo Channel we spotted the *Corsair* and headed towards it. Suddenly the killer whale, very much alive, rose alongside the boat. We taxied up to the boat with some anxiety as the whale roamed in different directions at the end of a six-hundred-foot line; we were not sure whether it would attack our small float plane.

Pat McGeer had managed to get there before me and he was standing on the fishing boat's deck with Joe and Sam, who briefly told me the story. A pod of killer whales had appeared, and one had moved close enough that Sam had taken a bead and fired the harpoon gun. At first, he thought he had missed his target. Cursing his luck, he started retrieving the line when Joe, who was standing behind him on the bluff, yelled at him to drop it before he got hurt—there was a whale on the line! The whale appeared to be stunned, and two others from the pod came to its aid, assisting it to the surface to breathe. (This is characteristic of many cetaceans, who tend to look after each other.) The men rushed to the *Corsair* and sped out to the whale, which by then was struggling vigorously and continued to do so for almost three hours.

Luckily it had quieted down by the time I arrived. As far as we could see, the harpoon had passed through the blubber in front of the whale's dorsal fin and the whale was relatively uninjured. I wavered over what to do. Put it out of its misery? It didn't seem very miserable. Sam and Joe were clearly growing attached to the whale and had no interest in becoming its executioners. Let it go, after all that effort and expense? I didn't relish explaining that one to the board or to the public. In the end, Pat McGeer's scientific enthusiasm carried the debate. He had looked forward to examining a whale's brain, he said, but think how much more could be learned with a live whale to observe instead of a dead one! Why, we could do electrocardiograms and electroencephalograms and bring in hydrophones and. . . . Our two harpoonists stoutly volunteered to sail the *Corsair* to Vancouver with their whale in tow.

I was more than sold on the scientific value of keeping the whale. But what in heaven's name, I asked, would we do with it once we got to Vancouver? McGeer came up with an answer to that one, too: why not see if Burrard Drydock would provide a temporary home for the whale? That led to my appeal to David Wallace, and with his agreement I had some breathing room to figure out what to do next.

As dusk began to fall on the narrow channel, I flew back aboard the seaplane to Vancouver. I spent the flight pondering my options. I was both anxious and exhilarated. I knew that this wonderful adventure would capture the imagination of the world as surely as it had captured that of our small group at East Point. Yet it was also fraught with danger, not only from the little-understood killer whale but from an even less understood animal: public opinion. My wife reminded me of that when I got home and told her what had happened. "Surely you're not going to bring that wounded whale back to Vancouver," she commented. Kathy was certain we would take some criticism for it. I added that to the list of possible problems but decided not to worry about it for the moment. There was no going back on this project now: I simply *had* to make it a success.

Our captive followed the *Corsair* like a dog on a leash throughout that night and the next morning. The weather was rough and neither Sam nor Joe slept during the night, but they didn't seem to care; the two were far more concerned about their whale than themselves. They timed its breathing as a way of monitoring its progress and even slowed down a few times when they thought it was tiring. By early afternoon they steamed into North Vancouver; I was there to greet them when they arrived and to watch the whale safely confined in a netted portion of a drydock. Exhausted as he was,

Sam was able to offer a wisecrack that was reported the next day in the papers: "*Now* can I have a free pass to the aquarium?" (I did better than that: I put him on the payroll as Moby Doll's feeder.)

Over the next few days Vancouver's attention was grabbed by front page headlines. As Kathy had predicted, there was immediate opposition to the capture, spearheaded by the local Humane Society leaders. In general, however, the public was fascinated by the captive killer whale. The story quickly spread beyond Vancouver to newspapers and television all over the world. Thinking the whale a female, we held a naming contest through the city's most popular radio station, and out of the hundreds of entries I chose the name Moby Doll.

In the meantime, our whale was getting medical care that most human patients would have envied. Pat McGeer quickly recruited a stellar team of scientific and medical colleagues to consult on the whale's health care program. The team included the UBC medical school's heads of clinical chemistry and bacteriology, and the heads of haematology and dermatology at St. Paul's Hospital. McGeer himself dropped everything to become the whale's personal physician. His first concern was to prevent the harpoon wound from getting infected. Using a hypodermic at the end of a ten-foot pole (because we were still afraid of the whale), he tried to give Moby Doll injections of antibiotics and liquid vitamins. Initially he had little success due to the toughness of her skin, but with ever larger hypodermics he finally succeeded in injecting her with 30 million units of penicillin and 2½ grams of vitamin B-1. Our main worry was that she refused to eat.

Once the harpoon had been cut off and the line removed, I invited the Humane Society representatives down to inspect the whale and her accommodations. The animal was now free to roam around her pen, which she did quite calmly. As I'd hoped, the Humane Society people were impressed by the medical team and the efforts we were making on the whale's behalf, and they made a public statement that they were satisfied with the conditions.

Moby was very vocal above the surface, with a range of squeals and whistles that we now know are common to killer whales. Underwater she was even better, as we found out when the navy donated some hydrophones so we could listen and record the sounds she made. I quickly got one of the recordings to the CBC, and within a few days Moby's vocalizing had been heard across Canada on the national radio network. Most interesting of all, we found that she occasionally "talked" with other killer whales who had apparently slipped into the harbour without anyone noticing.

The hoopla over Moby Doll pushed almost everything else out of my life in that first week. The media and the medical experts saw a great deal of the whale, but the general public had to rely on newspaper and radio reports.

That was frustrating to me; I was living and breathing this whale almost every hour of the day, and I wanted to share her. I made yet another request of David Wallace, and with his permission Burrard Drydock held a one-day open house for the public. Almost 20,000 people flocked to look at the killer whale and were deeply moved by the sight of this great animal. The public interest was broad and genuine.

Mindful of our imposition on Burrard Drydock, I scurried around trying to find a new home for the whale. Once again, connections from H. R. MacMillan and the *Marijean* provided the solution. Air Vice-Marshall Leigh Stevenson, with whom I had become friends on the *Marijean,* suggested we approach the military authorities about using their base at Jericho on Vancouver's English Bay. Somewhat doubtfully, I contacted the chief of staff of the B.C. area, Lt. Col. Bill Matthews, and was pleased when he immediately warmed to the idea that we might house Moby Doll in a pen at Jericho.

The Canadian military can move amazingly fast when it wants to. Within a day permission was granted to build a temporary enclosure adjoining the Jericho base's near-abandoned dock, even if that meant removing a number of its wooden pilings. The speed was largely due to Lt. Col. Matthews, an impressive-looking, big-voiced military man who displayed an amazing zest for the project. He was variously referred to by his men as Colonel Matthews, "Bull" Matthews or "Wild Bill" Matthews, depending upon the rank, circumstance or courage of the speaker. It turned out that Bill Matthews was a fun-lover and relished this new adventure. I suspect he was thoroughly bored by peacetime and enjoyed this bit of excitement. Matthews was quite happy to wreck the old dock and to scrounge all manner of construction materials for us.

Six divers and several officers came over from the naval base at Esquimalt to help with the construction, which was carried out in a mere eight days. The finished pen was seventy-five feet long and forty-five feet wide, and it varied in depth from ten to twenty-five feet as the tide rose and fell. It was no object of beauty, but I considered it beautiful enough—especially since it was constructed at little cost to the aquarium, with local companies and the military donating the construction materials and labour.

That left one major problem to solve: how to move Moby to her new home? Burrard Drydock and Jericho are about seven miles from each other at opposite sides of Vancouver's extensive harbour. Despite the whale's apparent docility we were still uncertain whether or not she might attack us, and she was no longer attached to a line. I fretted about this one for a few days until I spoke to David Wallace, who was wondering when he'd get his drydock back in operation. "That's not a problem at all," he said immediately.

"We'll simply haul the drydock across the harbour with the whale in it."
Poor David; not only was he losing $1000 a day (the normal charge for use
of the drydock) but his employees were so spellbound by their guest that
work was being disrupted. Still, he was a good sport about it and seemed as
fascinated as anyone else.

So, early one morning, the enormous drydock was pulled out into the
harbour by five tugs generously donated by Cates Towing, which for years
has done most of Vancouver's inner harbour towing. The navy provided an
escorting vessel, and the Harbour Police boats joined the parade and kept
sightseeing boats at bay. Our flotilla took four hours to sail the seven miles
from Burrard Drydock to the Jericho base. But then we had to wait another
four hours for the tide to rise high enough for the drydock's bow to nose its
way into the pen. On top of all this, once everything was in place, Moby
Doll refused to pass from the drydock into the pen. Sam and Vince Penfold
got into a skiff and tried to shepherd her forward, under the eyes of a noisy
crowd of VIPs, press, and military and aquarium personnel. To no avail. I
was at the end of my tether by this time and asked Matthews to clear
everyone not directly involved with the operation from the dock. This he
did in best military fashion by blasting everyone off with the pure force of
his voice.

It was another half hour before we forced Moby Doll into her new
home. It took a combination of Vince and Sam beating paddles on the
water, the siren from the police boat, and the raising of the drydock at the
far end to make her move. Once she was into her new quarters, David
Wallace quickly removed his drydock, probably fearing I'd find another
non-paying guest for it if he waited too long. He needn't have worried; I was
in no shape for anything else that day. I went home to bed, exhausted.

In the following days Moby Doll had callers from far and wide, some out
of scientific interest and others with more prosaic missions. As well as local
scientists, top marine scientists came from Harvard and Woods Hole. Ted
Griffin, the dynamic young owner-operator of the Seattle Aquarium, came
for a visit and swam in a wet suit along the perimeter of the dock to get the
best look he could at Moby. The biggest excitement came when Ken
Norris's successor at Marineland of the Pacific, David Brown, flew up from
Los Angeles to make us an offer of $20,000 for our whale. That touched off
a short bidding war: Victoria's Undersea Gardens announced it would
match Marineland's offer. David Brown coolly responded by saying that
Marineland would top *anyone's* offer, and he backed up the threat by raising
the ante to $25,000.

I was flattered at the attention of my peers, but I didn't want to sell.
Instead, I did my best to convince Vancouver of the desirability of giving

Moby Doll a permanent home where all could see her instead of this rotting dock. The city had various options, I told reporters in an interview, though each had its own difficulties. For about $200,000 we could expand the dolphin pond already under construction, but that would impinge upon the zoo's duck pond. Everyone knew that those blessed ducks were dear—nay, sacred—to the Park Board, so that might be difficult. On the other hand, we might try constructing something totally new somewhere on the shoreline of West Vancouver if we dared to think big. How much would "big" cost, the reporters asked? Oh, perhaps $500,000, I mused.

That was too big for mayor Bill Rathie, who addressed the whale question in City Council the following day. Why spend $500,000, our pragmatic mayor asked, when people who wanted to see killer whales had only to take a boat out into Georgia Strait? Mayor Rathie declared there was no question in his mind that we should sell while Marineland was still interested. He added, "If they can get $25,000 for only five days' work, I think the aquarium should maintain a permanent whale hunting expedition." The mayor's cash-register approach was attacked by a number of aquarium supporters as unbefitting the city's ambitions, both in council and in the letters pages of the daily newspapers. Having touched off the debate, I thought it wise to keep my head down and concentrate on other problems.

The main problem was that Moby Doll continued to fast. Concerned for her health, we netted and cautiously examined her. The team took a blood sample, and before letting his patient go Pat McGeer administered antibiotics, tranquillizers and vitamins. There was no obvious medical reason for her refusal to eat, so we began to wonder if the problem was the menu we were offering her. We tried a wide variety of fish, then fresh meat of many kinds and even poultry, but all were spurned. She may have eaten a fish or two while no one was watching, but it was hard to see in the brackish water.

What, we wondered, was the most tempting morsel we could offer her? I'd heard first-hand accounts from whalers who'd seen killer whales bite the tongues out of baleen whales. Anything seemed worth a try, so I phoned Western Canada Whaling Co. and soon received a gory package of blubber and whale tongue. Moby ignored it, just as she ignored a succulent (we hoped) octopus that Vince Penfold collected on a scuba dive especially for her.

Our failure was perplexing, because killer whales were known to feed on fish, octopus, seals, sea lions, porpoises and even large whales. What we didn't know at the time was that there are two very distinct populations of killer whales along the B.C. coast, residents and transients. The animals in the resident population prefer salmon, while the transients prefer warm-blooded prey. We only understood much later that Moby Doll was a resident and therefore a salmon-eating killer whale. Whale meat was probably as appetizing to her as a steak would be to a vegetarian.

Despite her refusal to eat, she seemed healthy both physically and mentally. After several weeks in our care she had perked up considerably, occasionally leaping out of the water in what seemed to be high spirits. She also developed something of a friendship with Sam, who spent hours at dockside trying to feed her. He took to whistling at her and found that she whistled back. Another helper taught her to turn over on her back so he could scratch her belly with a stiff broom. The press ate up every new story of Moby's activities and came back for more.

Our concerns about Moby's health returned when we discovered her skin was being affected by the water at Jericho, which has a high freshwater content from the nearby Fraser River. Her beautiful black-and-white coat was starting to sprout alarming patches of grey. Our team of medical experts agreed that the only way we could cure her fungus-infected skin was by moving her to saltier water. A new home was now not only desirable but essential, and I redoubled my efforts, lobbying anyone I thought could help us find a solution. My only bait was to invite people to visit Moby. This proved a pretty attractive offer: when you are the only person in the world who has a killer whale, you can pretty much call up whomever you want and be sure they'll accept your invitation to visit.

One of the most promising leads came from the West Vancouver Parks Board. Its chairman, Allan Williams, said he favoured a home for the whale in an abandoned fishery plant at Caulfeild or on the shore of Whytecliff Park. A careful lawyer who ten years later became the province's attorney general (and recently re-entered politics as a West Vancouver councillor), Williams told the press, "I personally think it would be a good thing for West Vancouver," but he added that all costs would be a matter for the Vancouver Aquarium Association. I wasted no time in inviting Williams down for a visit, never suspecting that he would become the first person to ever hand-feed a killer whale.

He came on September 9, almost two months after the whale's capture. The day before, Moby had eaten a fish that had been left on a line in the pen. One fish, and no more—it was very depressing. I casually asked Williams if he wanted to try feeding her, and while I was talking to some other visitors, he held out a lingcod suspended on a line. Miracle of miracles—she accepted it! Since she stayed by the dock with her mouth out of the water, Williams handed her another fish, which she daintily (for a killer whale) also swallowed. Then the greatest miracle: she ate the entire one hundred pounds of lingcod we had on hand at the dock.

Her fast was over. For the next month she ate about 120 pounds of grey cod, which we stuffed with vitamins and minerals, each day. We again tried out all kinds of food on her, discovering that she preferred fish to meat and soft-finned fish to spiny ones.

Despite the good news on the feeding front and the general good will in the community, it was proving impossible to get Moby Doll a home. For the moment, Stanley Park was clearly out; the duck pond could no more be moved from the west side of the aquarium than the Holy Sepulchre could be moved from Jerusalem. As well, the aquarium board was divided on the issue. Understandably, some of the more cautious members didn't like the idea of collecting large sums of money when there was no guarantee the whale would live for any great length of time. Even if the funds could be raised, we had no guarantee that an appropriate space would open up. The shores of West Vancouver were clearly the best place, but some residents got up petitions against our plans for a whale habitat. Nothing personal against Moby Doll herself, of course, but they objected strenuously to having their tranquil lives disturbed by what they saw as a noisy tourist attraction.

In any case, the question became academic on October 9. Her skin infection had been spreading, and she seemed to have lost the liveliness she had exhibited in the first months. On that awful day I was down at the dock for her feeding with Jean Southam, H.R.'s daughter. Moby ate her food, circled the pen slowly and submerged. We waited for her to come up, but she didn't. The minutes passed. I have never felt more helpless and forlorn in my life.

When it was clear she wasn't coming back up, everyone at the dock was devastated. It was hard to think clearly. At first I even kept the press at bay, refusing to let photographers into the dock area. After a few hours I came to my senses, but it still felt like inviting a pack of strangers into the front parlour after a death in the family. What were we going to do now? the reporters asked. With as much control as I had left, I replied that we intended to learn as much from her death as we had learned during the time she had been alive. Then I went home.

Two navy divers eventually dove to the bottom of the pen, found the body and secured a line around its flukes. A crane was brought in to haul it out, and it was at that moment that we finally knew: Moby Doll was actually a young male.

As the news got around, the whole city mourned. Moby Doll had touched the imagination of the entire community. The mysterious black-and-white stranger had gradually become familiar to average citizens. As well as changing public perceptions of killer whales in general, Moby had also revealed the species to have crowd-drawing potential far beyond those of dolphins and other small cetaceans.

We at the aquarium owed Moby a great deal. The whale had established us even more in the public mind as a local institution that dared to undertake exciting adventures. Over the next two years that good will helped greatly with the aquarium expansion. At the same time, the $25,000-dollar offer from Marineland signalled that this species' age of innocence was over. Aquariums and oceanariums all over the world wanted killer whales, and plans were afoot to capture them. Our experience with Moby Doll had allowed us to make great strides in understanding marine mammals, but at the same we had unwittingly opened the way to a new kind of commercialism.

My stock was very high in the closing months of 1964. The city named me Man of the Year and I spoke publicly as much as I could in those months, emphasizing that killer whales could be maintained in good condition in a Vancouver pool if the proper facilities could be provided. My international reputation had also risen steeply. When I went to Washington, D.C., in December for a meeting on the U.S. National Aquarium project, *National Geographic* invited me to write a piece about killer whales. We agreed that I would write an article about the next killer whale to be brought into an aquarium. As it turned out, however, Ted Griffin from Seattle would be the star of that story.

# 9
# Serious Men, Serious Women, Serious Money

I don't usually spend much time thinking about the past and wondering "what if." I am extremely happy with the way the Vancouver Aquarium has developed over the years and with the life it has let me lead. One of the proudest moments in my life was the opening of the expanded aquarium in March of 1967, and I always think back with pride and gratitude to the people who helped it happen. Yet remembering that event also brings back the memory of another, even more ambitious project that ultimately never saw the light of day, the U.S. National Aquarium in Washington. What would have happened, I wonder to myself, if I'd won the job of directing the National Aquarium? It was a big disappointment to me at the time, but not getting the job may have been the best thing after all.

The idea for a U.S. National Fisheries Center and Aquarium had been around for a long time and was finally authorized by Congress late in 1962.

The people behind the idea were thinking big: $10 million worth of aquarium, to be built in Washington, D.C., on the Potomac River and finished by 1967 or 1968. It had obtained the backing of John F. Kennedy, a strong supporter of science who, although most famous for his interest in space research, also recognized the importance of learning all we could about the oceans. The approval from Congress permitted the creation of a study team, and as someone who had started up an aquarium I was asked to join. It was an honour, and of course another opportunity to travel, so it took me about half a second to accept the invitation.

The year of 1964 found me in Washington several times for meetings of the study team. At that point, the momentum established by the late President Kennedy's interest was still in force, and the administration was still behind the project. An early meeting in April was chaired by no less than Dr. John C. Calhoun, science advisor to the secretary of the interior. The meeting was in the Commerce Department building on the Mall. Around the table were a lot of my Ichs and Herps buddies, including Earl Herald, the scholarly James Atz, "bad boys" Craig Phillips and Bill Kelley, and Sam Hinton, whom I'd last seen bowing to the prince and princess of Monaco.

During a break, F. G. Wood, Jr.—known to the profession as Woody—and I walked around the White House and then down to the Jefferson Memorial. The lagoon was surrounded by cherry trees in full blossom. As we walked, we chatted about the fact that some of our brother Ichs were moving around in interesting ways. Woody himself was a case in point: he had left Marine Studios in Florida to do research for the Navy Missile Site at Point Mugu, California. As the work was military, he couldn't give a lot of detail, but he was clearly very excited about it all and had been given a lot of resources and scope to look into the behaviour of dolphins and small whales. A decade later he wrote a book about the project called *Marine Mammals and Man*, in which he described projects such as training dolphins to help retrieve lost torpedoes. The research contributed a great deal of information about these animals' diving and navigational abilities. As we talked, a formation of Voodoo jet fighters flew overhead, as if to underline the presence of the military in scientific research. In fact, they were saluting General Douglas MacArthur, whose body was lying in state in the Capitol Building.

The first discussion at that study team meeting was budgetary. Through my work at the Vancouver Aquarium, I was getting used to dealing with tens and even hundreds of thousands of dollars, but this was something else again. Start with $10 million, we said: subtract something to pay for parking lots and surrounding grounds, and something more for architects' fees and other matters; now, how should the remaining funds be divided among exhibits, research facilities, administrative offices, theatre, dining areas and so forth?

Everyone knew how important the budgetary and administrative details were, but our real interest was new kinds of exhibits. Everyone agreed that the exhibits had to be outstanding, not just repetitive series of fish tanks. A concept took shape: at the beginning of the aquarium would be an "immersion sequence" to prepare and condition the visitor with appropriate sounds and images for the aquatic exhibits to come. After that, at least two of the major displays were to be thematic and sequential, like the new hall we were working on in Vancouver. One was given the working title of "The Living Stream," an exhibit that would follow the course of the Mississippi from its mountain headwaters to the Gulf of Mexico. The other was "The Shore to the Depths," which would present the changing marine environments as you go from the sea coast out into the Atlantic Ocean. And of course there had to be a huge whale tank, several smaller pools and galleries in which aquatic life could be systematically presented.

It was a terrific project, and whoever was appointed director would have a wonderful job ahead of him. I was interested, and I knew many of the other people at the table had hopes too. On my way to the airport I looked again at Washington, with its cherry trees and stately buildings, and wondered if I could be happy living and working there. The gracious, southern city was awfully tempting; Kathy had spent the war years there in the Women's Marine Corps and had spoken kindly of it. I had enjoyed visiting it during the war when my destroyer escort was in the Philadelphia shipyards for repair. I put my name into the hat to see what would happen.

Back in Vancouver I didn't have much time for daydreaming about other jobs, for things were popping on a number of fronts. The biggest single event was Moby Doll, who occupied the majority of my waking hours for four months. What was left over had to be divided between day-to-day administration and seeing to the aquarium's expansion. AEneas Bell-Irving was now the president of the association, and Bob McLaren had moved with his organizing skills and persuasive personality to the building committee. We had a vision now, a vision of the metamorphosis of our little aquarium into a magnificent, thematic living museum that would tell the story of British Columbia waters.

By January of the following year, the expansion was proceeding at full speed. The engineers David Leaney and Ted Maranda of D. W. Thomson Consultants Ltd. were in charge of designing the mechanical systems, and the job ahead of them was extremely complex. To begin with, we were making a number of customized additions to the four water systems inside the existing building. The alligators, crocodiles and other freshwater reptiles were getting gas-fired heaters to look after their supply of warm water, while the tropical freshwater fish were to be put on a separate recirculating system kept at a comfortable 75° F. Another series of tanks was set up to allow adjustable temperatures, depending on what type of residents moved in.

A warm saltwater system was planned for the bottlenose dolphins and the sea turtles. Since they required more filtration, the water in the dolphins' 24,000-gallon tank had to be changed every ninety minutes. A complete replacement would occur every week. The water for the tropical saltwater fish would pass through a sand filter and change every three hours; at the same time, new water would be constantly added to the recirculating system so that there would be a complete replacement once a month.

In the new addition, three main systems were to be put in: cool salt water for the outside porpoise pool, a separate cool saltwater system for the marine specimens, and a recirculating cool freshwater system for trout and salmon. Special systems had to be created for the labs, for the plankton feeders and for local reptiles and amphibians. And, of course, you couldn't forget freshwater systems for the most demanding specimens of all—human beings. All told, the expansion would require no less than twenty-eight different water systems.

Planning all this plumbing was fun; paying for it was less so. When the construction tenders came in it was clear that our original $750,000 budget had been optimistic—very optimistic. The lowest quote was just over a million dollars. A supreme fund-raising drive was in order, and we were extremely fortunate that exactly the right person for the job had just been introduced to the board by John Buchanan. The man was Ralph M. Shaw, destined to be one of the greatest presidents the aquarium has ever known.

Ralph was another benefit from our relationship with H. R. MacMillan, for he had, at sixty years old, just retired as vice-chairman and president of MacMillan Bloedel. Broad-shouldered and fit from exercise and his years in the forest industry, Ralph was (and remains) a gregarious character. He had a passion for excellence in any field and an astonishing array of friends: I was constantly surprised to find him in the company of up-and-coming artists and architects and some of the brighter lights in the legal profession. He brought with him not only world-class business skills, but a wide network of business associates, which aquarium fund-raising gave him an excuse to keep in touch with even after he was out of MacMillan Bloedel. His committee took aim at targets such as fishing, forestry and mining companies as well as downtown business corporations, and they mounted an astonishingly profit-able campaign.

Fund raising in the business community is an activity that I will forever associate with alcohol. Once the expansion campaign went into full swing I started to see a side of Vancouver that was new to me. About once a week, the fund-raising group would go to a private room in the Vancouver Club, one of the city's oldest bastions of business. This was the big time, and I felt flattered to be part of it. As we settled down to serious strategizing, out would come the liquor; ties would be loosened and jackets were slung over the backs of deep leather chairs.

"Okay," Shaw would say, "how about mining? We've only got $45,000 from them so far. . . ." The men would set their minds to who they knew, and how to get to people they didn't know, and what might be a realistic target for donations from that industry or group. John Simpson, the head of the great mining corporation Placer Development, was key to this process.

There was a peculiar rhythm to those sessions. Someone would talk for a little, and we'd all drink. Then someone else would say something, and we'd all drink. Or almost all of us: I tried my best to keep up, but after two drinks I couldn't drink any more, at least not without regretting it greatly. The others just kept going and, incredibly, got a lot of work done in the process. The fishing industry people—Ken Fraser, Ritchie Nelson, Jimmy Sinclair and John Buchanan—were all great fellows, big in the industry but quite varied in personality. H. R. MacMillan's son-in-law, John Lecky, was also a member of the group, giving us a direct pipeline to H.R. himself.

Back then there were few women in Vancouver who operated in the realm of money and power. Grace McCarthy was a notable exception, having joined our board and become a vice-president in the early 1960s. By and large, men planned and built and ran things; women taught and cared for people. As society has changed over the years so has the aquarium; we have been fortunate to have had many outstanding women both on staff and on the board, including four presidents.

But that was still some years ahead. In the early years, the greatest contribution by women to the aquarium was in volunteer and educational work. Typically for the times, married women often first came to us when their husbands became involved with the aquarium or when both took out memberships in the Aquarium Association. Joyce MacCrostie's long and valuable contribution to the aquarium began when she and her husband, Dr. Watson MacCrostie, took out memberships in the early days of the aquarium. For a while it was a toss-up for her whether she would volunteer for the aquarium or the Vancouver Art Gallery, where they were also members. Unluckily for the art gallery, she was "captured" by the aquarium's education program when we asked the Doctors' Wives Club to supply volunteers in 1962. Joyce's first job at the aquarium was guiding groups of schoolchildren, some seventy each day from various parts of the city. Soon after, she played an important role in our winning the 1962 plebiscite by getting the doctors' wives to distribute our brochures in medical offices throughout the city.

Joyce took a particular interest in opening the aquarium to disabled people, which led to our having ramps for wheelchairs long before it was standard practice. In the 1960s there were few public places that were willing or able to extend a hand to people with physical or mental disabilities. Wheelchairs and stretchers were difficult to accommodate in most buildings, and managers worried about public sensitivities, particularly to the presence of people whose disabilities were severe and visible. But from the beginning, the aquarium had welcomed group visits by chronic hospital patients. Our exhibits were classified as "recreational therapy" that thousands of mentally handicapped people were able to enjoy for years.

Another outstanding woman came to us when a well-known corporation lawyer named David Lawson joined the board of governors in 1962. His wife, Jane, was on the city's Junior League executive that year, and when I met her at a party I asked her if there was any possibility of the Junior League members giving guided tours at the aquarium. Jane was cagey: "They might if they are given a proper course," she replied. "They want to learn something; they don't want to just go in and serve soup." Soon after, I gave my first lecture on the aquarium specimens to fifteen Junior League members, who followed me around the place writing down the names of each fish. These young "society wives," as they were known in those days, were a smart and disciplined bunch. Both Jane and another Junior Leaguer named Mye Wright went on to become presidents of the aquarium.

The Junior League and groups like the Natural History Society were always good sources of volunteers. But we also got a lot of people, generally women, who had no particular affiliation, just an interest in community work or aquariums. Most male volunteers in those days were either students or pensioners; again, times have changed greatly, and as traditional roles have been turned on their heads and work schedules loosened up, the proportion of male volunteers has increased considerably.

Junior Leaguers or retired independents, we were glad to have them all. Those who volunteered as docents rapidly learned about the aquarium and its residents and became skilled at the ticklish business of keeping twenty or thirty children interested while making sure they learned something. They were so successful that the available time for visiting classes at the aquarium soon became full. Rather than stop and congratulate themselves, the volunteers and educational staff began an outreach program. The idea was to "take the seashore" to regular school classes, as well as to special groups like chronically ill children.

I frequently arrived at the aquarium in the morning to find a couple of docents carefully packing up a few animals and organizing the slides and posters they were taking out on their visits. Jane Lawson rusted out the back of her car with seawater and marine specimens that she splashed back and forth from the aquarium to the schools over the years. The highlight of these visits was always the presentation of live animals from the tide pools around Stanley Park. The kids loved picking up the starfish to examine their tubed feet, touching the sea urchins' sharp spines and feeling the soft-bodied sea cucumbers. Best of all was the chance to see a small octopus, even if it was only a preserved specimen in a bottle of formaldehyde.

All of this educational work increased Vancouver's appreciation of the aquarium and made the job of fund raising very much easier. Getting good press coverage is helpful, but actually touching families through their children is the best way to give yourself lasting public awareness. Ralph Shaw's committee was able to reap the benefits of this as it cast its nets widely in the city. I was amazed at their success in getting sponsorships for specific exhibits or facilities. Some came from high-profile sources already sympathetic to the aquarium, such as the *Province* newspaper's donation of new quarters for our reptile collection. But we also had generous contributions from less well-known groups such as the Japanese-Canadian Citizen's Association, which sponsored a beautifully designed jungle pool for our Mexican crocodiles. I very much doubt that such success would have been possible without the community awareness patiently created by the women volunteers.

By the end of the year, Ralph was able to report that a total of $242,000 had been collected in cash and pledges from corporations and individuals. The amazing thing was that he and his committee members were just warming up. "That was the advance gifts campaign," he told us at a board meeting. "Now we start the general campaign."

It was heady stuff, and it softened considerably my disappointment when I learned that I had not been selected for the job of director at the National Aquarium in Washington. The man who got the appointment was Warren Jensen Wisby, a professor of marine biology at the University of Miami in Florida. Wisby had an impressive background as a researcher, teacher and administrator and had even designed a laboratory building for his department in Miami. I knew him from the study team and was impressed by him—not that it made me feel any better.

As it turned out, however, the new aquarium was not to be. Because of its identification with President Kennedy, the National Aquarium was forever identified as a "Democratic project." According to Lou Garibaldi, the current director of the New York Aquarium, who laboured for a number of years on the project, the Republican administration killed the project; scuttlebutt had it that the funds were redirected to buy a couple of combat jets for Vietnam.

We moved into 1966 confident that the expanded Vancouver Aquarium would be completed in June of that year. As it happened, those hopes were dashed by two nasty labour disputes that had nothing to do with us.

The year began well. The first step of the expansion was to be the completion of the outdoor porpoise pool. This was a particular fund-raising coup, for the project was an expensive one and the sponsor was no less than the British Columbia Telephone Company. The planned pool was three times larger than any tank we'd ever had before. It would contain 125,000 gallons of salt water, circulated through diatomite filters every 135 minutes to keep it clean and clear. Visitors would view the pool from above the surface or through windows at a lower level reached by a ramp. By May, construction of the pool was almost finished and two dolphins that had been captured off the coast of California were waiting for us in a pool in Santa Monica.

Then came a city-wide strike by the glass workers' union that not only delayed the construction schedule but clobbered our admissions revenue. We had 10,000 fewer visitors that May than the 25,000 who had passed through our turnstiles during the same month the year before. It left us with a serious operating deficit, the first we'd had since we opened. It was also our first experience with protest "photo opportunities." The aquarium is a picturesque backdrop, and press photographers were far more likely to snap pictures of placard-wielding protesters in front of our entrance than on some nondescript city street.

The strike finished after a few weeks, but before we had time to recover a new one was upon us in June. This time it was a dispute between the municipal workers and the City. We weren't a municipally operated institution, but the park and the zoo were. The City and the Park Board actually made money during strikes because they did not pay their workers. We, on the other hand, lost money without compensating revenue. The striking workers picketed the park, and the construction unions working on the aquarium refused to cross the picket lines. Again, admissions plummeted. This was serious, because summer attendance is crucial to the aquarium. I had many a tense meeting with the finance committee and the accountant, for I couldn't lay off my hard-working employees or stop feeding the fish. At the same time, I was frequently on the phone to California. It was clear that we couldn't keep the white-sided dolphins waiting in Santa Barbara for very long, and indeed we lost our chance on one of them as time passed.

It was all getting to be too much. I'd been offered a much better paying job in New York a few months before and hadn't given it much thought. I was still smarting after not getting the National Aquarium, and in any case I really loved Vancouver and the aquarium here. But now I wondered if it was worth the stress. When I told a reporter friend that I was ready to quit, I was embarrassed when editorials appeared urging the City to take action in order not to lose me.

The strike finished on its own a few days later. I decided to stay, despite the ugly operating deficit we'd worked up and the arrival of a few more offers from other North American aquariums. I was still a U.S. citizen, and accepting the directorship of a major U.S. aquarium seemed like a natural thing to do. The only one that really would have tempted me, however, was the Shedd Aquarium in my hometown of Chicago, and that was never offered. Bill Braker had recently become its director and was doing far too good a job at the venerable institution for its board to even consider looking elsewhere.

In September our first dolphin arrived by air from California. Splasher was a six-foot-long Pacific white-sided (or striped) dolphin (*Lagenorhynchus obliquidens*) weighing 150 pounds. He was a striking animal with brilliant black, white and grey coloration. He was immediately given a training program by his keeper, Terry McLeod, and soon was performing for crowds of visitors. The dolphin feeding show took place four times a day during weekdays and six times a day on weekends and holidays. Splasher would leap twelve feet out of the water to take a fish from Terry's hand, do somersaults and hover half out of the water in a manoeuvre called tail-walking. He was spectacular, and the shows went over well with our visitors.

In December, two more white-sided dolphins arrived. Both were female, but for some reason Splasher didn't appreciate their presence in his pool. He finally selected one of them as his companion, and the other female tended to swim alone. The B.C. Tel Pool was officially opened two weeks after their arrival by the head of the phone company, Ernie Richardson, and his family. Splasher marked the occasion by eating his two companions' food and refusing to jump, but he soon returned to form. We owed him a lot, for he had drawn sufficient crowds during his short time with us to more than make up for the money lost during the strikes.

Splasher and his companions made a great deal of difference to our daily operations. For one thing, they ate a lot, each consuming approximately fifteen pounds of mackerel, herring and occasionally smelt a day. We carefully balanced their diet with added minerals and vitamins.

But, more important, they had a "cultural" effect on us. Dolphins are fascinating and terrifically attractive creatures, and everyone at the aquarium fell for these three, even those staff who had no direct contact with them. Any time something new happened in the dolphin pool—a crisis, the arrival of a new animal, a new type of behaviour—word would quickly get around and my office staff would magically disappear to see what was happening. I was right behind them, scurrying for the underwater windows.

It was a joyful moment when Splasher allowed aquarium staff to stroke and handle him freely for the first time. That happened about five months after he had taken up residence, the result of many patient hours of allowing Splasher to inspect the divers' hands and arms. It was the first sign of complete trust in his trainers. Within a few weeks Splasher became so affectionate that he would nibble on their fingers and roll on his back to be scratched.

Eventually Splasher entered a new phase—when he would not give the divers a moment's peace. He'd rub against them, nip them gently and even bunt them. These are all natural play actions of dolphins in the wild, but bunting can also be a weapon when used as a ramming manoeuvre against enemies such as sharks. After people got tired of getting bruised, they gave Splasher the message by firm vocal commands and the occasional gentle slap on the snout.

By February the construction was complete. The architect and engineers, interior designers and plumbing experts had done a magnificent job, but another task remained: we had one month to fill all the tanks with animals. It was a hectic time as specimens arrived from all over the world and existing residents tried out new quarters.

The alligators had a luxurious new home where the old aquarium entrance had been. It seemed not so long ago that the two animals had been a mere eighteen inches; now they were almost ten feet long. Their beautifully decorated new pool had been sponsored by the family of the late George Cunningham, the urbane and much admired alderman who for ten years was a member and chairman of the board of governors. Almost twenty feet long, the pool was maintained at a constant 82° F by a "package" hot water heater supported by a new filter. Now that the male alligator was an adult, he bellowed in rage each night when he heard the blast of Stanley Park's nine o'clock gun. He thought it was a competing male, not one of the city's most distinctive soundmarks.

Once again, my brother Ichs were exceedingly generous. Earl Herald sent us two spotted leopard sharks from the Steinhart in San Francisco. Don Wilkie, who by now was director of the T. Wayland Vaughan Aquarium in La Jolla, sent a representative collection of southern California fish and invertebrates. Vince Penfold and Gil Hewlett spearheaded our local collecting efforts, spending a great deal of time in boats or underwater in scuba gear. And the local divers and fisherfolk contributed a constant stream of specimens, from a sixty-pound lingcod to a box full of hairy crabs.

Just as it had eleven years before, it rained on March 15 when we opened the new wing. Nonetheless, the aquarium looked marvellous. Looking at its sparkling perfection, from the colourful galleries to the polished terrazzo

Carl Lietze (*right*), seen here with Fisheries Minister James Sinclair around 1956, was the driving force behind the plan to build the Vancouver Aquarium. *VANCOUVER SUN* PHOTO

My professor, Bill Hoar, shown here in 1990, leaned out the window one day in 1954 to ask me if I would like to go to Mexico—the next day. MURRAY NEWMAN PHOTO

We started as a small aquarium, nestled among the trees of Stanley Park.  Bill Hoar photo

What a difference a decade or so makes: the entrance of the aquarium in 1967 after our great expansion.

Bob McLaren's 1962 board of governors. *Front row, left to right*: Bob McLaren, Fraser Bruce, Grace McCarthy, Harry Duker, R. T. Jackson. *Middle row, left to right*: D. B. McGougan, K. Campbell, R. E. Walker, W. A. Clemens, F. R. Butler, E.V. Gray. *Back row, left to right*: AE. Bell Irving, D. E. Miller, R. E. Wootton, A. C. Peck, G. T. Cunningham, Murray Newman

Fish scientist Cas Lindsey lured me to British Columbia in 1953 with his yarns about salmonid research in the Cariboo region. T. G. Northcote photo

Smithsonian expert John Widener (*left*) and long-time aquarium volunteer Joe Bauer prepare a mould of the 12-foot manta ray caught during a cruise in Mexico on H. R. MacMillan's yacht, the *Marijean*, in 1962. BILL CUNNINGHAM/*VANCOUVER PROVINCE* PHOTO

Fisherman, conservationist and author Rod Haig-Brown (*left*) wrote the story and artist Rudy Kovach designed the exhibits for the new British Columbia galleries opened in 1967. MURRAY NEWMAN PHOTO

Don Wilkie nets Billy Wong's stingray in a 1961 expedition to Tomales Bay, California. Wilkie went on to become the director of the Scripps Institution's Stephen Birch Aquarium-Museum in California. MURRAY NEWMAN PHOTO

Diving near Gambier Island from our none-too-buoyant collecting boat, the *Aquarius*. MURRAY NEWMAN PHOTO

Dr. Pat McGeer administers penicillin to Moby Doll in 1964. The long hypodermic shows how much killer whales frightened everyone before Moby gave the world its first chance to know one. VINCE PENFOLD PHOTO

Lt. Col. Bill Matthews. A happy warrior, he roared with laughter when I told him that the Department of Defence was investigating the "irregular" use of military property to accommodate a killer whale.
P.V. THOMAS PHOTO

My wife, Kathy, seen here with a sunflower starfish, was our first volunteer docent.
MURRAY NEWMAN PHOTO

Jock Maclean, King of the Octopuses, during a collecting expedition.
MURRAY NEWMAN PHOTO

A basking shark harpooned off Vancouver Island in 1962. Murray Newman photo

The model of the basking shark now hangs from the ceiling of the aquarium.
Murray Newman photo

Earl Herald of the Steinhart Aquarium with a tank that was typical of his style as an aquarist.

Spencer Tinker, of the Waikiki Aquarium, helped us get started in 1956.

Folksinger and "fish guy" Sam Hinton of the T. Wayland Vaughan Aquarium in California, with his wife, Leslie, in 1960.

Joyce MacCrostie joined us as a volunteer in the 1960s and became president in 1981.
PHOTO COURTESY JOYCE MACCROSTIE

Werner Schroeder, the great director of the Berlin Aquarium, with a tiny friend.
PHOTO COURTESY BERLIN AQUARIUM

Ken Norris—aquarist, whale scientist and role model—and I examine a sperm whale tooth around 1958. DON TIMBRELL/*VANCOUVER SUN* PHOTO

Time to grow: the aquarium just before our great expansion under Ralph Shaw.

Schoolkids came by the thousands, just as Grace
McCarthy had said they would, after we distributed
"fish cards" throughout B.C. schools in the early 1960s.

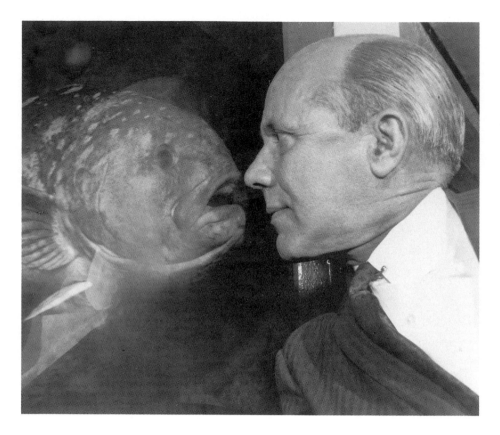

Aquarium president Ralph Shaw admiring Mister E., the skilfish, the aquarium's first media star, in 1967. GORDON SEDAWIE/*VANCOUVER PROVINCE* PHOTO

Skana being moved in a sling, shortly after we bought her from Ted Griffin in 1967.
MURRAY NEWMAN PHOTO

In the late 1960s, Ralph Shaw was worried about Skana's rapid growth in the B.C.Tel Pool.
MURRAY NEWMAN PHOTO

Future curator Gil Hewlett during Skana's medical examination. MURRAY NEWMAN PHOTO

Jane Lawson (van Roggen) distributing banners on the
occasion of the opening of the whale pool in 1971.
MURRAY NEWMAN PHOTO

"Prime Minister, I'd like you to meet Skana." Pierre Trudeau, Skana and trainer Klaus Michaelis at the opening of the new killer whale pool in 1971. PHOTOGRAPHER UNKNOWN

floors, none of the visitors knew that artists and aquarists had worked around the clock the day before to finish the job.

The B.C. Hall of Fishes was everything I'd hoped it would be. Its tanks were arranged sequentially, exhibiting the aquatic organisms found in the open North Pacific Ocean to the shores of Vancouver Island through the straits to the mainland and then into the various freshwater habitats of British Columbia. Sandstone and fibreglass had been used liberally to create realistic-looking habitats, and the famous author and conservationist Roderick Haig-Brown had written a narrative on the "Waters of British Columbia" that we presented on graphic panels. The Rufe Gibbs Hall led off from the B.C. Hall of Fishes and presented a comprehensive salmon and trout story. It had hatching troughs, nursery tanks and a beautiful simulated stream in which sockeye salmon were spawning a few months later. Rudy Kovach, the extremely creative designer introduced to us by the Hudson's Bay Company executive Aubrey Peck, designed a curved wall with a map showing the Fraser River Estuary and the transition area for migratory salmon. Artist Gladys Clawson designed an end wall to the Rufe Gibbs Hall showing the five species of Pacific salmon against a map of the North Pacific.

Out of sight but constituting more than half of the building were a series of spaces for special purposes. Across the back were laboratories with their own saltwater and freshwater systems for biological research. Next to the labs was a small library for staff and visiting scientists. Penetrating deeply into the building was a service entrance large enough for our collecting truck and complete with a receiving tank, water connections, food preparation room, walk-in freezer, storage rooms, holding tanks and connecting corridors to work spaces throughout the building.

Down in the basement, Chief Engineer Gerry Wanstall had a new glass-walled office. From his desk, he could survey his domain of power panels, pumps, filters, air conditioning equipment, air compressors and a jungle of other complex but beautifully organized machinery. The new education area had its own entrance and lobby with the Aldyen Hamber Student Laboratory on one side and the Fishermen's Union Aquatic Nature Centre on the other.

Ralph Shaw and his fund raisers had done us proud, having collected almost $650,000. The total bill for the expansion came to almost twice the $750,000 originally estimated for the job. Without a doubt, we had one of the finest aquariums in the world, both functionally and aesthetically. Yet within a few months it would be too small, and Ralph Shaw would be off and running to find new funds for us.

Moby Doll had just been a portent of the future. The whales were coming, and the aquarium would never be the same again.

# 10
# A Bouquet of Orcas

My first chance at a replacement for Moby Doll arrived on a June morning in 1965. I was up to my eyeballs in plans for new expansion when my secretary put through a phone call that made me drop everything else.

"This is Bob McGarvey," said a strong, confident voice. "Me and Bill Lechkobit got a couple of killer whales for sale up here in Namu. Twenty-five thousand dollars each. You want 'em?"

My first reaction was to silently curse Marineland and the highly publicized offer they'd made for Moby Doll the year before—it was obviously regarded now as the going price for a killer whale. But of course I wanted them. The question was, how inflexible were these men going to be about their price? And who was I going to be bidding against?

I quickly got the answer to both questions. A sterling example of the tough, independent fishermen who trawl or gillnet along the North Pacific coast, McGarvey was no pushover. He described the situation. Namu is one of the small cannery towns that dot the coast from Vancouver to Alaska. The two whales, a twenty-two-foot bull and a ten-foot calf, had wandered into a small bay with a narrow mouth. McGarvey and Lechkobit had put some nets across the mouth of the bay and were now putting in calls to Vancouver, Los Angeles, New York, California and Seattle—in short, to every aquarium known to have an interest in owning a killer whale. If no one came up with a suitable price, McGarvey told me, he and Lechkobit were prepared to cut their nets and let the orcas go free.

"Why don't I fly up to Namu right away and we'll talk about it," I said as soothingly as I could. A few rapid phone calls failed to turn up any major money. Still, I wasn't unduly worried. The main thing, I thought, was to get up there before any other aquarium did.

A friend from one of the local fishing companies generously offered a ride up to Namu in his company's plane, and on the 280-mile flight over the mountains, inlets and islands of coastal British Columbia I was charmed as always by the beauty of this wonderful province. Thinking our main problems would be the technical ones of transporting the whales south, I spent my time calculating what boats and equipment I should ask Bob McLaren to "borrow" from the Department of Fisheries and the fishing companies who had been so generous in the past.

When we arrived in the little fishing village, I strolled out on the dock to talk to the two fishermen, taking a bottle of whiskey out of my pack so we could share a congenial drink. The bearded McGarvey and the clean-shaven Lechkobit declined the drink. That was when I knew I was in trouble; these fellows definitely meant business. I was even more troubled when they took me out in their boat to look at the whales. They were magnificent specimens, but it seemed clear to me that the fragile nets wouldn't keep them in the bay if they were determined to escape. Although the larger whale was clearly too big for us, I thought it might be possible to accommodate the smaller one. But I had to work fast.

I flew back to Vancouver in time for a black tie banquet in the beautiful Bayshore Inn to honour H. R. MacMillan. H.R. had been very generous in the recent past so I didn't want to bother him again. I looked through the crowd for a likely donor and immediately spotted Leon Koerner. Excellent, I thought: the Koerner Foundation had put up some of the money for the Moby Doll expedition. I cornered him in the lobby and described the humiliation Vancouver would endure if the new killer whales went to Seattle or, worse, to California. He resisted my entreaties, as did the two or three other people I spoke to.

The next day I had to endure a stream of reports from Namu as the Seattle Aquarium's Ted Griffin and then the Marineland team arrived in the little cannery town. My fears about the security of the bay were confirmed when the smaller whale, the most desirable of the two from an aquarium's point of view, escaped. Marineland dropped out of the bidding at that point; they judged it unlikely that the remaining whale could be held long enough for proper transportation to be arranged.

That left Ted Griffin, who before leaving Seattle had managed to round up $8000 from the merchants of the Pier 56 area. I'm told he actually flew up with the bills in paper bags, along with a couple of bottles of Scotch. (I never did find out if the fishermen preferred his brand of Scotch to mine.)

Blond, wiry and quick of movement, Ted had been one of the first people to feed Moby Doll the year before. Unlike myself and my peer Ichs and Herps, he was an entrepreneur rather than a biologist, and he had developed the privately owned Seattle Aquarium with his own money and talent. At Namu he dove along the netting to examine the captive whales, then courageously entered the enclosure. He seemed to be entirely without fear of these potentially dangerous beasts.

I was very jealous of Ted's success in buying the whale, but I put the best public face on it I could. Besides congratulating him publicly, I sent him my newest staff member, biologist Gil Hewlett, to assist with transporting the whale to Seattle. The voyage down, with the whale in an enclosure Ted built himself and hauled behind a tugboat, was a two-week epic that included the convoy's being shadowed by a pod of orcas. On his arrival with his whale, now named Namu, Ted became the hero of Seattle. He got a huge amount of press and even wrote the article about killer whales for *National Geographic* that I had originally been commissioned to write.

I went down for a visit one day, and I arrived as Ted was being filmed by a crew from Metro Goldwyn Mayer headed by Ivan Tors, the man who directed the "Flipper" and "Seahunt" T.V. series. It was an amazing spectacle as the wet-suited Ted swam with Namu and rode on his back, holding the tall dorsal fin. It made me realize that a totally new perception was coming about, one that saw killer whales as large, friendly dolphins.

Ted was very much on a roll in those days. He soon started a company to collect killer whales for aquariums, operating with considerable success in the waters of Puget Sound. One of his first captives was Shamu, a small female that he sold to the Sea World oceanarium in San Diego. Shamu proved to be an amazingly quick study, learning to leap clear out of water on command, shake hands with her trainer and even allow the trainer to put his head into her open mouth. She became an instant hit with enormous drawing power.

It was too bad about losing out to Ted, but the expansion was in full swing and I was very busy. The aquarium now had a new president. Ralph Shaw's fund raising and general comportment as a board member had been so impressive that he was unanimously voted president when AEneas Bell-Irving died during his second year of office in the fall of 1966. AEneas had been much loved and his death was totally unexpected.

When Ralph took over, the aquarium entered a new era. Suddenly we seemed to have enough money to hire the staff we needed, to stop *worrying* about how to pay for everything and even to do things with a little style. With Ralph at the helm, anything seemed possible. So when Ted Griffin called in early March of 1967, offering to sell us one of the several killer whales he'd recently captured in Puget Sound, Bob McLaren and I immediately flew to Seattle to look at them.

Ted had captured an entire pod of fifteen whales, two of which had drowned in his nets. (Public reaction to the number of killer whale deaths in his expeditions was one of the things that eventually drove Ted out of business. But that was years away.) He planned to release the adults, which were too big for any existing aquarium. Of the remaining five, two had already been purchased by Sea World of San Diego, and he planned to keep two. That left one for us, if we were interested. The whales seemed in good health, although they weren't eating yet. I was confident that Ralph Shaw would favour the idea, so I asked about Ted's terms, told him I'd be in touch very soon and went back to Vancouver.

It was a terrible time for a heavy decision to be made, since we were only a week away from opening the new expansion and things were very hectic. Nonetheless, Ralph Shaw unhesitatingly called a special meeting of the board to consider the purchase. Ralph introduced the matter and gave me the floor. I argued that if we could get the money together, we would be able give the whale a good home in our new dolphin pool. Its 125,000 gallons were spacious compared to the quarters of many other captive orcas; in San Diego, for instance, Shamu the killer whale was quartered in a pool with a mere 80,000 gallons.

Moreover, the whale would actually be in Vancouver the following week: Ted Griffin was going to exhibit it at the boat show in the Pacific National Exhibition. We did not have to say definitely that we wanted the whale until the last day of the Boat Show. The asking price was $15,000 down and $1,000 per month for one year thereafter.

The discussion that followed was heated. Some of the board members felt strongly that it was too risky: they were being asked to commit a lot of money, yet who knew how long the whale would stay alive? And didn't we have enough on our plate with the new wing about to be opened? The debate went around the table until Bob McLaren moved that the board give its approval to go ahead and negotiate for the killer whale at a price of up to $27,000 and subject to an appraisal of its health. Pat McGeer, the brain researcher who had been Moby Doll's personal physician, seconded the motion. I held my breath as the vote was called: five to five. Once again, there was no hesitation from Ralph Shaw, who as president cast the sixth and deciding vote in favour. Ralph was always ready for adventure.

Walter the Whale arrived in Vancouver on the back of a flatbed truck resting in a carefully prepared supporting structure. The whale was lifted by crane into a temporary pool, thirty-five feet in diameter and eight feet deep, on the PNE grounds, where it lived in artificial seawater throughout the two weeks of the Boat Show. Ted drained the pool every other day, eased a hose into the whale's mouth and pumped a mixture of herring and fresh water into its stomach. Despite the small pool, the whale thrived. It began feeding on herring and lingcod offered to it at the pool's edge and squealed at the curious visitors.

Ted finally accepted our bid of $22,000. We would pay $5000 on delivery of the whale, another $5000 sixty days from the date of and $1000 per month for twelve months. If the whale died before the payments were completed, the payments would cease. He was easy to bargain with as he was pleased to find a home for the whale so convenient to the Boat Show. Besides, he had worked out his techniques and was confident that he could catch more whales.

On the day the Boat Show closed, we moved Splasher and the other two dolphins to the smaller dolphin pool within the H. R. MacMillan Tropical Gallery. Ted drove the whale to the aquarium, where it was lifted in a sling by a mobile crane and deposited gently into the B.C. Tel Pool. The whale was ours.

At first we were worried about the whale's skin, which appeared to be sloughing badly. Remembering the problems that Moby Doll had with fungus and lesions, our assistant engineer John Rawle volunteered to swim with the new whale and scrub its skin with a brush underwater. The whale seemed to like this very much.

Once again, Vancouver went whale-crazy, taking the new resident to its heart. Crowds lined up to see the whale, which closer examination revealed to be a female. "Walter" clearly wouldn't do any more, so we quickly held a name-the-whale contest and received an astonishing 5971 submissions: twenty-five two-column pages of single-spaced, typewritten names.

The winning submission, Skana, was proposed by the six-year-old son of a North Vancouver man who had a boat of that name. *S'quana* is the word for killer whale in the language of the Haida Indians who inhabit the Queen Charlotte Islands (which are today known by their traditional name of Haida Gwaii). A Haida name seemed especially appropriate, for the killer whale figures prominently in the totems and legends of these First Nations people.

Knowing that orcas are sociable animals, we decided to try putting Diana, one of our white-sided dolphins, in with Skana and brought her to the B.C. Tel Pool by stretcher from the 24,000-gallon tank in the H. R. MacMillan Tropical Gallery. With a great flip of her tail, Skana began to chase the dolphin around the pool, and we were afraid we would lose Diana. Vince Penfold tossed in some fish, however, and both animals settled down.

A few weeks later we decided that we'd better do a thorough examination of Skana. "Operation Whale-down" began with engineer Gerry Wanstall lowering the water in the pool. Skana quickly felt the change and began to swim around her pool, squealing excitedly. As the depth of the pool was reduced from twelve to four feet, Vince and Gil put on their wet suits and waded in to restrain the whale. We'd already seen Ted Griffin handling her like this, and we knew that cetaceans tend to stay quiet and passive if they are stranded or artificially grounded. True to form, Skana showed no aggressiveness towards the two men, despite the considerable mental stress the situation must have caused her. We placed a smooth plastic sheet beneath her and supported her head, flippers and flukes with foam pads. Another staff member kept her wet with spray from a garden hose. The dolphin Diana stayed comfortably in a stretcher while all this was going on.

At a nod from Vince, a team of medical specialists organized by Pat McGeer entered the pool and went to work. They took blood samples for analysis and gave her a vaccine injection. Opening her mouth with a hose they gave her an anti-roundworm medicine, for by now we knew that this parasite was common in cetaceans. McGeer and his colleagues were interested in recording a whale's heart rate and, using equipment especially designed for Skana, they took an electrocardiogram.

While all this work proceeded, we took complete measurements of the whale so that we would be able to follow her growth rate over time. Skana was truly a beautiful specimen, fourteen feet, five inches from nose to tail-fluke notch. Her dorsal fin was twenty-one inches high, her tale flukes forty-eight inches wide and her "waistline" (girth at the widest part of her body) was a svelte ten feet, seven inches.

Even before all of the work was finished, we started filling the pool again, and the animals began to float on the rising water. Vince and Gil stayed with Skana until there was enough depth for her to swim again. It seems incredible, but she behaved as if nothing had happened. She even ate a substantial supper of fish soon afterwards, always a good sign.

In the weeks that followed, Skana began to work with her keepers Terry McLeod and Doug Muir to learn a few tricks. One of the first was to roll over and extend her flipper upward for a firm, if wet, handshake. The most impressive trick was to leap out of the water and touch the end of a pole about eight feet above the surface. The splash from this manoeuvre was so tremendous that we were reluctant to train her to leap any higher. Sometimes, however, she leapt clear out of the water, from sheer exuberance it seemed to us.

In training Skana, Terry and Doug used the basic method that has been used with performing animals for decades. In essence, the trainer has to establish a goal and then begin working the animal towards it. Any action in the general direction of the goal is rewarded; once the idea is understood by the animal, the trainer narrows the goal until the desired goal is reached. The job is much easier if the animal naturally likes to do the activity, such as jumping in the case of orcas.

Skana quickly learned the meaning of the training whistle, which was to confirm that she had performed the required behaviours. Terry and Doug began by touching her nose with the rubber-tipped pole and rewarding her with a fish whenever she touched it by herself. She figured that one out quickly, so they moved to a more complicated task: they held the pole above the water in the middle of the pool but only gave her the fish if she came to get it by the feeding platform. It took a little longer, but again Skana figured it out. From there, the progression was quick as the pole was raised higher and higher above the water.

Once Skana realized that her trainers wanted her to jump, she joined in the game with enthusiasm and would launch herself clear of the water like a black-and-white missile. From there, she learned to retrieve a ball, vocalize above the water and even help push the feeding platform into a locked position at poolside. The tricks appeared to make her life more interesting, and we planned to keep adding to her repertoire to prevent her from getting bored.

On the other hand, sometimes Skana didn't feel like working. On those occasions, she communicated her annoyance by slapping her tail or flippers loudly and by spitting water—something an orca can do with some force if she wants. Younger whales generally like to work, but as they get older they get moodier.

The tricks fit in with the exhibition plans of the aquarium, but I also wanted the local scientific community to benefit from Skana's presence. A team of researchers from the aquarium and UBC carried out a detailed behavioral study of Skana, a project that involved observing her at set intervals around the clock. We also brought in some high-quality recording equipment to get her vocalizing on tape.

Our staff enjoyed diving with Skana. She clearly liked the companionship and happily let them hitch a free ride holding on to her dorsal fin from time to time. Her most endearing habit was "holding hands" with the divers, an activity she initiated herself by squeezing the diver's hand between her flipper and her body. Once she had a firm grip, she would swim slowly about the pool.

We clearly needed a separate space for training, observing and holding our animals for treatment when the necessity arose, and we made plans to build one. The new pool was fifty feet long and held 80,000 gallons of seawater. We built it at the northwest corner of the building behind a ten-foot-high fence to give the whales some privacy. Since this new pool was at a distance from the B.C. Tel Pool, it was necessary to move animals very carefully in stretchers carried by mobile cranes.

About this time, one of the most . . . perhaps I should say *vivid* characters ever to work in the aquarium arrived fresh from the Psychology Department at UCLA. The idea of inviting a psychologist to study the whale sprang from the fertile mind of Pat McGeer, who felt we had enough zoologists around the place and proposed that we involve other kinds of scientists. Pat had heard about a promising young New Zealand psychologist named Paul Spong who was studying the central nervous systems of primates, a subject that concerned Pat professionally. At the time, Spong was investigating epilepsy in apes, but Pat thought he might be persuaded to take an interest in whales.

The idea seemed a bit far out for us, since our interest was mainly natural history, but Pat was very persuasive. After some debate, the board of governors agreed to pay half of Dr. Spong's salary on a contract basis for two years, and Pat arranged for a contract at UBC to pay the rest. Spong's research objective, as the terms of his contract put it, was to investigate "problem-solving behaviour and intelligence in the porpoise and killer whale."

When he arrived in Vancouver, we discovered Paul Spong to be a slightly built, articulate man with a soft voice, a dry sense of humour and a deep interest in whales. It wasn't long before he'd decided that the aquarium and Skana were far more interesting than UBC and apes. And little wonder, for we provided him with a lab, a bright young assistant named Don White, expensive electronic equipment and what turned out to be a whole new life.

Since quite a lot of work had already been done on vocalization and acoustics in cetaceans, Paul said he would like to begin with a study of Skana's visual acuity. He would test her ability to differentiate between one and two lines. As the two parallel lines were brought closer and closer together, it would become harder and harder for the whale to tell whether there were two lines or only one. He and his assistant worked very hard on this problem and finally determined that Skana's vision, both above and below water, was about as good as a cat's vision in air. While a cat's acuity is only mediocre, the whale's ability to see equally well above and below the surface surprised them.

These experiments were taking place at a time when a great cultural revolution was occurring among the baby boomers, the generation born during and following World War II. The face of Vancouver had changed, seemingly overnight, with the arrival of thousands of young hippies. The flower children were everywhere you looked, camping in the parks and filling the streets. It was also the time of opposition to the Vietnam war, and many of these young people were Americans dodging the draft or protesting the war by coming to Canada.

This irresistible human force ran into an immovable object in the form of Vancouver's mayor Tom Campbell. Known as Tom Terrific (after the cartoon character) by his fans, Campbell disliked the hippies with a passion, and he tried all he could to get them off the city's streets, including some heavy-handed use of the police. He did nothing by half and was extremely direct, as I found out one night at a reception when he asked me to become director of the Vancouver Museum. "How much are you making?" he demanded without a trace of embarrassment. Somewhat taken aback, I told him. "Oh, we can give you a big raise," he declared, "much more than you make at the aquarium." I thanked him but declined the offer; Vancouver's museums were operated by the City and their professional staff were always in trouble.

There was a huge polarization going on in Vancouver, and while I pursued the aquarium's objectives among the political and financial elites, Paul Spong became more and more involved with the counterculture. Relaxing in the smoke and chemistry of the time, he let his hair and beard grow. Not for him the formality of suits, neckties and board meetings and the stultification of the older generation. He wore beads and a beret like that of Che Guevara, hero of the Cuban revolution. He also often used the high-tech stereo equipment supplied by the aquarium for acoustic research to play the increasingly revolutionary music of the times.

My staff were mostly a pretty clean-cut bunch of people, and they weren't sure what to make of Paul. He often worked late hours in the aquarium, and I sometimes got worried notes from the janitorial staff about his nocturnal activities. Still, his research seemed worthwhile during that first year, and an alternative lifestyle didn't seem anything to make a fuss about.

Admissions took another enormous leap upwards with the arrival of Skana, just as they had the year before when our first dolphin arrived. Orcas are wonderful animals, quite irresistible.

On a chilly February afternoon in 1968 a pod of killer whales entered Pender Harbour north of Vancouver and swam into Gunboat Bay. A local fisherman named Cecil Reid got in touch with Vince Penfold at the aquarium, who suggested they lay a seine net across the narrows to hold the whales until we could get there. A few hours later, a crestfallen Cecil phoned back: while the men were trying to stretch a net in the strong tidal current, they had had to watch all the whales escape—right under the boats.

Pender Harbour was an inlet with many islands, coves and small bays. Its mouth was fairly narrow and the waters within were quiet and protected, yet clean from the ever-changing effect of the powerful tides. Herring and anchovies lived there in great schools. These attracted salmon, and the salmon attracted fishermen and killer whales.

Around Pender Harbour were several communities, notably Madeira Park and Garden Bay. Local people travelled back and forth in small boats and even the children went to school by boat. It was, and is, a kind of British Columbian Venice where water and boats are more common than roads and cars.

In the late sixties Pender Harbour attracted many young American Vietnam war protesters who built crude huts in campsites on the shores and hills surrounding the area. These blended in with the abandoned Indian cedar shacks, bleached silver grey over the ages, on the islands in the harbour. At night, campfires ringed the waters and there was much music and conviviality.

A few days later, Cecil was back on the phone: the whales had returned, this time to Garden Bay, where Cecil and his crew set a seine across the mouth. Vince chartered a plane and took Paul Spong with him to see the whales. As they flew in through a rain shower, they could see the figure of a swimming whale within the concentric circles of two seine nets. Landing nearby, they found only one whale left in the bay. The rest had escaped. The remaining whale, about sixteen feet long, had not attempted to swim over the cork line that floated on the surface.

In the late afternoon a floating "herring pond" was towed to the site and placed inside the outer net. The herring pond was a sixty-six-foot square of four logs chained together, from which was suspended a herring web bag (essentially a large net) eighteen feet deep. As the preparations began, the whale circled close by, watching the men work. It would not voluntarily swim into the pond, despite the ton of succulent live herring placed there to tempt it. The team eventually "swept" the whale in with a short length of gill net; despite these actions, the orca remained remarkably calm, exhibiting no obvious fear or panic.

Later on Ralph Shaw and I arrived by seaplane and, after some amiable consultation with Cecil Reid and his friends, we agreed to purchase the animal for $5000 on the basis that the whale be maintained at Pender Harbour. We arranged for the animal to stay in the pen at a marina in Garden Bay.

The animal started to feed within the first two weeks of capture, the shortest period yet for a captive killer whale. It ate 130 pounds of herring each day, fortified by a cocktail of vitamin supplements. Six weeks after its capture, Terry McLeod started training it, and he found it to be very responsive.

Four months later, Cecil and his Pender Harbour friends captured seven more killer whales. The whales had entered Garden Bay, blowing and snorting, around 8:30 on a warm May evening. The fishermen had worked all night laying their nets across the bay, gradually encircling the animals in a smaller and smaller area. The pod included a fine bull about twenty feet long, four cows and two calves. A brisk bit of international business followed that left Cecil and his friends considerably richer.

First and best-equipped of the international customers was John Prescott, curator of Marineland of the Pacific, who arrived twenty-four hours later. After a couple of days of preparation, John went into action. With a nine-man crew of local fisherman and a twenty-six-ton crane, he took a mere ninety minutes to scoop two whales out of the water and into a semi-trailer. Within twelve hours the whales had flown to Los Angeles on a Flying Tiger cargo plane and were swimming in one of Marineland's big pools.

We are grateful to John, for he singlehandedly performed a rescue mission when he noticed that one of the calves hadn't come up for air. This occasionally happens to cetaceans; they seem to pass out in moments of stress and can drown. In Ken Norris's research on the death of dolphins in the purse nets of tuna boats, he found that many of them simply dropped to the bottom of the net without attempting to escape, thus drowning. John plunged into the water, managing to wake the baby up and bring it back to the surface. For the next forty-eight hours we harnessed a "scotchman" float to the little whale to keep him afloat; eventually he was given the name Hyak, and he became a star resident at the aquarium for the next twenty-three years.

In the next few days, three more whales went by air to various California aquariums. The Vancouver Aquarium purchased the large bull and the calf that John rescued. This meant we now had four killer whales, Skana and the three in Pender Harbour. It was a wonderful opportunity for research, and we decided to open a branch operation of the aquarium in Pender Harbour to carry it out. The main part of the new research station was a viewing platform, from which visitors could watch our staff work with the whales in a floating pen.

A few weeks after the naming, however, the largest whale elected for independence and found an opening in his enclosure. On the one hand, his escape was sad, as he was the largest marine mammal in captivity at the time, and it would have been fascinating to watch the social relationships between him and the other whales. On the other hand, there was some relief at not having to pay for the 250 pounds of herring he ate each day.

During the summer months, the station attracted as many as 1200 visitors a day. Three hours away from Vancouver by highway and ferry, it was a perfect day trip. The residents of Pender Harbour were very helpful with the project, and in return the local economy got a shot in the arm. Even more whales were caught by the fishermen and were sold to aquariums in Los Angeles, Niagara Falls, Japan and England. At that time we had no idea what the population of orcas on the B.C. coast actually numbered, but I began to get uneasy about it. If there were over a thousand orcas on the coast, as it was thought at the time, capturing ten or twenty calves didn't make a huge difference to the population. If the numbers were less, then the Pender Island fishermen might be creating a conservation problem, especially since Ted Griffin was also collecting further south in Puget Sound. It was only a few years before we knew more, and regulations were put in place both here and in the U.S.A.

I also had an administrative problem brewing. We were overreaching ourselves in trying to create a new research station and a new collection of whales while at the same time building a major aquarium in Vancouver and undertaking an expedition to the High Arctic. We were juggling many balls at the same time and it was only a matter of time before we had to put one down—or drop it.

Paul Spong was the scientist in charge at Pender Harbour, and he soon put his countercultural stamp on it. I retain a clear visual memory of flying into Pender Harbour one morning on a float plane to view the whales. As the plane swooped towards the water, I could see a young girl playing a flute as she sat on the edge of a fishing boat near the whales. The whales were clearly interested in all kinds of sounds, and Paul had taken to playing various kinds of recorded music to them and inviting musician friends to play to them live. The research area was often a scene of bells, gongs and exotic stringed instruments and of people who dressed like Paul. I was increasingly concerned about what was going on, not least because some of the instruments were ending up in the water where the whales might swallow them. On the other hand, Paul was getting towards the end of his contract, and I thought I could just wait him out.

Meanwhile, back at the aquarium, Skana was growing fast. She was now seventeen feet long and it was clear that she would soon be too big to be comfortable in the 125,000-gallon B.C. Tel Pool. The baby Hyak had been transferred to the aquarium's research pool, and he was also growing fast. At some point we hoped to bring the two of them together, but to do so bigger quarters were definitely needed. I proposed this to the board, and towards the end of 1968 they authorized me to get the architects working on plans for an additional pool. I wanted the new pool to be at least three times larger than the B.C. Tel Pool, which would get new residents: the belugas Bela and Lugosi, which had come to the aquarium shortly after Skana.

As all of this activity progressed, the eccentric behaviour of Paul Spong was causing increasing difficulty at the aquarium. He was by this time convinced that Skana was suffering from sensory deprivation, and he declared that such deprivation caused whales to become silent in aquariums. (This was clearly not the case, for Skana vocalized frequently.) His opinion was that Skana should be released and so should the Pender Harbour whales.

Soon after, the last of the Pender Harbour whales escaped from its pen. That didn't bother me greatly, as it happened; the research coming out of the place was minimal, and the whales were very expensive to feed. It was winter, and few people were making the trip up to see the whales, so the costs were not mitigated at all by admissions. We closed down the Pender Harbour Research Station with few regrets. Three Pender Harbour fishing families—the Reids, the Camerons and the Goldrups—had had a brief bonanza from the sale of whales. However, when killer whales ceased to enter Pender Harbour, the fishermen went back to their chief occupation, catching salmon.

The end of the Spong saga at the aquarium came in June of 1969. Paul had gone public with his opinion that Skana should be set free. That was his opinion, and I wasn't about to tell him he couldn't hold it. But neither was I going to renew his contract. We informed him of this, and I also gave orders to the staff that I didn't want Paul working directly with Skana or bringing his musician friends in with him either.

A few days later, there was Paul on the front page of the newspapers. He'd shown up at the aquarium's front doors with a stack of musical and electronic instruments, demanding entry so he could swim nude with Skana and play her more music. Paul held an impromptu press conference sitting cross-legged and shaggy-haired on a rug covered with countercultural para-phernalia. He announced he was going to set up an organization called LOOF (Legion of *Orcinus orca* Friends) and added, "Dr. Newman gets upset because he thinks his public image is being ruined. I've always liked Dr. Newman, but he's just a bit dull."

In the years that followed, Paul gave up his university connection and became one of the founders of Greenpeace. He moved to Hansen Island off Alert Bay and became an active spokesman for whale conservation. Smooth and articulate as ever, Paul continues to advocate the release of captive whales and gives an excellent "clip" to reporters who call him whenever they want something negative said about the Vancouver Aquarium.

# 11
# White Whales from the North

Killer whales are spectacular, but belugas (*Delphinapterus leucas*) are endearing. Their mouths are permanently curved into what looks like a smile, and their white, comical heads bob up and down at the people watching through the tank windows. The beluga's natural pace is a relaxed mosey; if there were flowers in the ocean, belugas would stop to smell them.

Belugas differ from killer whales in far more than colouring and temperament. They have no dorsal fins, and they are surprisingly supple and flexible. They can turn their heads and bend and twist their rather lumpy, fatty bodies in a way impossible for the streamlined, athletic killer whale. As well, their foreheads bulge into a "melon" that swells and changes shape in a strangely affecting way as the beluga examines something (actually, the melon is probably connected with their acoustic "sonar" rather than with their thinking processes).

In summer, these small white whales can be found along Canada's Arctic coast, in Hudson Bay, along the Siberian and Alaskan coasts in the Pacific and as far south as the mouth of the St. Lawrence River on the Atlantic Coast. When born, the calf is grey in colour, but as it matures it becomes snowy white. Belugas are five or six feet long at birth and grow to a length of about sixteen feet. They eat fish such as smelt and Arctic cod but also invertebrates such as shrimp and squid.

The history of human treatment of beluga whales is a bloody one, particularly in Hudson Bay. Prior to the arrival of the Europeans in the Churchill area, local Inuit hunters harpooned belugas to feed their families and their sled dogs, as did the native Cree people of the Nelson River area. As early as 1689, British whalers were in Hudson Bay. When a Hudson's Bay Company post was established in Churchill in 1717, whale oil was used to light the lamps in the buildings. The explorer Samuel Hearne reported that in some successful years eight to thirteen tons of beluga oil were sent back to Britain. Both British and American whalers operated in Hudson Bay from the 1800s up until the First World War. Towards the end of this period beluga hides were sold as well. The hides were laid out to rot, and when the outer skin sloughed off, they were cleaned, scraped and pegged out to dry, then shipped to England as commercial porpoise hides.

The old Hudson's Bay Company whaling operations were closed down in 1931. Wishing to stimulate employment among local people, the national Department of Fisheries took over the management of the beluga fishery in 1949. It set up the Adanac Whale and Fish Products Company in Churchill, where it constructed various buildings and put the word out that belugas were once again in demand. Local people paid one dollar each for a licence to hunt belugas. Throughout the 1950s they slaughtered 450 whales a year. In 1965 Churchill Whale Products Limited took over, selling its highest grade beluga oil for $15 a gallon. Lower grade oil, used for margarine, sold for ninety cents a gallon, and *muktuk*, the skin and outer layers, sold for ten cents a pound in fifty-pound bags. Efforts were made to produce higher-priced products such as canned meat, but the discovery of high levels of mercury in the flesh of the beluga made this impossible. Commercial whaling then declined, but the government, again concerned about local employment, encouraged "sport" hunting, in which outside hunters engaged local guides and the animals were killed with rifles. This activity was not very profitable and ultimately it was limited to local residents, who continue to shoot a certain number of animals for their own purposes under regulation by the federal government.

The first belugas collected by a modern aquarium were captured by Carleton Ray of the New York Aquarium in 1961. In August of that year, Carleton flew to Bristol Bay on Alaska's southwest coast. Working with a local fisherman he managed to capture two adult females and a male calf, which he flew 3700 miles to New York in a converted B-17 bomber. At first, the belugas would only eat live killifish, a great problem since the killifish were very small and the whales required hundreds of them a day. Finally, however, the animals adjusted to more easily obtainable food and survived very well in the various pools that were built for them on the aquarium grounds.

I had always found belugas among the most enjoyable animals on exhibit whenever I went to the New York Aquarium, and I was very interested in getting some for Vancouver. I had my hands full with Skana and the Pender Island whales in the fall of 1967 when I heard that a couple of belugas had been captured in Alaska. Did I want them? Of course I did, but with Skana in the B.C. Tel Pool we only had the thirty-five-foot dolphin tank in the MacMillan Tropical Gallery. That was a bit small for belugas, but if it was only temporary perhaps we should say yes. I talked it over with Ralph Shaw, who was already committed to creating more space for orcas, and he discussed it with the finance committee. They decided that in the scheme of the planned expansion the cost was minimal and the benefits would probably be great. Once again, as he did so many times during his years with the aquarium, Ralph told me, "Go ahead with it, Murray."

Next day, Vince Penfold, aquarist Bob Cant and I were flying northwest aboard a small, twin-engine Beechcraft bound for King Salmon, Alaska. Along with us was Alan Best, the curator of the Stanley Park Zoo. I was pleased to have Alan with me, for as an experienced animal collector he was wise about the care of wild animals in the field.

It was not until we were well on our way that I fully appreciated just how distant our destination was—as far west as Hawaii and just opposite Siberia, about 1800 miles from Vancouver. The air was beautifully clear as we flew up Georgia Strait and over Johnstone Strait. We soared past huge snow-covered mountains and over deep, narrow inlets, their shores forested with evergreens and their waters milky from melting glaciers. The city of Prince Rupert slid past on our right and then we entered American air space over the islands of the Alaska Panhandle.

After twelve hours in the air we flew over Cook Inlet and the Alaska

Peninsula, then landed at a large American Air Force base at King Salmon, near Naknek. To our surprise there was a motel, a restaurant and a fine general store, all very close to the plane. The light of the following morning revealed flat terrain with numerous potholes and scrubby vegetation, including small aspens with flaming yellow leaves. The temperature was about 50° F and very pleasant. Powerful jet fighter planes were landing, slowed by their drag chutes as they roared in, while others belched orange flames as they took off.

Our instructions were to go to the *Kathy Lee,* a thirty-two-foot fishing boat that we found tied to a jetty along the banks of a river near the air field. There in the boat's flooded, open hold were the ten-foot female beluga and a seven-and-a-half-foot male calf, which had been captured about a week earlier. It was a sad sight: the fishermen were inexperienced in the care of the animals and the belugas were in poor shape, moving very sluggishly in the green, putrid water. After examining them Vince said that they appeared to be free of disease but had been lacerated, probably by the roller at the stern of the boat as they were winched on board. I decided to buy them and to get them out of there as soon as possible.

While Vince injected the animals with penicillin and vitamins, Bob Cant took the gear out of the plane and began blowing up air mattresses to prepare a bed for the female on the floor of the plane, from which all the seats had been removed. The belugas were too big to be transported at the same time, so two flights would be required in our small aircraft. We decided that Vince and Bob would stay for a few days while Alan Best and I returned on the first flight with the female. Alan constructed a wooden frame from which the whale's sling could be suspended within the plane. Meanwhile, several sergeants from the United States Air Force arrived at the jetty with a mobile crane and a flatbed truck.

With the crane it was easy to fix a sling under the whale and lift her out of the hold. We drove her to the air field and, with great effort and the co-operation of fifteen or more airmen, she was eased into the plane through its double doors. With any captive animal, time is of the essence, so we immediately took off on our long, smelly return flight.

There are several major problems to consider when transporting cetaceans. One of the most serious is overheating. Whales regulate their body heat with a special system of blood vessels in the tail, pectoral fins and other areas of the body where there is little blubber. The system consists of shunts through which the animal can pass large amounts of blood if it requires cooling or, conversely, keep the blood away from these areas to keep warm. When the whale is out of water, a rise in temperature can easily be fatal, for air does not conduct heat away as fast as cold, moving water. Since our beluga was equipped to live in water that normally did not exceed 45° F, the pilot did not heat the plane's cabin which remained around 40° F throughout the flight.

A second problem is to support the whale in a relatively comfortable position while still giving it maximum freedom to breathe. With small whales a sling is a very satisfactory method, but with larger whales the pressure of the body mass against the sling is very great. Tilting the animal to one side in its sling takes pressure off the rib cage and allows the chest to expand relatively easily in at least one direction. In this position the animal can often be rocked in the sling, helping to relieve any discomfort.

The final problem relates to the skin. Whale skin is totally unlike anything else; it has the texture of neoprene rubber but is almost as brittle as a soft pencil eraser. Since water is too heavy to carry in even small amounts, you must try to simulate a water environment. An underliner is rigged under the sling and water is sprayed or sponged continuously over the skin. This procedure can be very tedious on a long trip, and the flight from Alaska was very long. The beluga took it remarkably well and did not struggle. All the way back to Vancouver she was very vocal, and her whistling and chortling seemed to us to be very hopeful signs.

After thirteen hours of flying into a head wind, the plane finally arrived in Vancouver at 5:00 A.M. on Saturday, September 16. A sleepy aquarium crew was waiting for us, and with the assistance of an Air Canada fork lift the whale was transferred to a truck. Back at the aquarium she was placed in the inside mammal pool.

Bob and Vince arrived with the second whale on Monday. As soon as the calf was placed near the edge of the pool, the two whales began a verbal barrage, with one vocalizing and the other answering immediately. As we gently lowered the calf into the pool, the cow became wildly excited, pushing the staff members away with her soft snout and rubbing the calf vigorously from snout to tail flukes. After giving him a complete rubdown, she buoyed all 340 pounds of him onto her snout and carefully swam with him around the pool. As Gil Hewlett commented, the sight was enough to raise a lump in everyone's throat.

Because the two whales had not eaten for approximately nine days, we force-fed them a diet of emulsified herring and water supplemented with vitamins. A long flexible rubber tube and pump were used to move the liquid from a bucket into their four-chambered stomachs. The cow received about ten pounds and the calf about one pound. This feeding went on for two days, and we kept them under round-the-clock observation. The calf attempted to nurse several times, but the cow did not seem to co-operate.

At the end of two days the animals continued to ignore all food presented to them, whether live or dead. It was time to take the initiative, and on Wednesday morning the water in the pool was lowered to about three feet. Gil Hewlett and another staff member entered in wet suits. One held the cow securely about the midriff with a flannel bed sheet while the other waved a fresh herring in front of her mouth. She would have nothing to do with it. Then Gil gently opened her mouth and rubbed the herring around—still no good. This continued for about an hour, during which time the cow shook her head violently and bucked. The whole thing seemed hopeless until the cow, annoyed at having the herring stuck in her mouth, forcibly blew it about six feet through the water. Someone noted, however, that immediately after blowing out, she sucked in vigorously. So Gil grasped the herring firmly when she forced water out and released it when she sucked in. The morsel sailed down her throat. Using this method they were able to feed her about eight pounds. Then, it was back to force-feeding her with up to forty pounds of vitamin-enriched food each day.

The baby beluga thrived in his new home, taking on 152 pounds by December. Whenever we fed the calf, the cow stayed right by his side or underneath him, continually caressing or nuzzling his entire body. Every so often she would grasp one of the feeder's legs with utmost care as if to say, "Be careful with my baby." She sometimes piggy-backed him for hours in the pool. She also seemed quite unafraid of divers and often rubbed against their smooth wet suits. The calf was also a gentle creature, although quite stubborn at times. One of his favourite tricks while we were feeding the cow was to nibble softly on the divers' boots.

When mother and baby animals are obtained it is usually the baby that is difficult to feed, but in this case it was the other way around. Finally, we discovered that the cow had a gum infection and an abscessed tooth. Realizing that we needed a professional veterinarian to help us with these valuable animals, we brought in Dr. Roberta Hartman. Though Dr. Hartman was a dog and cat veterinarian, she was undaunted by whales. The tooth was removed and the infection treated, but mama still refused to eat. The lack of food and liquid intake caused her to become dehydrated, so intravenous feedings administered through veins in the cow's flukes were begun on a daily basis. They included dextrose, saline and amino acids in proper proportions with her body fluids. These liquids were supplemented with antibiotics, minerals and multiple vitamins, including large doses of vitamins C and B12. At the end of a week of intravenous feedings the mother beluga began to take small amounts of food on her own, then increasing amounts until she was eating normally.

Now that we had killer whales, dolphins and belugas in our collection, it seemed appropriate to try to round it out with one of the least understood of the cetaceans, one that had never before been held by an aquarium: the narwhal. This small arctic whale is found mainly in Baffin Bay and contiguous waters. It is famous for the long slender tusk present only in adult males. In the Middle Ages this tusk was attributed to an imaginary animal known as the unicorn, and Queen Elizabeth 1 is reported to have considered a narwhal tusk to be one of her most cherished possessions. Actually, the horn is really the left incisor tusk of the narwhal and the only tooth present in the male. The female has no teeth at all. These small whales reach a maximum length of about fifteen feet, and the tusk extends another eight feet in a large male.

Our first narwhal expedition, mounted in August 1968, was mostly an exploratory project. No narwhal had ever been captured alive, and the board had authorised an expedition to Baffin Island to determine the possibility of acquiring several narwhals for Vancouver. Alan Best was again one of the group, along with Pat McGeer and David Lawson, then a vice-president of the aquarium board.

Our interest was stimulated by the work of the Fisheries Research Board out of their Sainte-Anne-de-Bellevue lab in Quebec. Again the government was interested in assisting the native people in capturing small whales, and sixty or so narwhals had been netted and autopsied for scientific analysis. We spent a week visiting likely spots around Pond Inlet on the north end of Baffin Island, camping out part of the time and seeing a lot of wildlife. Perhaps most important, we made some friends in Pond Inlet, then a village of about four hundred Inuit and seven or eight families of southern Canadians. One of the Inuit was a powerfully built man named Kyak, owner and skipper of the *Bylot,* a forty-foot Lunenburg fishing boat that was the largest permanent vessel in the Arctic. Because of the ice, it could only be operated for one month of the year. Kyak was a man greatly respected in the area, and he had been an RCMP special constable for twenty-six years. In 1967 Kyak received Canada's highest award, Companion of the Order of Canada, for his outstanding work in training young RCMP officers in northern survival. We also met the Panipakoocho brothers, Arreak and Ely, who became our guide and interpreter respectively, and another Inuk named Bunnee Katchok, a fine stone carver and artist.

With them, we visited a number of sites, the most beautiful of which was Koluktoo Bay, a sort of northern Shangri-la. Warm in the arctic summer sun, it was surrounded by beautiful mountains, green valleys and glacial-fed brooks. The waters were filled with narwhals, ringed seals and silvery Arctic char, all apparently feeding on the abundant crustaceans in the bay. Alan Best was delighted with the place, and he returned with a pair of beautiful snowy owls for the zoo.

I returned from the trip without any narwhals but with a much clearer idea of what it would take to capture some. Unfortunately, part of that clarity concerned the cost: it was going to be expensive, and the aquarium association's fund-raising efforts were almost entirely focussed on the new killer whale pool. I tried to organize an expedition for the summer of 1969 but couldn't get the money together. Nonetheless, I continued to talk about the project as much as I could, and one day I was rewarded by a phone call from Jim Graham.

Jim and his wife, Isabelle, had heard me speak about our narwhal trip at a meeting of the Commonwealth Society. Unlike almost everyone else in the room, they had actually seen narwhals close up. Incredibly, Jim and Isabelle had just recently unpacked their pup tent and packsacks after a four-thousand-mile trip that had taken in some of the most isolated settlements in the world, including the Indian village of Old Crow in the Yukon and the arctic settlements of Inuvik, Sachs Harbour, Resolute Bay and Arctic Bay. At their final stop in Pond Inlet they had seen narwhals and heard from local residents that the Vancouver Aquarium had been there the year before. When they returned to Vancouver, they decided to see if they could help the aquarium collect its narwhals.

Jim was a self-made man who had started work fresh out of high school in 1934, operating a tiny foundry with his father. Canny and extremely methodical, he had built the foundry into one of the city's largest by 1968, when he sold the business. He and Isabelle had only been married a few years when I met them, and they were clearly delighted with each other. Free of financial worries and with the energy and health to enjoy their new freedom, they were interested in seeing the world and in supporting projects that they liked. It has been the Vancouver Aquarium's good fortune that they have liked us since they first came into our lives in 1969.

With the basic financing assured by the Grahams, my staff and I began detailed planning for the trip. Our objective was to capture five young narwhals and bring them back alive to the aquarium for study and exhibition. Since there would be no supplies for hundreds of miles, we had to take everything with us: nets, cradles, slings, inflatable boats, outboard motors, tents, camping equipment, food and other supplies. I sent word to Kyak, Bunnee and Ely in Pond Inlet and arranged for them and the *Bylot* to join us.

The team grew as the departure date approached. The members of the original expedition signed on, with Alan Best bringing along his biologist son, Robin, and a log salvager friend named Ed Lee. Ralph Shaw, the aquarium president, came along with his son, Ralph Jr. (known to everyone as Ralphie), as did one of the youngest members of the aquarium staff, Chris Angus. Everyone was assigned a job, including the Grahams, who were put in charge of radio communication along with David Lawson.

We came in two waves, the first arriving from Resolute Bay on August 1. Our base was Baffinland Iron Camp, chosen because it had an airstrip that we remembered from the previous expedition. Perhaps "airstrip" is dignifying it somewhat; it was relatively flat, free of boulders and long enough for a sizeable aircraft to land on.

During the first week a thirty-knot wind blew each day out of the north and the water was too rough for much travel. On August 8, when the second group came in on a Twin Otter, some of us boarded the plane to fly over to the village of Pond Inlet. During the flight we made a sweep over Koluktoo Bay. It was as starkly beautiful as ever, and even from the air we could see that it was rich in marine life. We counted about three hundred narwhals swimming in small groups around the drifting ice.

We established a second camp at Koluktoo Bay on the following day, just in time for the arrival of the *Bylot*. The camp began to resemble a small village; along with Kyak and Bunnee Katchok, the boat was carrying Kyak's eighteen-year-old son, the twelve- and nine-year-old sons of our pilot, and two more Pond Inlet men. This new camp was made up of two cabin tents, several small tents, a toilet tent and a bath tent. Our cooking facilities consisted of Coleman stoves set up outside in the open air. A stream running through the camp served as a source of drinking water.

Setting our nets was the first order of collecting business. They were 150 feet long and 30 feet deep, with a mesh of 18 inches. Earlier whale studies indicated that a mesh of this size would reduce the whales' ability to detect a net with echolocation (their natural sonar). We anchored the end of each net out in the water with rocks and tied the other end to the shore. Once the nets were set, someone watched them at all times so we could remove animals before they were hurt. The twenty-four-hour watch was also necessary to protect the nets from the drifting ice pans and icebergs, which weighed anywhere from one to a thousand tons. The constant dragging in and resetting of the nets proved to be a tiring chore. At least visibility wasn't a big problem, for the season of the celebrated midnight sun was upon us.

Although about five hundred narwhals must have swum past the camp in the first few days, it took a week before we made a capture. A sixteen-foot male with a six-foot tusk became entangled in a net. The catch was exciting, but with a weight of four thousand pounds the whale was too large for transportation to Vancouver. Robin, Chris and Ralphie untangled the narwhal, put harnesses on him and were able to guide him through the water fairly easily. The whale was not aggressive and he did not use his tusk as a weapon. The young men discovered that the narwhal seemed to enjoy having his back rubbed and became very passive when they rubbed his skin. We measured and photographed the animal, then released him.

Meanwhile, at Grise Fiord, far to the north on Ellesmere Island, a group of Inuit hunters had captured a young male narwhal. These Inuit normally shot whales for food, but Corporal Al Kirbyson of the RCMP had heard we were looking for narwhals and notified us that the Inuit collectors wanted to sell the whale they had caught. After a meeting in our camp, Jim Graham said he would buy it for the aquarium.

Chris and I made the three-hour flight to Grise Fiord to have a look at the nine-foot narwhal calf. Corporal Kirbyson had been taking good care of the whale, which was feeding on sculpins while tethered by his flukes to a three-hundred-foot line in the ocean. This animal, named Keelaluga, seemed in very good health and sported a four-inch tusk. I agreed to buy him from the Eskimo Co-op. Chris and I assembled the contraption he had brought with us, a metal frame on wheels that resembled a giant baby carriage. The young narwhal was eased onto a sling that was moved onto the carriage. The men of the village then helped us wheel the carriage up to the airstrip.

Chris and I flew to Resolute, where we and the narwhal hitched a ride on a huge military Hercules plane to Edmonton. After transferring the narwhal to a chartered DC-6 propeller plane, we headed out over the Rockies, flying as low as possible so that the narwhal would not be hurt by the low pressure at higher altitudes. Packed in ice and sprayed with water, the whale weathered the flight well. On our arrival in Vancouver we were greeted with flashing cameras and crowds of reporters. It was all front page news, and we were even featured in *Time* magazine. We were heros—but the real heroism was taking place three thousand miles to the northeast in Koluktoo Bay.

The group had netted two adult female narwhals and three calves, a good start (we hoped) for a breeding colony, since we now had the male from Grise Fiord. Once it had been decided to take the animals the crew moved with all possible haste. They simply abandoned the camp, leaving tents, inflatables, outboard motors and other equipment for the local people. (This became the basis of the sportfishing camp that the co-op established in following years.) If the animals were to survive, it was imperative that they reach Vancouver in the shortest possible length of time. With a great deal of effort and two sleepless nights, the group transported the narwhals twenty miles down Milne Inlet to the shore near the airstrip. Their labours far from over, they then had to cover a half mile of soft sandy beach to the airstrip.

An old Bristol Freighter aircraft arrived the next day to take the team out. It took fourteen hours to load the plane. The team worked extraordinarily hard, neglecting their own health in order to see to the needs of the animals.

Then began the twenty-hour flight to Vancouver in a plane almost totally stripped down inside, with no seats and no insulation from noise or cold. During the long journey, the job of checking respiration rates of the whales was taken up by Isabelle Graham. With killer whales, breathing in transit is considered normal down to one breath every thirty seconds; the adult narwhals breathed about once every twenty seconds. The calves breathed much faster, and the intervals seemed to relate to their size; the largest calf breathed every six to ten seconds, and the smaller one never held its breath for longer than six seconds.

The team slept (or tried to sleep) in relays, with those who were awake spending most of their time watering the whales. After a stop in Yellowknife, where they picked up 1600 pounds of ice for the last half of the journey, the plane was so overloaded that the new pilot and his ground agent threw out much of the gear. It took some pleading even for the aquarium personnel to be allowed back on the airplane.

On arrival at Vancouver more than half the party went to the aquarium to help in any way they could, although they were too tired to be very functional. They watched as each narwhal passed by the aquarium's veterinarian, who administered antibiotics and took blood samples. None of the narwhals showed any symptoms of having gotten cramps in the sling, a common aftereffect of sling transport. Dr. Roberta Hartman devoted her total attention to the animals while Pat McGeer organized a council of medical volunteers to assist.

Despite the great efforts of our veterinarian, medical consultants and staff, the three calves soon died of pneumonia. We suspected the warmer water in Vancouver was an underlying cause of death, although our arctic belugas were doing fine under the same conditions, but cooler water was not obtainable. When it became obvious the babies were sick, an oxygen tent, antibiotics and steroids were administered in an attempt to save their lives.

The adult narwhals showed no symptoms of lung disease, but two months after capture the smaller cow died. Blood analysis indicated that death was due to bacterial infection. The larger cow died a couple of weeks later. Blood tests indicated infection there also.

Keelaluga, the last of the six narwhals obtained during the summer, died on December 26, 1970. He was a young male, nine feet, seven inches long, and weighed approximately 900 pounds. While in captivity, he had been active and healthy, eating about fifty pounds of fish a day. On autopsy, he was found to have an abscessed lung. His death came as a great surprise and shock to the aquarium staff.

It was evident that the problems of exhibiting narwhals were both medical and technical: we needed a refrigerated seawater system. We decided not to collect any more narwhals but continued to seek scientific information about them over the years.

In contrast with the delicate narwhals, our belugas, Bela and Lugosi, thrived in the aquarium. The recovery of the female was a tribute to the energies and skills of our veterinarians Roberta Hartman and Allan MacNeill. Once the female had her tooth and gum problems cured, she started eating up to forty pounds of herring daily, while the calf consumed fifteen pounds of herring plus whatever fish he managed to steal from the female. One day we were fascinated to see her undertake some "parental discipline" with the calf. It consisted of a rapid exhalation of bubbles accompanied by loud squealing and frequently quick nips on the side. The calf learned his lesson and kept a safe distance away at feeding times.

The calf rapidly developed a distinct personality and appeared to be a comedian at heart. He spent much of his time by the pool windows making faces at the people outside. The staff often commented that he seemed to be laughing at the strange creatures on the other side of the glass. His tremendous capacity for food earned him a nickname, "the Blimp." Bela remained fairly timid by comparison with the sociable Lugosi. However, both liked to be scratched or rubbed. The calf especially would roll over with a happy look on his face, allowing us to scratch his belly.

One of the most interesting things about the belugas was the amount and variety of sounds they were able to produce. The sounds could be deafening when not muffled by the water and ranged from a high-pitched squeal, which the cow used to scold the calf, to a series of rapid low-frequency clicks that were audible, even through the thick glass, as a buzzing sound. Frequently during feedings the calf would vocalize in a very disgusted manner if he decided he was not being fed quickly enough.

Although at first we believed the animals to be a young cow and her calf, we surmised later that they were probably siblings—a brother and sister pair—with approximately two years' difference in their ages. This conclusion was based on Arctic studies by scientists and detailed growth histories and observations of our animals. Our staff came to feel that Bela was not old enough to be Lugosi's mother.

Our success with the orcas and belugas created international recognition for the Vancouver Aquarium, although the loss of the narwhals was a great disappointment. It also raised my professional profile once again, netting me an attractive offer from Chicago's Brookfield Zoo. I was tempted, but Ralph Shaw organized a small get-together at his home to persuade me to stay, and included in the group was my professor Bill Hoar, our designer Rudy Kovach and my ever-supportive governor Bob McLaren. Kathy and I realized that we had become too attached to British Columbia and our good friends here to think about leaving. Not long afterwards, I became a Canadian citizen, as had Kathy a few years before.

# 12
# More Than a Fishbowl

An aquarium is something like an iceberg: most of it is hidden from view. While much of my job was spent in public activities, the steadiest source of satisfaction came from working "below the surface" with my staff and watching them and the volunteers carry out the thousands of tasks that keep an aquarium running. By the early 1970s we had a collection of people that almost rivalled our collection of animals for variety. Sometimes, when I tired of the paperwork on my desk or wanted to escape the telephone, I would recharge my batteries by taking a stroll through the aquarium to see what was going on.

If I started my walkabout in the morning, before the doors opened to regular visitors, I would often come across a five-foot monitor lizard named Dinny being taken for his morning constitutional on the floor of the Tropical Gallery by our reptile specialist Bob Marshall. In his mid-fifties at the time, Bob Marshall was a patient, friendly man. The old entrance area (now part of the Graham Amazon Gallery) had become a veritable apartment house for reptiles, a two-storey affair with many glass-fronted cases, most equipped with small swimming pools for their residents. The Women's Auxiliary became very involved with reptile maintenance as volunteers, so I would often find one of these women assisting Bob in opening the cases, helping the turtles and water monitors out onto the floor and taking them for a walk around the gallery.

Dinny was a major celebrity of the reptile section, and he got his name because of his resemblance to a dinosaur. He was actually a water monitor (*Varanus salvator*), a very impressive specimen with his long neck, strong jaws, whiplike tail and well-developed legs. In nature, the water monitor feeds on fish, crabs, frogs, birds, rats and even decaying meat, but Dinny received more refined fare in the aquarium: chicken heads, raw and boiled eggs, horse heart and vitamin supplements. He ate with great relish, not chewing like iguanas and other lizards but swallowing whole like a snake. Dinny had other snakelike characteristics as well, most notably a long forked tongue that he continuously flicked in and out. The monitor is the only lizard that uses its tongue the way snakes do, as a chemical receptor for tracking prey and general orientation. In spite of his formidable fighting equipment, Dinny became extremely tame and was easily handled.

Monitors are among the most active of reptiles, adapted to climb trees, swim and dig burrows. As they require exercise to maintain good condition, we decided he should have an opportunity to roam around. So every morning Bob strapped a small dog harness and leash around Dinny's front quarters and tethered him by a long cord in the reptile section. Dinny generally spent an hour observing all the other reptilian residents, checking particularly on the crocodiles and alligators. Later, he would climb back into his tank unescorted, submerging himself contentedly in the 80° F water after the coolness of the tiles on the gallery floor.

If I wandered by the aquarium kitchen on Wednesdays and weekends, I would generally find Bob Marshall there preparing luscious "salads" for his smaller reptiles—lettuce, celery, apples, grapes, tomatoes, cottage cheese, hard-boiled eggs and dog food.

Preparing food and feeding the animals is a never-ending job in an aquarium. I have a list from 1971 that details these totals for the previous year: 60 tons of herring; 2½ tons of whole lingcod; a ton of California jacksmelt; three tons of horse heart; 1000 pounds each of cooked shrimp and brine shrimp; two tons of local smelt; 1600 pounds of rockfish fillets, and 400 pounds of chicken heads. That was just the meat—there were also tons of vegetables, dog food, eggs, trout pellets and various other foods used to supplement animal diets.

The mammals' diets accounted for a large percentage of the herring and lingcod. At that time, Skana and Hyak ate 180 pounds of herring each day, or about 32 tons in a year. The two beluga whales ate 14 tons of herring a year; Diana, the Pacific white-sided dolphin, almost 3 tons, and the seals 7 tons. The remainder of the herring and lingcod was eaten by various fish and reptiles. The mammals also required supplementary vitamin pills—*Geviral-T* capsules (multiple vitamins), ascorbic acid tablets and vitamin B1, which we hid in the mouths of the herring.

The meat came to us frozen and was stored in our large freezers near the two truck entrances. Large amounts had to be thawed each week. At any given moment you might find two or three aquarists in the kitchen cutting up herring, shrimp and horse heart into pieces of different shapes and sizes corresponding to the sizes of the mouths to be fed.

Some of our more ferocious residents would cheerfully have eaten each other if we hadn't taken steps to prevent this. Take the five American crocodiles that we collected in a 1962 expedition to Mexico aboard the *Marijean*. In ten years they had grown from fourteen inches to the five feet, two inches of the largest, a male who was ironically known as Cuddles.

In July, one of the crocodiles died. An autopsy showed that the stomach contained $3.04 in pennies plus assorted items such as buttons, rocks, marbles and flash bulb cubes. This was the result of the public's using the pool as a wishing well or throwing things at the crocodiles to get them to move, a danger to animals in all zoos and aquariums. We suspected this massive bolus to have blocked passage of food and tried giving a purgative to one of the remaining crocodiles. A stool was passed, but no foreign material was eliminated and the animal still refused to eat.

At this point Dr. Roberta Hartman decided to X-ray the crocodiles. Gil and Bob Marshall tied the five-foot creatures' jaws together firmly with soft rope and took them by truck to the Cove Animal Clinic. Sure enough, the X-rays revealed a mass the size of a grapefruit in Cuddles and smaller masses in the others. It was decided that Cuddles should be operated on to remove the obstruction.

General anaesthetics are relatively ineffective on crocodilians. Because Cuddles was cold-blooded, we decided to use ice to decrease his metabolism to a minimum for the operation. The crocodile was slowly cooled down over a period of half a day, at the end of which he reacted only when his eyelid was touched. In Dr. Hartman's operating room, which rivalled any found in a hospital, Cuddles was strapped to the operating table on his back. Everyone present in the room wore a sterilized mask, and Dr. Hartman wore the green robe, cap, mask and gloves of a surgeon.

She began the operation with a vertical incision between the tough plates of the abdominal wall, followed by a cut through the stomach wall. Once through, she reached her gloved hand into the stomach and brought out a handful of pennies. Then another, and another, until over three pounds of pennies, flash bulbs, buttons, marbles and one expended rifle shell were extracted.

Once the stomach was emptied, an antibiotic tablet was dropped in and the wall was carefully sutured. Next came the most difficult step—the suturing of the hard outer skin. Dr. Hartman used a large curved needle and braided stainless steel wire, with buttons as anchors to pull the sutures tight (this also gave a very fashionable touch to the operation). She finished the job with a plastic spray to seal the incision.

More than one of those in attendance wondered at this point if the animal was still alive, but no one dared ask since everything had gone so well. There was absolutely no reaction from the crocodile as warm towels were placed around his heart and neck region. These were replaced every few minutes for a half an hour or so and still there was no reaction. Then—hooray!—an eyeball rotated. The patient was alive and Dr. Hartman was a hero.

Cuddles stayed at the hospital for several days and within a week began accepting food. In six weeks he was eating ravenously and frequently tried climbing the railing of his pool to get at the turtles in the adjoining pen.

Sometimes my wanderings in the aquarium took me to the basement, where Gerry Wanstall's engineering department had its nerve centre. Gerry had been part of the staff when the aquarium opened in 1956, and he had been a key participant in the 1967 expansion and the addition of the whale pool in 1971. In fact, there was nothing in the aquarium that he hadn't had a hand in building or maintaining. What *had* changed between 1956 and the early 1970s was the size of the department. In the beginning it was a one-man operation; now Gerry had three staff members to help him control the aquarium's millions of gallons of water, dozens of pumps, and complex arrangement of pipes, valves, water heaters and reservoirs.

Gerry's number two man at the time was John Rawle, who had started with us as a floor boy. After finishing school, he worked as an aquarist and reptile keeper before being transferred to engineering in 1967. Extremely handy at the cleaning of filters, the testing of water and the maintenance of equipment, John had another important qualification: he was a qualified first-aider. During the busy summer months he was often called upon to take care of a wide range of minor injuries, usually caused by fainting or falling. Some people claimed that looking at the fish with their noses close to the glass caused them to get dizzy and faint. Others fell on the concrete steps around the whale deck. We were always installing additional railings to try to minimize falling.

John was far from the only aquarium staffer who began as a floor boy. It was an excellent way for someone interested in the field to get some experience. There were not many of these positions open, and they were highly prized. We were besieged not only by high school students for a chance at one of these jobs but also by parents pleading on their offsprings' behalf.

Any time I went for one of my walks, I would be sure to come across a floor boy or two in their red shirts and white slacks, hard at work with a dustpan and broom. Their numbers increased in proportion to the increase in visitors as the busy summer months approached. Most were either in their final high school years or the early years of university. The prerequisites for the job were an interest in marine life, the ability to work with the public and cope with difficult situations, and a sense of humour.

We gave them no formal training since the jobs they are formally hired to do are quite basic. The floors had to be kept free of water, candy wrappers and popcorn, and tank glass free of condensation. There were also washrooms to be attended, light bulbs to be changed and potential accidents to be guarded against. These were staggering tasks on a busy, humid day when there could be over 1500 people in the aquarium at a time.

Security at night was always a concern, but we had a marvellous couple living in the caretaker suite from 1976 to 1989. Ernie and Eileen Neal were responsible for security during evening rental parties and then on through the night and early morning. Probably the worst intrusion they ever had to deal with was the late-night arrival of a deranged man who shattered a number of windows and trashed the gift shop before the police arrived.

In those days before feminism changed so many aspects of how we live and work, there were no floor girls, and conversely there were no male guides. The guides were an innovation begun in 1967 in response to our much enlarged building. We needed staff on the floor looking after the public and we were looking for ways to expand our educational role. We were concerned not only about teaching schoolchildren but about reaching the general public who came to visit. Lectures and special programs touched a relatively small number of people; we decided to try training some guides who could narrate the marine mammal presentation and talk to the public about the other exhibits.

We selected six UBC students. I started their training with some lectures, after which Vince Penfold and Gil Hewlett took them on a detailed tour of the aquarium. They also were given uniforms, with sailor collars and navy miniskirts and fishnet stockings. Though they looked great, the fishnet stockings became a bone of contention because the guides found them very uncomfortable. Still, the young women were good sports about it and wore the stockings for that first summer.

The guides were an instant success. There were usually three at work at any given time, each covering a different area. They delivered lectures, answered thousands of questions and operated the video cameras that B.C. Tel mounted over the B.C. Tel Pool so that people throughout the aquarium could watch the dolphins on video monitors. Some even swam with the dolphins.

Just as some of the floor boys continued in the aquarium business, so did some of the guides. One of these was a young biologist named Stefani Nerheim, who as Stefani Hewlett (she and Gil took a shine to each other and got married) rose to manager of public affairs in the aquarium. Energetic and articulate, she became famous for her public programs and her publications.

Occasionally aquarium staff became "parents" to orphaned animals. That happened to Gil and Stefani with the arrival of an orphan harbour seal who soon was given the name of Maggie.

Every year between June and August, the aquarium receives several young harbour seals. These are generally orphaned youngsters whose mothers either have been killed or have deserted them. Harbour seals are the most common seal in our area and are ubiquitous in northern seas. They tend to frequent sheltered coves and bays, and generation after generation will stay in the same area. The females start pupping around early summer in lagoons or protected bays. The pups, weighing about twenty pounds, are able to swim at birth and generally nurse in the water, the mother hauling the youngster below the water level at the first sign of danger.

Adult seals feed on herring, rockfish, salmon, groundfish and shellfish. For this reason they are often shot at by fishermen, both commercial and recreational, who feel the seals threaten their fishing success. By the time the little ones come to us they are generally emaciated and may be suffering from pneumonia or any number of ailments. Our success rate at keeping the orphans alive was very good, however, once we had settled on a feeding formula consisting of calcium caseinate, salmon oil, water, salt, glucose, cod liver oil and emulsified herring.

Maggie arrived in July, one week old and very thin at about fifteen pounds. She also appeared to have an ear infection. A fisherman had found her crying and helpless on a rock in North Vancouver where her mother had abandoned her (most likely because she was ill). Stefani insisted that she and Gil take Maggie home to insure round-the-clock care, and so the little seal joined the Hewletts' menagerie of a large adolescent Weimaraner dog and a little kitten. Gil confessed to being somewhat reluctant in the beginning, but the seal fit right in, began gaining weight rapidly and was soon following her "parents" around like a small dog. They began by feeding her every four hours during the day and once at night and gave her an oral penicillin to clear up the ear infection.

Within a week Maggie was exploring the back garden with energy and interest and excavating large holes in the flower beds. For hours she would scoop away at the earth with her mole-like front flippers, causing devastation among the Hewletts' petunias and marigolds. After about a month, Maggie was well enough to return to the aquarium. There she shared a pool with another seal about two weeks older than herself and thrived over many years.

If my walkabout through the aquarium happened around midmorning I would almost certainly have a chance to mingle with a couple of herds of schoolchildren, for by the early 1970s our education program played host to over 12,000 students a year. Two thirds of these were grade five students who came to view the aquarium displays; the rest were grade eleven biology students who came to use the Aldyen Hamber Student Laboratory. Looking after these kids were 140 volunteer docents who took a five-week preparation course in September and worked under the supervision of our education supervisor Sharon Proctor.

I heard about Sharon when I began to look for a new education supervisor in 1967. She was an outstanding biology student working towards her Ph.D. at Stanford University's Hopkin's Marine Station near Monterey. When I had a chance to interview her for the job, we talked for a while about feather boas—not the article of clothing but the marine plant, a kind of kelp (*Egregia menziesii*) that she was researching for her thesis.

Sharon talked of her research with eloquence and enthusiasm but indicated she wanted to work with people rather than scientific projects alone. I decided she'd fit in perfectly at the aquarium. And she did. Her twin focus on biological science and people created one of the best educational programs of any zoological institution that I knew about.

Watching Sharon and her team of docents in action was always a pick-me-up for me, so when I was feeling particularly martyred by my administrative duties I'd duck into the Aldyen Hamber laboratory to see what they were up to. I was very proud of this teaching lab featuring fifteen shallow pans and a small community tank with flowing salt water. Its focus is on local intertidal creatures such as starfish, sea urchins, sea anemones, hermit crabs and marine worms. We had conceived it as a hands-on teaching space. Sharon structured the handling so students would relate the "feel" of an animal to its environment and life along the shore.

Sharon argued in favour of having high-quality equipment in the lab, so we persuaded John Buchanan, who by then had retired as chairman of B.C. Packers, to raise the funds. For many of the kids, the most exciting part of the lab visit was the chance to use one of the Spencer-AO binocular research microscopes that we purchased with the funds that John raised.

I loved to watch the children peer through the scopes and see their faces change as a whole world suddenly opened up before their eyes. I knew that thrill well and still feel it when I see the surface of a sea urchin revealed as a busy jungle of fluted spines, with beaks on stalks opening and closing, and elastic tube feet (podia) extending out towards me. Under the microscope, a crab can be seen to have continuously moving appendages that send water currents over its gills; a featherlike marine invertebrate called a hydroid sports hundreds of tiny polyps that look like miniature sea anemones; the decorator crab is discovered to carry on its back a forest of tiny hydroids, algae, sponges and sea squirts. It is a fascinating experience to see these living forms up close, and the kids chattered excitedly as they made new discoveries.

Sharon had her own ideas about the experiences children should have in coming to the aquarium. She wanted the visit to be an exciting extension of school learning, and she designed her programs to illustrate with real life examples the things the children were learning in class. Sharon was always exploring new ways to capture the attention and imagination of our young visitors. One of the most successful was an education program called "Sharks!", which introduced grade four students to the study of these amazing creatures.

After watching the 1:00 P.M. killer whale show, the classes moved inside to our shark tank in the MacMillan Tropical Gallery, where they observed the lemon sharks and nurse sharks swimming ceaselessly in the tank. As they stared wide-eyed at the tank, a docent described the differences between sharks and bony fishes, the sharks' senses of smell and vision, their appetites, and the specific animals in the tank. At this point the class was divided into three groups, and the children sat in semicircles on the floor. Since we felt such a young age group needed "props" to touch and handle in order to hold their attention, we passed around shark jaws, shark skin ("Ooo, it's like sandpaper!" was the inevitable comment) and fossilized shark teeth. The *pièce de résistance* was always the "saw" of that strange-looking relative of the shark, the sawfish.

The programs got ever more ambitious. Sharon and her team created a whale study program for grades ten to twelve, that also began with the 1:00 P.M. killer whale show. The spectacle of Skana, Hyak and the dolphins performing their leaps and showing off their streamlined bodies gave the youngsters an appreciation of the magnificent grace of these animals before they settled down to some serious questions. The rest of the program took place in the underwater viewing area, often with Skana and Hyak peering curiously at the students through the windows.

The program covered anatomy, physiology and the different species of whales. Again, props were used as much as possible during breaks from the docents' lectures. Skulls of whales and terrestrial animals were there to be compared, but also samples of commercial whale products: sperm soap, ambergris (the base material of perfume), canned whale meat, jelly powder, fertilizer, blood powder (rich in nitrates), insulin and spermaceti (used in lighting and lubrication) were all displayed and set the stage for a discussion of whaling. Using a slide show, the docent reviewed whaling's bloody history, from the traditional methods of the Inuit and the Nootka Indians to the development of the harpoon gun.

The lecture then turned to the present day, when many species are threatened with extinction. Feedback from the students on whaling was animated, and they expressed concern about whaling and sympathy for the individual whales. Thousands of students went through this program over several years and were sensitized to the need for conservation of these great animals.

If it happened to be early afternoon on the second Wednesday of the month, I could always drop in on a meeting of the Women's Auxiliary. These volunteers amazed me with their energy, for they always had a number of projects on the go. The largest ongoing one was the education program, which they helped to organize and manage, but they also contributed funds to the

Junior Library, assisted in the production of the newsletter, enrolled new members into the aquarium association, booked visiting school classes, and guided disabled children and adults through the aquarium. For many years they even arranged fund-raising "Skana Parties" with fashion shows where models wore beautiful dresses in killer whale colours—black and white. All of this significantly assisted the financing of our education activities.

No matter where I decided to wander or what kind of mood I was in, I almost always looked in on the aquarists and the marine mammal staff. By this time, Billy Wong was the chief aquarist and the central figure in the daily operation of the aquarium, a sort of daytime operations manager of the entire upstairs building. As chief aquarist, he was directly responsible for the people who kept everything alive (except for the marine mammals). This complex task involved scheduling staff, ordering food, equipment and medical supplies, controlling maintenance and implementing security. It was the kind of work that never stopped. Since the aquarium is open every day of the year, Billy was always juggling things to try to meet staff and material needs from day to day. His office was in the food preparation room where, through the glass wall, he could keep his eye on everyone coming and going in the adjoining service area.

Billy's hard-working assistant chief aquarist was Andy Lamb, a biology graduate from the University of British Columbia. Andy was another of those who came to us in 1966 as a floor boy, and worked his way up. In the 1980s, he wrote an excellent book, *Coastal Fishes of the Pacific Northwest,* which was illustrated with the superb underwater photographs of another staffer, Philip Edgell.

In addition to his work as an aquarist, Andy was in charge of the aquarium's collecting operations. This meant going out to B.C. rivers, lakes and streams for freshwater specimens, as well as collecting marine animals using our twenty-eight-foot vessel *Nautichthys,* which replaced the unpredictable *Aquarius.* Andy and his colleagues kept the *Nautichthys* busy. In 1970 alone it sailed on eighteen expeditions in local waters, trawling, setting lines for sharks and diving.

I was always impressed with the way Billy and his colleagues handled the arrival of specimens from any major collecting expedition. In 1971, for instance, after our two beluga whales were moved outside to the B.C. Tel Pool from the old Fred Brown Pool, we decided to make their indoor tank into a tropical Caribbean display. I took an expedition to Florida to collect specimens, accompanied by Andy Lamb, a young aquarist named Tim Low, our governor Dave Lawson and Dave's friend Senator John Nichol.

Our group went to Grassy Key, about one hundred miles south of Miami, where Gerrit Klay operated a place he called the Shark-Quarium.

Gerry had developed a successful method of shipping sharks over long distances, and he had agreed to get us some lemon sharks (*Negaprion brevirostris*) and a nurse shark (*Ginglymostoma cirratum*). Tim Low worked closely with Gerry to learn as much as possible about his methods. Tim learned that Gerry's success in shipping these fish was to ride with them and occasionally "massage" them in their tanks to help their blood circulation in the cramped quarters. We did some collecting of our own by beach seining and diving, and we returned from our ten-day trip with many fine specimens.

Meanwhile, back in Vancouver, Billy Wong and the others were busy renovating the Fred Brown Pool for its new inhabitants. They installed new lighting, changed the water system and even added a rockery to give the smaller fish places in which to hide. With the renovations complete, they netted and quickly carried over most of the aquarium's existing Caribbean specimens, such as triggerfish, jacks and Nassau groupers. Moving our large brown jewfish (a kind of grouper) and two nurse sharks was more complicated; they had to be anaesthetized to make them easier to handle. As anticipated, the fish were soon comfortable in their new tank. The large spotted groupers spent most of their time among the rocks while the eleven silvery jacks moved in formation in the open water.

When we arrived from Florida with our specimens, most of the new fish stayed in holding tanks until it was clear that they were healthy. The new nurse shark and three lemon sharks were immediately placed in the pool and started feeding the following day. A few days later, however, Billy reported that our jack population had dropped to eight. After ten days only one remained, the largest of the original school. Luckily, the sharks had settled down by that time and the residents of the tank lived together "happily ever after." Or almost ever after; for some reason the queen triggerfish, a chunky little fish with a small mouth and big teeth, decided to start biting the sharks and the jewfish on the tail and had to be banished to another tank.

If I walked from the Tropical Gallery out the big glass doors on the aquarium's west side, I left Billy Wong's ichthyological empire and entered the domain of chief trainer Klaus Michaelis, who was responsible for the aquarium's marine mammals, from the three-ton Skana to the youngest harbour seal pups. Klaus had been born in Berlin, Germany, and from a young age had balanced an avid interest in plants and animals with an equally strong interest in music. He studied at the Berlin Conservatory of Music for several years and worked around circuses before coming to Canada in 1954.

When he joined the aquarium staff in 1967, Klaus had worked with everything from dogs to African lions in zoos and circuses. But he started with us as a tropical marine aquarist under Billy Wong. At the time, we were feeding the fish twice a week, and some of the tropical marine fish were not doing as well as they might have. Klaus insisted that they should be fed every day, perhaps even several times a day. After all, he argued, in nature, coral reef fish are continually nibbling over the surface of the substrate and darting up to feed on particles in the water. We started feeding more often, the fish did better, and I promoted Klaus to assistant chief aquarist. He became involved with feeding baby seals as they were brought into the aquarium and then began assisting with Skana. In 1970 he became our chief trainer, having developed a special relationship with Skana, who always performed best when Klaus was conducting the whale show.

Klaus believed it was important to build up a strong rapport with each animal, and whenever possible he assigned one person to each seal, sea lion or whale. This person could be a staff trainer or a volunteer docent; it didn't matter so long as the person took a direct and intimate interest in his or her assigned animal. The results of Klaus's training techniques were obvious. He trained the staff as well as the whales, and the thirteen years that Skana starred at the aquarium with Klaus as chief trainer may have been our best years.

Billy and Klaus and their staffs came from many different backgrounds, and this diversity brought a wide range of experience and skills into the aquarium. Through their efforts and those of the carefully supervised volunteers, the aquarium maintained one of the healthiest specimen collections and lowest mortality rates of any major aquarium in the world.

In this aspect of the aquarium as in most of the others, the help of volunteers was essential. I met new ones every time I visited a different part of the building. Two who stick very firmly in my mind from this period were the young women that Klaus put in charge of feeding Samson and Josie, our two Steller sea lion pups (*Eumetopias jubata*). The pups arrived in the summer of 1970, two days after being caught in the sea lion rookery on Triangle Island north of Vancouver Island.

The Steller sea lion is a massive animal named for Georg Steller, the German naturalist on the historic Bering expedition of 1741, and it is native to the coast of Alaska and British Columbia. Full grown, a male can weigh up to 2700 pounds. Females are considerably smaller at around 450 pounds.

When Samson and Josie arrived, however, they weighed only forty-nine and thirty-five pounds respectively. About three feet in length, they had thick brown fur and large eyes and flippers. Their outstanding characteristic was probably their cry, a deep-throated "aaahhk" that sounded like a cross between an after-dinner belch and the "baa" of a sheep. (I often wondered what Stanley Park visitors must have thought of the rude noises emanating from inside the aquarium fence.) We built them a special pen outside in the aquarium's research/training area, with a tank containing 1200 gallons of seawater for them to swim in.

From the time of their arrival, the pups were cared for by two university students named Kim Culler and Meg MacNeill (Meg was the daughter of our vet Allan MacNeill). Kim and Meg fed them during the first summer, mixing their special formula and spending many hours each day in the pen with them. In the wild, such babies nurse for at least nine months. The young animal doesn't "suckle"; rather, the mother squirts milk into its mouth. This means a young Steller can't easily be taught to suck from a bottle, so initially Samson and Josie were tube-fed on formula by their volunteer mothers. A tube was inserted into the stomach via the mouth, and while one person held the pup, the other pumped the food down. The formula consisted of herring, soybean-base formula for human babies, salmon oil (generously supplied by B.C. Packers), cod liver oil, calcium caseinate, salt tablets and various vitamin supplements. These ingredients were combined in an electric blender.

Tube-feeding is very traumatic for an animal like a sea lion. Aware that feeding should be the most satisfying experience in the day for a pup, Kim and Meg decided they would have to change methods if they were to establish any rapport with Samson and Josie. They had noted that after each feeding, Samson would suck on their fingers. Taking advantage of this, they began pouring the sticky, strong-smelling formula on their fingers, hoping that Sam would become accustomed to the taste of the formula. As they hoped, he eventually took a few ounces of food from a bottle. That was a success, but not a total one: since a mother sea lion's nipples barely protrude from the flat surface of her hide, the girls had to hold their fingers tightly around the nipple on the bottle to simulate the mother's body. It was very awkward.

Soon after Samson started bottle-sucking, Josie began fastening her mouth to his ear each time the bottle was produced, sucking vigorously. Again, Kim and Meg poured formula on the area being sucked (poor Samson!), and soon Josie too accepted the bottle.

At the end of the summer, Josie weighed fifty-eight pounds, while Samson tipped the scales at seventy-five pounds. Kim and Meg returned to school, but Kim continued to care for the pair on weekends. On weekdays, they were fed by the staff or by a team of docents who also spent many hours a day sitting with the babies, letting them "chew" on their fingers or rub against them—in other words, providing them with company.

Stellers are not often seen in zoos or aquariums both because they are so huge that they require enormous facilities and because their belligerent nature is not amenable to training. Moreover, in captivity, they must have human companionship in order to remain tame and responsive. Rain or shine, I could count on finding a docent or two outside by the pups' tank, feeding and playing with them throughout the winter. Each docent devoted one day a week to this work, and each was greeted by loud "baas" from both pups as she entered the research area to feed them.

In the wild, Steller sea lions nurse for nine months to a year and complete weaning takes about four months. At the aquarium, Samson and Josie were weaned at the age of about six months. Sam changed from his formula quite suddenly. One day he was feeding from a bottle; the next day he was happy to throw back whole herring—a fine Christmas gift for the staff and volunteers! Josie, however, was on the formula for another month.

Josie often blew into the bottle, sending a fine spray of formula over the docent and everything else around her. By this time the formula consisted of blenderized herring, salmon oil, warm water and various vitamin supplements. It was a smelly potion, and the hapless volunteer would carry around quite a fragrance after her day at the aquarium. Worse, if there were lumps in the formula or the formula was made a little too thick, Josie would simply refuse to swallow it. Instead, she would open her mouth and violently shake her head from side to side, sending the odoriferous mixture in every direction.

Once the pups were weaned, the job of the volunteers was over, and the docents turned to feeding other animals. Klaus and his staff took over the care of Sam and Josie, training them to emerge from the research area into the public view. Sam adapted to this very rapidly and each day would waddle alongside Klaus up to the stone wall behind the whale pool deck. There he would mount a box and show off his table manners for the spectators. Josie was less of a performer. She'd timidly poke her head from behind the fence and upon seeing the people hastily scuttle back out of sight.

After two years of loving care, Sam and Josie had grown into awesomely powerful animals. Sam weighed 900 pounds, and with his broad forehead and huge chest was assuming the characteristic appearance of a bull. Josie had reached 225 pounds, with more delicate features than Sam. They were growing to the point where it would be difficult to accommodate them any more, so after much searching we finally found a new home for them at the Mystic Marine Life Aquarium in Connecticut where Steve Spotte, the director, built them a large, new residence.

By walking down the hallway from my office across the back of the aquarium, I would cross yet another invisible boundary and enter the realm of the scientists. Research was always very strong at our aquarium, and it was overseen by a research committee headed for many years by the eminent oceanographer Dr. Michael Waldichuk.

In the early 1970s some of the most interesting work was being done by Dr. Allan MacNeill, who had become the aquarium veterinary consultant after Dr. Hartman returned to her dog and cat hospital. White-haired, friendly and congenitally skeptical, Al MacNeill was a government veterinarian with a full-time job in the agricultural laboratories where he worked in animal pathology. He spent his weekends at the aquarium emphasizing good hygiene, good record-keeping, quarantine of sick animals and excellent nutrition.

A visit to Allan in the lab usually resulted in an enthusiastic discussion about one or all of the projects he had going. One day it might be his observations on a new species of lungworm isolated in narwhals; another time it might be the haematology (the blood composition) of our small cetaceans, anaesthesia techniques for use on small reptiles, or his disease survey on fish mortalities in the aquarium. I could always find several students at work alongside the established scientists in the lab, too. They were usually from the zoology or biology departments at UBC.

At any time during the walk I might run into the lights, power cords and other gear of a camera crew, for the 1970s saw us get into television in a big way. We were used to television news crews for exhibit openings and other events, but whole programs or series were something else again. One of our first projects was a four-part series for CBC called "The Water World," which was filmed in the aquarium over a period of two months. The series contrasted two types of aquariums: the home tank and the Vancouver Aquarium. One of the best of these segments took the viewer behind the scenes with Billy Wong and his staff as they cleaned the tanks, removed sick fish and did some underwater gardening. While the television work was somewhat disruptive to the staff and the public, it provided an element of excitement that both groups enjoyed.

My greatest involvement with television came in 1973 when I hosted a CBC series called "Wonders of the Aquarium World" with Bob Switzer. The twenty-two programs were produced and broadcast by the local CBC affiliate CBUT, and they allowed me to present everything from collecting in the South Pacific to the mechanical operation of our building in Stanley Park. It was great fun for me and an opportunity to learn some new skills, including handling a movie camera.

Predictably, however, the aquarium's top television performer was Skana. I was completing the "Wonders" series when a Toronto advertising agency called to ask if they could use one of our killer whales for a Timex watch "Torture Test." These well-known television commercials featured a Timex water-resistant watch being put through severe and unusual punishment to illustrate its durability. The agency wanted to strap a watch to

Skana's tail and have her go through a series of exercises. Typical, I thought to myself: upstaged once again by a killer whale. Still, I readily agreed since the television exposure promised to be massive.

Skana seemed happy to co-operate, even with a large "watch band" on one of her flukes. Klaus and his staff spent two busy days with the television crew filming the commercial in the large whale pool. As a scientist with a great attachment to experimental validity, I was pleased to note that the ad was totally authentic, with no film editing or substitution of watches; the down side, of course, was that it took an endless number of retakes to get exactly the details desired for the sixty-second commercial. Still, Skana didn't seem to mind and Klaus took it in his stride. The finished commercial duly appeared on television screens all over the world. As for the watch, Klaus got to keep it and wore it till it died—two weeks after the filming.

Sometimes my walkabout came towards the end of the day, when I was about to go home. If I decided to leave the building through the front doors, the last people I'd see were the staff and volunteers in the Clamshell, our gift shop. The Clamshell was the brainchild of another great woman leader to emerge in the aquarium association, Mye Wright. Like Jane Lawson, Mye came to us from the Junior League and quickly took on more and more responsibility. After serving as president of the Women's Auxiliary, she joined the board of governors and became the first woman president of the aquarium association. Her death in the mid-seventies was a great and tragically premature loss.

Mye was like Ralph Shaw in her passion for excellence. Until she arrived on the scene, our shop was little more than a small souvenir counter offering tourist keepsakes and a few aquarium-related items. Mye argued fiercely that we should upgrade to a full-fledged store with high-quality merchandise. That meant a more expensive line of goods, and I worried both about the appropriateness of costly merchandise and the effect that higher prices might have on revenue. Mye eventually prevailed and brought in Joan Ballou, another quality-minded person from the Women's Auxiliary, to become the Clamshell's manager. They expanded the shop and achieved a seasonal balance: during the summer they emphasized souvenirs for tourists, while during the winter they went "up-market" with B.C. Indian crafts, Eskimo carvings and high-quality crafts by local artists and potters. The new formula was very successful, and the revenue became more and more important to the overall operation of the aquarium.

The Clamshell was partly a volunteer operation in winter, with the Women's Auxiliary helping with the selection of sales items and working in the store. The volunteers enjoyed working in the Clamshell because of the pleasant environment and good people there. In the high-volume summer, it was staffed entirely with paid workers.

After a word or two with the Clamshell ladies, I would walk out the doors towards the Stanley Park Zoo, then turn back for a final look. With its high, classically proportioned entrance hall, the aquarium was now an impressive sight, a quantum leap beyond the modest building we'd opened in 1956. Yet as I looked at it in those reflective moments, I didn't really see a building. The essence of the aquarium was not glass or concrete or cash registers but people: the staff, the board, the scientists and the many volunteers and members. It had always been that way at the Vancouver Aquarium, and I hope it always will be.

# 13
# Side Trip for a Coelacanth

Members' tours are one of the things I've enjoyed most during my time at the aquarium, but they have their stressful moments. I remember a tour member saying, "I feel a bit dizzy," while on a hike in Papua New Guinea some years ago. We happened to be wading knee-deep in a swamp near the Sepik River at the time, some hours upriver from the lodge where we were staying. It seemed the member, an enthusiastic fellow who had gone with us on a previous tour to the Arctic, had a pacemaker he'd neglected to tell me about.

As he started keeling over into the mud, I may have wondered briefly about the wisdom of taking some of the aquarium's most valued supporters (and Vancouver's most illustrious citizens) into quite so exotic a setting. Luckily the tour included my friend Dr. Aki Horii, who was wading right behind us. Even more luckily, when we got back to the lodge we discovered that it was host to a conference of heart specialists from New York. The member survived and has cheerfully gone on to new adventures since then.

The truth is that the aquarium owes a great deal of its success to members' tours, which are always led by staff members. A biologist might call it a perfect example of symbiosis. The members get wonderful and not overly expensive trips to unfamiliar places; the accompanying aquarium staff can familiarize themselves with new habitats and often do some collecting at very little cost, and also they have an opportunity to bond with supporters of the aquarium. I first started thinking seriously about members' tours during the late 1960s, after H.R. MacMillan sold his yacht, the *Marijean*.

Our expeditions were eco-tours long before the term was coined by the travel industry. The key was to provide an interesting experience to the members while not putting them into too much danger or discomfort, especially given the fact that many of them were older people.

On a Vancouver Aquarium tour to Uganda in November 1971, Jim and Isabelle Graham sponsored an impromptu side trip to the Comoro Islands to see if we could catch a coelacanth (pronounced "see-la-canth").

The 1971 tour was my first visit to Africa. The tour started in South Africa, with an itinerary that took us by plane, van and boat through Rhodesia, Zambia, Tanzania, Kenya and Uganda. A distinguished group of fifteen members had signed on. One was Phae Collins, the daughter of H. R. MacMillan's fellow timber baron W. J. Van Dusen, whose family has continued to support our efforts. Another was Bert Hoffmeister, the affable MacMillan Bloedel chairman who had been one of the most distinguished commanders of the Canadian forces in World War II. Rounding out the roster were the Grahams, their appetites for collecting recently whetted by the narwhal expedition to the Arctic.

As our party travelled through Africa, my mind feasted on the possibilities for showing the people of Vancouver the natural wonders of this fabulous continent. I imagined African habitats in the aquarium with freshwater fish, terrestrial vegetation, birds and perhaps reptiles, amphibians and some small mammals. I can't remember if I also imagined where the money was to come from.

One of our early stops was the Durban Aquarium on South Africa's east coast. There we heard Acting Director John Wallace describe his ambitions for exhibiting one of the world's most enigmatic fish, the coelacanth. Like Earl Herald at the Steinhart Aquarium in San Francisco, Wallace had constructed a special tank in hopes that a coelacanth would present itself. The truth, however, was that neither his people nor any other aquarists in the world had been successful in capturing one of these strange animals alive.

Coelacanths are well known to paleontologists. Their fossilized remains are abundant in ancient rock formations, appearing first about 400 million years ago. Often referred to as missing links between land and marine animals, they had lungs and sported fins with fleshy bases, which contained jointed series of bones. The ancient forms of the coelacanth originated in freshwater lakes, and some eventually took up life in the oceans. Since their fossils do not exist in geological formations less than 60 million years old, it was assumed they were extinct until December 22, 1938. That was the day that Marjorie Courtenay-Latimer, the young curator of the East London Natural History Museum in South Africa, discovered a five-foot-long pale blue fish in the catch of a trawler. She contacted an eminent ichthyologist in Grahamstown named J. L. B. Smith, and he confirmed that this unique specimen was indeed a coelacanth. Hard as it was to believe, this ancient form of life still existed in the ocean.

Scientists worldwide were fascinated by this discovery. Smith officially named the new genus and species *Latimeria chalumnae* in honour of both Courtenay-Latimer and the Chalumna River, off the mouth of which the catch had been made. He desperately wanted to obtain additional specimens and offered a reward of a hundred pounds to any fisherman along the South African Coast who might obtain one for him. But World War II intervened and another specimen was not obtained until December 20, 1952, when one was caught in the Indian Ocean off the Comoro Islands between Madagascar and Africa. By the end of 1971, sixty-nine specimens had been captured and distributed to various museums throughout the world. All but the first one had been collected in the Comoro Islands, and none had stayed alive for longer than ten hours after being caught.

Like any student of the undersea world, I knew something about coelacanths. One of the main fish books for my graduate ichthyology course was a volume by J. L. B. Smith in which he had described the coelacanth at some length. After the visit to the Durban Aquarium, I started talking to anyone who would listen about the coelacanth and the possibility of eventually acquiring one for Vancouver.

Twenty years later, Jim Graham tells people of his suspicion that I had been cooking up the idea of a coelacanth shopping trip long before we got to Africa, although Durban was the first place he heard me talk about it—in other words, that Durban was the bait to my hook. He may be right. I remember trying to describe to the group just how you would go about capturing a coelacanth: it lived in deep water, so you'd have to find a way to let it adapt slowly to the rising temperature and decreasing pressure as you brought it up. As a former foundryman, Jim has always liked technical challenges, and he seemed intrigued by both the problem and the prey.

Meanwhile, the tour proceeded without a hitch. The final leg was a trip by van across Uganda to Murcheson Falls, where we slept in tents along the bank of the Nile. In the morning we woke to find a hippo wandering among the tents; luckily this caused more delight than alarm among the members. Later that day, a large riverboat took us upstream to the magnificent falls. Along the banks were large Nile crocodiles, some sunning themselves with their mouths open. White egrets walked boldly among them. In the water were many hippos, washed clean so that the pink marking around their eyes and muzzles was clearly visible from where we stood on the boat.

Throughout the tour, I continued to talk about the coelacanth, and by the time we got to Uganda, the Grahams had made a decision. The aquarium would get its coelacanth if they had anything to do with it—and they would, because not only would they provide the funds, they'd go along to the Comoro Islands with me to do the collecting. Jim proceeded to plan our project meticulously, and he continued to manage it very efficiently throughout.

We knew that coelacanths lived in deep water, possibly in the cool region below the thermocline where temperatures are around 54° F. If they were caught on hook and line they would have to be brought up through temperatures and lower pressures that would be harmful to them. The solution I thought of was to build a cage. Once caught, the coelacanth could be put in the cage and quickly lowered back down into the depths where it could remain cool and comfortable until we brought it up slowly for transfer to new quarters.

After saying good-bye to the rest of the tour group, the Grahams and I flew to Nairobi, where we had talked with the Canadian trade commissioner about our project. In the bustling Nairobi market we bought chicken wire, pliers, line, a child's wading pool, window screening, thermometers and fishing equipment. Then we left for Tanzania. On our arrival at the airport in Dar es Salaam we were stopped briefly by customs officials, whose furrowed brows and whispered conversations among themselves indicated deep suspicion of our motives in carrying such insurrectional supplies.

Shortly after arriving in Dar es Salaam we were invited for drinks at the home of Canadian High Commissioner Jim Barker. There we met a French couple who were very familiar with the Comoros, which at that time was a French colony. They told us that if we were to succeed in getting a coelacanth, we must get in touch with one Monsieur LeBret, the most influential man in the islands. Not only was he part-owner of the local airline, but he had other, more mysterious interests, the couple intimated. And by the way, they said, be careful with coelacanths: they are bright blue when they first come out of the water and can fin themselves across the boat deck to bite you the way an angry dog would.

With that encouraging information, we flew the next day for the Comoros in an old DC-3. Our stewardess was a striking young Danish woman who, after a little casual conversation, told us she lived in a rooming house on Grande Comore Island where there was a freezer "filled with coelacanths." How could that be possible? we asked. She shrugged; although the government was nominally in charge of all specimens captured, private citizens were interested in them also. Evidently, these fish were outside the official tabulation and sold on a black market.

Two and a half hours after takeoff, our plane circled the dark volcanic island crowned by Mount Karthala, one of the largest craters in Africa. Below us we could see plantations and the dhow-filled harbour of Moroni, the capital town on Grande Comore, with its narrow winding alleys, colourful market and handsome mosques. We soon were installed in a very pleasant French resort called Maloudja. Outside the hotel a man played with a brown lemur, a friendly, primitive primate with a long furry tail. Inside, on the wall of the dining room was a mounted coelacanth. All in all, the omens seemed good. We had nine days to catch a coelacanth.

Jim went into action, hiring a jeep for transport and a bespectacled young Comoran named Salim as our interpreter. The next morning, we headed out on the rocky road to Iconi, the village off whose shores most coelacanths had been caught.

As we drove over the pitted road, Grande Comore revealed itself to be the right kind of place to be associated with the survival of ancient animals. Exceedingly remote and isolated, it combines striking contrasts. The contour of the island drops precipitously into the abyssal depths of a brilliant blue ocean. In fact, the island is really the top of a gigantic mountain that rises from the ocean bottom thousands of metres below the surface. Its peak, Mount Karthala, is an active volcano whose lava flows scar the land with black cinder swathes that extend down to the coast, where they form black sand beaches. The surface of the island is packed with ugly craters, some of which are filled with water to form round, steep-sided lakes. Gigantic, thick-trunked baobab trees stretch grotesquely skyward. Mosquitoes swarm in the shadows of the pandanus trees and the coconut and banana palms, while large fruit bats fly overhead or roost in the trees. The air is filled with the smell of perfume from the ylang-ylang blossoms.

The village of Iconi proved to be a particularly beautiful place. It had a handsome white mosque and pleasant buildings of whitewashed coral laid out along the black lava shore of the brilliant blue ocean. The men of the village wore long flowing white robes; in accordance with their Moslem faith, the women covered their faces with colourful gowns or cloaks, leaving only their eyes visible to the outside world. The presence of Isabelle in her Western dress didn't seem to bother anyone; she was very sensitive to the local people and treated everyone with the same dignified but natural friendliness, and they respected her, despite her costume.

Salim took us to the village chief, Mohammed Ali Chabani, and we walked with him down to a hut on the beach for a chat with the village's most successful fishermen. All had caught coelacanths, but it turned out that the coelacanth was of less interest to them than another deep-water fish—a species they called "nyessa" (*Ruvettus pretiosus*). This rich, oily, fish has important medicinal properties; its oil is an effective purgative rather like castor oil and it is also used as a salve for insect bites. Like the coelacanth, it lives near the bottom and can only be caught at certain times of the night. It is when the fishermen go out to catch nyessa that they sometimes catch coelacanths. The best period to catch the coelacanth is from January to March, when the intense heat of the austral summer is cooled occasionally by torrential rains and the odd cyclone.

With dramatic gestures, the Iconians described how they went out fishing in their small dugout canoes, stabilized with outriggers. Starting at about nine o'clock at night, they paddled to favourite spots 1000 to 6600 feet offshore and fished all night with hand lines. Since the fish lived close to the bottom, the lines were weighted with rocks to take them down and rigged in such a way that the stones would be released when fish took the bait.

The Comoran government paid a fisherman about $200 for turning in a coelacanth, an amount equal to J. L. B. Smith's original reward of a hundred South African pounds. Although this sum far exceeded the average annual income of the fishermen, they were more interested in edible fish found close to the surface. Their gear was generally inadequate for deep-water fishing and, in any case, food was a higher priority than money.

We also learned why most coelacanths die soon after being caught. Since the big, muscular fish had the unpleasant habit of snapping at the fishermen with large, tooth-filled mouths and could waddle alarmingly fast on their fins, the fishermen took the precaution of beating the fish over the head with clubs—as fishermen do all over the world. Jim soon hired the chief and his ten best fishermen to fish for us every night as long as we were there. Although it was November, not the best month for coelacanth, we would try anyway.

Back at our hotel we found an invitation to have drinks with Monsieur LeBret in his Moroni office. He proved to be a smooth and confident man, and the meeting was positive. Was it possible for a coelacanth to be acquired for the aquarium? Eminently possible, Monsieur LeBret assured us, especially given our strategy of hiring the fishermen of Iconi. Should that not work out, a preserved coelacanth would cost $800 and perhaps a few incidental expenses. He would try to get us an interview with the president of the Comoros to expedite matters. But, LeBret warned us, we would have to deal with the French colonial bureaucracy as well as the Comorans.

With Salim to interpret for us, we started our bureaucratic odyssey in the office of the first secretary of the High Commission of the Republic of France, a Monsieur Delabrousse. So far as the High Commission was concerned, he said, there was no impediment to our mission. We could take a coelacanth away with us—if we caught two and left the second one there. However, we must also visit the office of Monsieur Picard, the director of agriculture.

This we did. Monsieur Picard was less helpful. Permission to catch such a valuable fish on such short notice? Impossible. It would be necessary to request and obtain formal authorization from Paris. Without it? Unthinkable. Perhaps we would like to join in the international expedition scheduled for next year, in which the French National Museum was a participant.

It was a sombre little band of Canadians who left Monsieur Picard's office that afternoon. And one angry Comoran: our interpreter Salim was voluble in his indignation about French highhandedness. Authorization from Paris indeed! This was the naked face of imperialism, he sputtered, an affront to the dignity of Comorans. He took it as his personal challenge to help us outmanoeuvre the bureaucracy, and from that moment on he was an enthusiastic member of the team.

Next stop was a government warehouse, where we were shown a dozen rusting galvanized metal "coffins" containing coelacanths preserved in formalin fluid. We were permitted to peer into the boxes and look at the strange, lobed fins, large eyes and scattering of white scales among the large dark blue scales covering their bodies, all dyed rust-brown by the deteriorating metal containers. Could one of these specimens be acquired for display in the Vancouver Aquarium? Jim inquired of the official who received us. Impossible. They were all previously spoken for. We could return to Vancouver and apply for the next available fish if we wished.

Dejected by our preliminary rounds with the local bureaucracy, Jim and I went out in an outrigger canoe to take temperature readings about one mile off our resort. A coelacanth had been caught there in 1958. The temperature at the surface was a warm 79° F; six hundred feet below it was only five degrees lower. That sounded promising; perhaps the problem of controlling temperatures for a live specimen might not be so difficult.

The next day began in the nearby jungle, where we cut down thick bamboo for the construction of our cage. Then we made a shopping trip to Moroni. Jim had done some calculations; our cage needed bamboo staves two to three inches in diameter, half-inch steel rods that could be made into hoops, hinged ends and wire netting. It would measure four by eight feet when finished, ample room for the largest imaginable coelacanth. We bought the necessary materials and some new fishing lines for the fishermen.

Back in Iconi, Jim and Isabelle set to work making the cages and covering them with blue fly screen. The villagers were keenly interested in the project and quickly became possessive of the huge blue cages, arguing fiercely among themselves over who would help with the construction. It was hot work, the temperature being about 92° F.

When the cages were finished, we gathered the fishermen together for another talk. With Salim interpreting, I explained that despite its nasty temperament the coelacanth was delicate. So it was essential to treat the live fish carefully and *not* to hit it over the head. Once the fish was taken off the hook, it had to be put in the cage and lowered immediately to a cool depth.

Since the fish is nocturnal, it had to be kept in the dark. As a final touch, we supplied the fishermen with flashlights.

Then we drove back to Moroni, where another message was waiting from LeBret. The president of Grande Comore, the Sultan Said Ibrahim, would see us the next day. We felt very hopeful on the morning of the interview as LeBret accompanied us to the palace and into the presence of the Sultan, an aristocratic Arab of great dignity.

LeBret interpreted, and the meeting with His Excellency went well. He had no objections to our quest. Clearly, our major problem was going to be the Republic of France—and the coelacanth, which as the days passed (and the bills mounted) was proving to be elusive.

Jim decided to increase our chances for success by giving the fishermen a powerful incentive. The deal was this: the fisherman who caught a healthy, active coelacanth that remained alive for at least a week would get an all-expense paid trip to Mecca. We had researched this; charter flights were readily available and could be joined for a reasonable cost by any Moslem wishing to go on the *haj*, or religious pilgrimage. All Moslems are supposed to make this trip before they die, so the fishermen were extremely excited by the chance to become *hajji* and fished every night with great intensity.

We also decided to open a second front in the campaign when we discovered that coelacanths were sometimes caught off a small, isolated fishing village called Bouni at the other end of the island. It was a rough ride over a rocky road full of hills and gulches. Beneath the perfectly formed archways of Bouni's whitewashed buildings, we discussed the project with the local chief Abdalla Mohammed and his fishermen. Like the people of Iconi, they were captivated by the project and the Mecca offer. On the rough lava rocks of the shore, another bright blue cage was constructed.

Now we had two villages at opposite ends of the island fishing for us. We visited them almost every day, although travel was tiring on those terrible roads. The bills added up at an astonishing rate. Iconi, being more accustomed to white westerners, had a more businesslike attitude to the enterprise—which is to say that Chief Chabani was more creative about finding things for Jim to pay for. (Four years later I got a plaintive postcard from the Steinhart Aquarium's director John McCosker, who was in Grande Comore on what proved to be another difficult but fascinating coelacanth hunt. "Dave Powell and I are considering opening an aquarium in Iconi with Chief Chabani as Chairman of our Board of Trustees," he wrote in exasperation. "Care to serve as a consultant?")

Just in case we didn't get our live specimen, we kept up our efforts to obtain a preserved one. Permission was required not only to buy the fish but to export it, preserved or live. Every meeting seemed to present a new technical, financial or political problem, and we had to be ever mindful of the competing interests and regulations of the French and Comoran governments. The greatest official opposition continued to come from the office of Monsieur Picard at the agriculture bureau. Luckily, we were not without allies ourselves.

On the international front, we enlisted the help of the Canadian high commissioner in Dar es Salaam, who sent cables to the minister of agriculture in France. On the local front, LeBret and Salim followed up all the contacts they had in the local government. Salim's major coup was to get us an interview with the Comoran minister of agriculture, who was only too happy to expedite our petition once he understood that Monsieur Picard was against it.

As the documents and cables and payments came together, the unfortunate Monsieur Picard found himself outflanked and overruled. It was a happy afternoon when we left the agriculture office with our official permission to obtain a specimen. No one savoured the triumph more than Salim.

We went back to the warehouse and selected the largest specimen there. It was a female weighing 170 pounds and measuring five feet, three inches, which had been captured earlier that year a mile off the island of Anjouan at a depth of 990 feet. Once in possession of our rust-coloured treasure, we had it welded into a formalin-filled galvanized case and enclosed in a hardwood box. The total weight was almost 600 pounds.

Time ran out for the fishermen. Our departure date arrived without any success in either Iconi or Bouni. Disappointed but not empty-handed, we said our good-byes and made our final payments in both villages.

Following an emotional good-bye to Salim, we flew to the mainland, where we had to wait for a few hours in the airport of Dar es Salaam. After so much effort, we were afraid of having our precious cargo stolen. Jim, who is tall and powerfully built, stretched himself out on the coffinlike box until it was time to embark.

Back in Vancouver we put the fish on display in a handsome glass tank filled with clear isopropyl alcohol and framed with bronze. It is very impressive—the third-largest coelacanth ever captured. Since the two larger ones reside in the comparative anatomy laboratory at the Natural History Museum of Paris, ours was the largest ever placed on public display.

So well displayed is our coelacanth that some people never quite understand that it is dead. One elderly visitor was heard to say, "It's cruel to keep such a large fish in such a tiny container. Why don't they give it a larger tank?"

In his book *Living Fossil,* Keith S. Thomson expresses concern that aquariums are placing too much pressure on the apparently small population of coelacanths. The truth is that none have been caught by aquariums. The great majority of coelacanths have been bought by scientists, research laboratories or museums. I have to smile at Thomson's account of an international expedition that arrived in Iconi the year after we did. The participants were no less than Britain's Royal Society, the American National Academy of Sciences, France's National Museum of Natural History and *National Geographic* magazine. A fisherman who had worked with us caught a coelacanth at 2:00 A.M. less than a mile from the shore of Iconi and placed it in our beautiful blue cage. Thomson describes this as a "primitive cage," assuming that it was built by the villagers. Primitive or not, it kept the fish alive long enough to be transferred to a fibreglass tank where it could be filmed. Dr. Thomson states, "After the stunning success of 1972, groups from many institutions—the California Academy of Sciences, the Vancouver Public Aquarium and the New York Aquarium, for example—made expeditions to the Comores and obtained frozen and preserved specimens."

At least he puts us in good company, even if he does not realize that they followed us rather than the other way around.

# 14

# At Home
# with Skana and Hyak

The prime minister of Canada removed his coat, revealing a natty striped shirt. Then he donned rubber boots and nimbly jumped down onto our immaculate new whale feeding platform. Skana, Hyak and the dolphin Diana had just put on a tremendous show to mark the opening of their new pool. Now our chief trainer Klaus Michaelis was offering Pierre Elliot Trudeau a piece of herring with which to reward Skana, who waited expectantly with her sleek head out of the water at the side of the pool.

As he grasped the fish in his hand and bent over the water, Mr. Trudeau got a close-up view of Skana's forty-four cone-shaped teeth and large pink tongue. When I saw the prime minister pause for a moment, I suddenly wondered if he was considering a novel way of dealing with the more fractious members of his caucus. I banished this unworthy thought from my mind as he dropped first one and then several more chunks of fish down Skana's gullet. Then, at a sign from Klaus, Skana silently slipped back into the water and swam off with her pool mates in the best killer whale habitat yet created by an aquarium.

The new habitat contained two pools, a main pool for the whales to live in and a smaller holding pool adjacent to it in the northwest corner. The main pool was ninety-two feet long, forty-eight feet wide and eighteen feet deep in the centre. With a combined capacity of approximately 400,000 gallons, the pools gave the animals more than three times the total volume of their previous home in the B.C. Tel Pool. The two new pools were connected by a short passage covered by an attractive bridge, from which the aquarium staff could manipulate a hydraulically operated gate to allow the transfer of animals from one pool to the other. Actually, there were two gates, one solid and one of stainless steel mesh. When it became necessary to drain either the holding pool or the main pool, the solid gate could be closed and the desired water level maintained in the other pool. Normally, the watertight gate was left open with the steel mesh gate forming the barrier.

Skana and Hyak had moved into their new $1.4-million home a few weeks earlier. The move took four hours, as we drained the B.C. Tel Pool and hoisted the whales by crane from the old pool to their new one. While in transit the whales were measured and weighed, and veterinarian Allan MacNeill took blood samples. At ten years of age, Skana now weighed 5500 pounds and measured about twenty feet in length; the five-year-old Hyak weighed 3000 pounds and was sixteen feet long. The whole aquarium staff came out to watch the transfer.

Once in the holding pool the two began feeding immediately, to our great relief. When the gate separating the pools was opened, Hyak entered the main pool. Skana refused to swim into the larger pool, however, and resisted our efforts to get her to do so for three days. Finally she relented and entered her new home with assistance from aquarium divers. Having spent the greater part of her youth in the B.C. Tel Pool, she found it a little difficult to become accustomed to her new surroundings. We moved Diana the dolphin to the new pool a few days later in a stretcher, and in a few months two other Pacific white-sided dolphins joined her there.

It was through the leadership of Ralph Shaw that the magnificent new pool became a reality. With the arrival of Skana and Hyak, our $1.5-million expansion in 1967 had become almost instantly insufficient in size. We had been prepared for dolphins, but not two growing killer whales and the audiences who thronged to see them. A lesser man might have thrown up his hands at the task of raising new millions so soon after the completion of a major fund-raising campaign, but Ralph accepted the challenge with the enthusiasm of a champion thoroughbred facing a new starting gate.

He settled on an approach taken from his years in business: the sale of debentures. These, he told the board members, would generate our capital requirements without appealing to the taxpayers and would allow supporters of the aquarium to assist us by lending (not donating) the money. After much discussion in the finance committee, the aquarium association authorized the issue of $1.2 million's worth of income debentures, paying 7 per cent per annum and maturing in fifteen years. The entire issue was sold, and twelve years later the debentures were completely paid off.

The construction job was equally difficult, but for very different reasons. The toughest task was installing the thirty three-inch-thick Plexiglas windows along the pool's eastern side. We had contacted glass and aquarium experts from various parts of the world for advice about how to overcome the immense technical challenges: the Plexiglas had to withstand great pressure and be optically acceptable, and we also had to combat the problem of condensation.

Variations in thickness of these pieces of Plexiglas, together with warpage, made it impossible to use prefabricated, fitted neoprene gaskets. Cold, wet weather complicated the problem by preventing the sealants from adhering properly. Our contractor finally suspended a plastic curtain within the pool so that the frames of the windows could be warmed while the work was taking place. This sped up the curing of the sealant.

The new habitat was a hit with the public, bumping up our attendance by yet another quantum leap. That was gratifying, but I was even happier with the learning opportunity it afforded us, for we were now able to observe the behavioural patterns of a mixed group of cetaceans: Skana, Hyak, and the dolphins Diana, Thetis and Apollo. A few months after the pool opened, Susan Hoffer and her partner Robyn Woodward did a number of round-the-clock recordings of the animals' activities. Working in six-hour shifts, the two women stayed glued to the underwater windows monitoring what was going on in the pool in three general areas: solitary behaviour, social interaction and the dominance hierarchy.

One of the most interesting observations made by other researchers had been the importance of tactile stimulation for captive cetaceans. Susan found this to be true of our animals, for each was frequently observed rubbing itself against the sides and floor of the tank. Often the animals would swim slowly with their genital areas touching wall or floor.

Physical contact was also part of their social interactions. The animals usually swam together in varying combinations for five or ten minutes after each show. When swimming together, their bodies or flippers usually touched. Often the dolphins moved actively around Hyak, each rubbing its body or head against his body, and these interactions were frequently sexual, though they stopped short of mating. Occasionally Hyak and Skana swam together with their genital areas in contact.

One of the most interesting actions involved Hyak, who would sink to the floor of the tank where he'd lie belly down, waiting for another animal to arrive. Most often it was Diana or Thetis (or occasionally both) who would join him down there, rubbing their heads and bodies against his fins or other body parts. It wasn't clear if this was part of a courtship pattern or just a reflection of their need for tactile stimulation, but there was little question about what was going on when Skana joined him on the bottom. Then the rubbing was mutual, and they nuzzled each other all over their bodies.

Sex play among aquarium dolphins was well known to aquarium professionals. When Marineland of the Pacific opened in California in 1954, Ken Norris and David Brown remarked about it often. When female dolphins were not receptive, male dolphins frequently rubbed their erect genitals on objects in their pools. When the females were receptive, they tended to be aggressively sexual with the males, chasing them and rubbing their bodies against them. In the Vancouver Aquarium the public was amazed by the sexual behaviour of Skana and Hyak and often were very excited by what they saw, pointing and shouting.

Hyak and Diana spent most of their time playing by themselves or with each other. Whenever an object, even something as small as a feather or a piece of paper, fell into the pool, the two would spend time vying for it. It was amazing to see Diana attempting to steal something from the much bigger Hyak's mouth. If nothing else was available, they would scrape bits off the vandex coating of the tank and play with that.

Most types of social order are based on some kind of dominance hierarchy, and we certainly saw one among our cetaceans. As might be expected, the killer whales dominated the tank, and Skana was the dominant animal. She often broke up the interactions of the other animals, and if some particularly fascinating object was thrown into the pool, it was she who always got it. Nonetheless, very little aggression was observed among our killer whales and dolphins. Occasionally we would note new scars on the dolphins' bodies, which by their size could usually be traced to one of the killer whales. We would also see dolphin tooth marks on the whales. The dolphins did not totally fit into the social hierarchy of the killer whales. The dolphins were much faster and seemed to behave according to their own rules. For instance, when all the others were resting, Diana would sometimes take it upon herself to play social director. She would swim rapidly around the whales in circles, which usually had the effect of stimulating them to start moving again.

Sometimes the dolphins would anger Skana and she would chase them and try to bite them. This was particularly so in the early days with Splasher, our first dolphin, who was very aggressive. One morning we found Splasher at the surface of the pool, dying. Apparently he had been crushed against the side of the habitat and had sustained mortal injuries, probably as a result of being chased by Skana.

Though the early shows were similar to those in the oceanariums, we never did go in much for the circuslike "ride 'em" performances. Over the years our whale shows became more and more naturalistic. (In the 1990s we stopped them altogether, but I'll return to that later.) Our training methods also changed as we became more sophisticated in our understanding of whale psychology. In the early days, our training methods were the traditional ones of positive and negative reinforcement. In its simplest form, positive reinforcement involved blowing a whistle, then giving the animal a fish when it did what the trainer wanted. Negative reinforcement, or "discipline," was somewhat more complicated, given that we were dealing with an animal weighing 3000 pounds. Withholding a piece of herring was one option, but surprisingly the most effective chastisement was for the trainer to turn his back on Skana when she failed to perform properly. She didn't like losing his attention.

In fact, Skana seemed to enjoy performing before an audience, more than any other whale we've ever had. If the stands were crowded and people were clapping loudly, she'd jump higher than on a slow day. For most of her thirteen years in the aquarium, she rarely refused to perform so long as the routine remained exactly the same. Since Hyak was under her dominance, at least in the early years, he always followed along and did what Skana did. In fact, she made him do it, often biting him if he failed.

If something in the routine changed, however, Skana often became upset, especially as she grew older. For that reason, her trainers rarely tried to teach her anything new. Once, when Klaus was trying to teach her to roll over and present her belly above the water, she expressed her displeasure by clamping her jaws on his head—gently, but enough for a little warning—when he leaned over to give her a herring.

The whales clearly formed attachments to certain people and also came to dislike certain others, sometimes for reasons we couldn't identify. Odd as it sounds, Skana didn't seem to like thin people. She did like Klaus and Jeremy FitzGibbon—both of them robust, stocky men—and as time went on she tended not to accept food from anybody else. (Thank goodness she was relatively young when the slender Pierre Trudeau was invited to feed her.)

Sometimes we learned things about them by accident. There was the day the trainers discovered that Hyak could recognize images in a book—from the other side of a tank window! Jeremy was standing in front of a window with a model of a salmon, when Hyak came close to the window and appeared to be very interested. Jeremy and Klaus were intrigued, and they started showing him pictures from an illustrated book. It was quite a sight: the whale with his eyeball completely against the window, looking through three inches of Plexiglas at a book. Hyak was clearly only interested in the pictures of killer whales, dolphins or fish that looked like salmon. With any other type of animal, he drifted away from the window, but killer whale pictures brought him back close to the glass.

In the beginning, Hyak was so interested that he would stay by the glass as long as he could hold his breath, perhaps ten minutes. After a while he would get bored, but they could bring him back with a new picture. Jeremy said that the whale would even wait in the morning for him to arrive: "As soon as you opened that door, he'd be there squeaking at you to get out a book for him or turn the page."

A researcher from UBC heard about our bookish orca and came to do a small research project. Eventually she found that Hyak was most attracted by the particular shadings of killer whales rather than their shape. An outline of a killer whale wouldn't interest him, but killer-whale-like markings would. Although no other whale showed as much interest in printed or sketched images, White Wings (the newly named Pacific white-sided dolphin who had originally been called Diana) occasionally did. Once, Jeremy and Klaus put a large poster up against the glass showing every species of dolphin and whale, and White Wings went up and down the row looking at each one.

While there was a great deal of good killer whale research undertaken in aquariums during the 1970s, the great demand for orcas was undoubtably fuelled by their potential as spectator attractions. Up until the early 1970s, all of the captive specimens had originated from the inside waters of southern British Columbia and northern Washington State. By 1972, about sixty orcas had been captured with nets by outfits like Ted Griffin's company, and they had been bought by seventeen different aquariums or oceanariums in various parts of the world. The growing "market" showed signs of demanding up to twenty whales a year.

Many ordinary citizens had become uneasy about the situation and begun to press for regulation of the numbers captured. The government of Canada made a first step in 1970, passing a law to protect orcas from harassment and requiring a permit to be issued to anyone who wanted to capture one. Washington State followed suit in 1971.

However, since all of this was done without any concrete idea of the number of killer whales in the area, no one knew what the permit quota should be. I was pleased when our old friend Mike Bigg became involved with an international project to find out how many orcas there were on the coast. In 1971 the Fisheries Research Board of Canada and its equivalents in Washington State, Oregon, California and Alaska began a four-year study. Mike was in charge of the Canadian part of the study.

When Mike first spoke to me about the project, I suggested that they try a one-day census, just as national governments do periodically. The problem with trying to do a count over a longer period of time was the fact that orcas are extremely rapid swimmers. A pod may travel over a hundred miles in twenty-four hours. With a one-day census, it would be far easier to avoid double-counting. Moreover, after my years of fruitful co-operation with fisherfolk and other marine people, as well as the different official agencies, I thought the researchers could enlist their help as census takers. Michael liked the idea, as did the various partners in the research.

The study design that was finally adopted contained two parts. The first part, which included two census efforts in successive years, aimed to establish the basic numbers. The second two years of the study would be devoted to understanding to what extent the whales were migratory. Observers were asked to watch for killer whales throughout the year.

As I'd hoped, the various marine organizations operating on the coast were more than willing to co-operate on the census. Thousands of questionnaires were sent out to commercial fishing associations, ferries, airlines, tugs, patrol vessels, yacht clubs, lighthouses and many other groups. Each questionnaire asked the observers four basic questions about any group of killer whales they might see: Where was this group seen? How many individuals were in the group? In what direction was the group travelling? What was the date and time of the sighting? The project was widely publicized by post office posters, mailed notices, newspapers, radio broadcasts and government weather broadcasting stations.

The first census was held on July 26, 1971, a Monday. That date was chosen carefully with various factors in mind. Statistically, it had the best chance of good weather and therefore of good visibility for whale sightings, and many people could be counted on to be out on the water enjoying the weather. The partner agencies agreed that a weekday was preferable so that the numerous commercial marine organizations would be among the participants.

After the results were tallied and analyzed, the count was as follows: 360 different killer whales were seen in British Columbia, 114 in Washington State, none in Oregon, 13 in California and 62 in southeastern Alaska. That made a total of 549. Pods containing as few as 2 and as many as 25 individuals were reported, all within twenty miles of shore. Fully 60 per cent were seen on the eastern side of Vancouver Island or in northern Puget Sound.

Scientists have now identified 650 killer whales off the coast of B.C., and there are perhaps double that number when you include American waters.

So that first census was a pretty remarkable effort. Moreover, it was one of the first of many excellent research projects on wild orcas that would be done either with the help of the aquarium or by people associated with us. One of the most important tools in this research has been the camera, for it has allowed scientists to catalogue the orcas by their dorsal fins and other markings and thus identify them with great certainty. Another tool has been the hydrophone, which has allowed us to record and analyze the sounds the animals make.

Perhaps the single most important finding in the 1970s was the discovery that there were two different types of killer whale in our waters. The difference was not biological but in the way the whales "make their living" and in their social systems.

One type are known as "transients" because their pods move over great distances. The transients eat warm-blooded prey such as seals, sea lions, porpoises and minke whales. Autopsies on transients washed up on shore have found sea birds and deer in their stomachs, and once the remains of a pig was found in the stomach of an orca in the Queen Charlottes. None of the stomachs have contained fish bones.

The other type are known as "residents." These live in large and apparently stable family groups and eat only fish.

Perhaps three hundred of the thirteen hundred killer whales living within twenty or thirty miles of the Pacific coast are transients. Orcas are also found far offshore and in fact are probably the most widely distributed animal in the oceans. They have been seen almost everywhere, though not with the same frequency. For instance, they are rarely found in tropical waters. The largest population is probably around the Antarctic. It is not certain whether this division between fish-eating residents and mammal-eating transients is typical all over the world. It may be that in areas where it is difficult to find enough to eat, the animals rely on a great diversity of prey and a variety of strategies for catching their dinners.

John Ford, the aquarium's resident whale scientist, told me recently of killer whales off the coast of Argentina that have a very specialized hunting technique for catching sea lion pups in shallow water—a technique that sometimes results in the orcas stranding themselves. The interesting thing is that this hunting of pups occurs for only a few months of each year. The rest of the time these whales move up and down the coast feeding opportunistically on a variety of prey, and they even steal fish from fishermen's nets. Photos that have caught them "in the act" verify that these are the same whales who go after the sea lion pups on a different part of the coast.

Transients are harder to study than residents because their social structure seems looser. It is hard to know if an animal has died or simply started

travelling on its own. The social system of residents seems essentially permanent: the only way into the group is to be born into it, and the only way out
is to die. This fact makes it easier to estimate mortality and other characteristics of the pods. Based on recent observations, the resident population seems
to be increasing somewhere between 2 and 3 per cent a year. Some find this
surprising because overall stocks of salmon (their main food) are not increasing. It may be that the residents are reproducing faster because of the sixty-five
animals taken for aquariums up until the early 1970s. Another explanation
may be that there are fewer deaths from fishermen shooting them.

If true, this latter explanation is another example of how quickly
attitudes towards killer whales have changed over the decades since we
captured Moby Doll in 1964. After years of people seeing and studying killer
whales both in aquariums and in the field, there is a distinct social revulsion
against shooting them, an activity once very common. John and his colleagues still see bullet wounds in orcas on our coast, and clearly some
fishermen still feel the whales to be competitors for fish. Recently in Alaska's
Prince William Sound a group of about thirty killer whales started stealing
black cod or sablefish from long line boats in the area. The fishermen
responded with rifles. As many as eight animals were killed, and most of the
survivors have scars.

People often ask aquarium staff how intelligent killer whales are and are
never fully satisfied with the answer (which may vary according to the
opinions of our very individual staff members!). The fact is that scientists
don't agree even on how to evaluate human intelligence—just think of the
controversies over I.Q. tests, and the influences of culture and environment,
and the role of memory.

Like any responsible scientist, John Ford is careful when asked a question like this, even after fifteen years of studying orcas both in the aquarium
and in the wild. When I brought up the question of intelligence in our
conversations during the writing of this book, he started out by saying that
while perceptive and capable of innovation, orcas are not intelligent in any
way that resembles human intelligence. For instance, they don't seem to
communicate about past or present events, or to process abstract ideas as
humans do. Then, as John got deeper into this topic which is so close to his
heart, I saw once again that ability to empathize with the objects of study
that distinguishes a good animal scientist. For this reason, I've quoted him
verbatim from our taped conversation:

> How does a killer whale perceive its environment? We're so
> dependent on our eyes. Of course, we think about places as we
> travel and we can see vast distances. But killer whales cannot see

very far because of the opacity and lack of clarity in water. Sometimes they'll lift their heads above water so they can look around, but generally they're underwater where they simply cannot see. They live in a dark, cold, wet world. What would their perception be like? How would they remember as they swam from the coast of California to the coast of British Columbia? How would they know where they were?

I think the answer is that they don't, and that's why the transient types turn up in the oddest places. They go into Indian Arm [near the city of Vancouver] or Vancouver harbour and these kinds of places, basically sneaking around looking for prey.

Transients seem to use sonar very sparingly. They travel in silence and I think they use passive listening, just listening to surf noise, the natural sounds of an area. Nearly every place has its own ambient noise. They're cuing on these things to know whether they're way inland or along the exposed coast and so on. They don't want to alert their potential prey to their presence with sounds. Lance Barrett-Lennard, a research associate here at the aquarium and one of my graduate students at UBC, is looking at this. He's found that they make what he calls "cryptic clicks." They'll make just one click and that will provide them perhaps with an echo enough to navigate without alerting the prey to their presence.

The resident types, I believe, are quite different animals. They are creatures of tradition. They live in their kinship group that is a long-term lineage. They learn the routines as they grow up in that group. Perhaps certain groups learn that in April or May it's time to go to the central coast and start working up Berg and Dean channels looking for the Bella Coola run of spring salmon. When that peters out, the next place to go is down the coast towards Johnstone Strait and exploit the fish in that area.

You can see these kinds of traditions, I think, in the dialects that the different groups have—which you don't see in the transients. There is a behavioural tradition for each lineage. You see it in the rubbing behaviour that is a very strong tradition in certain resident groups and not in others. I imagine that every location on the coast probably has a slightly different acoustic signature, just by the tones, the echoes they get back from their social sounds, their calls and their sonar. We can detect by listening in places like a river estuary, where it's shallow and muddy, that the sound is very different than in Johnstone Strait, which is deep and quite narrow. I believe as the animals go past certain landmarks, through a combination of just listening and through their sonar they have a pretty good idea of exactly where they are.

When I listen to someone like John Ford and hear about the new work being done in or through the aquarium by our young research associates, I am proud of the contribution we have been able to make through our cetacean program. We started small and flew blind because so little was known. Our facilities were inadequate by today's standards, but then again there *were* no standards—in fact, we were part of making them. Each new killer whale habitat that we built was a great leap forward from what had been done before, both in the comfort and stimulation we could offer the animals and in the opportunities to learn more about them.

The killer whale habitat that Pierre Trudeau opened for us was a milestone in habitat design in many ways. However, there was a bit of unfinished business that remained for several years after the opening. The design had included a new boardroom with windows onto the pool. Unfortunately (but typically) we were short of funds at the end of the construction, and since it was not essential to the care of the whales, we sacrificed finishing the room. It was bare of furnishings, an echoing concrete space enlivened only by its marvellous view into the whale pool.

It seemed a shame that the project Ralph Shaw had devoted so much of his time and talent to financing remained unfinished. After Ralph had stepped down from the presidency of the aquarium association, our old friend John Buchanan stepped in. An aquarium founder and friend of H. R. MacMillan, Buchanan agreed to raise the funds that would convert the unfinished space into an elegant room. We decided to name the room after Ralph in recognition of his great contribution.

When I first spoke to him about the project, John expressed some trepidation about raising the money. "I've been in so many fund-raising campaigns," he said. "People run when they see me coming." Nevertheless, he soon came back to us with $65,000 raised from Ralph's many friends, enough to make it one of the most attractive boardrooms in Vancouver. (I'm not the only one to say so: the most recent accolade I've seen came from *Vancouver Magazine*'s 1990 Best and Worst listings, in which the Ralph Shaw Room was named Best Boardroom in Vancouver.)

Since that time we've had hundreds of board and other meetings there. Many times I've looked up to see the streamlined form of an orca appear by the windows, staring in as the business of the aquarium was being discussed.

Though it has been a great temptation, I have always resisted making an amendment to the minutes:

> Present: The meeting was attended by Ralph Shaw, Jean Southam, Murray Newman, Jane Lawson, Skana (ex officio). . . .

# 15

# Please Don't Feed the Scientists

It was as a marine scientist that I came to Vancouver in the first place, and it was scientists like Cas Lindsey, Bill Hoar and Ian McTaggart Cowan who were the main forces in bringing me here. Science is where I started, and I try to encourage any bright young person I meet to think hard about the marine sciences when she or he is thinking about careers. When I was a student, I was powerfully attracted by Cas Lindsey's stories about his salmonid research in the Cariboo region, and I soon discovered that the reality was even better than the stories. In the early 1950s I drove up with Cas several times to see the research he was doing on trout, and it was my introduction to the interior of this splendid province. We'd leave early in the morning to take the Trans-Canada Highway up the Fraser Valley, passing the tranquil green farmland with its dairy herds and admiring the evenly spaced mountains framing both sides of the narrowing valley. Farther to the south rose the towering peak of Mount Baker in nearby Washington State, and to the north you could see the steep slopes of the rugged Garibaldi range. At the village of Hope you went into the canyon as the mountains closed in on either side. The highway became a narrow road; at certain points you had to drive out on narrow wooden platforms over the canyon, an exciting proposition since there was only room for one car.

And then you emerged from the canyon into a totally different climate and landscape: a desert with sagebrush, mountains shimmering off in the distance and, in springtime, an enchanting vista of purple and yellow flowers everywhere. But we'd press on and after about five hours arrive in Cache Creek and the land of huge cattle ranches. Cas was pursuing his research just east of Clinton, a cowboy town with a splendid hotel built of logs and a well-deserved reputation for great parties.

Cas's research dealt with the question of why different trout species swam in different directions (i.e., upstream or downstream) in different river systems. It was research you had to get your hands—and feet, and frequently all of your body—dirty to perform. Cas and his colleagues and students lived in tents, and they spent a lot of time building enclosures and dams to conduct their experiments. The research was mainly of interest to science, but it had a practical application since the provincial government stocked many Cariboo waters and it was important to know what the trout would do once introduced to new lakes or streams.

Perhaps the greatest single recruiting device for the marine sciences is a public aquarium. In North America, it was probably the New York Aquarium that most strongly established the principle that a public aquarium can significantly participate in scientific research. During the past sixty years literally hundreds of scientific papers have been published by the staff and their collaborators on subjects ranging from taxonomy and animal behaviour to genetics and biochemistry. The scientists included such great names as Charles Breder, Charles Townsend, William Beebe, Christopher Coates, Myron Gordon, James Atz, Carleton Ray and Father George Ruggieri, S.J.

The emphasis on science permeated the entire hierarchy of the institution. For instance, Ross Nigrelli was associated with the New York Aquarium for more than thirty years as pathologist, then as director of the Department of Marine Biochemistry and Ecology, and then as director of the entire aquarium. He also ran the splendid new Osborn Laboratories of Marine Sciences attached to the New York Aquarium. Most of the world's aquariums have had a scientific side to them. The London Aquarium was usually headed up by a scientist such as my friend Dr. Gwynne Vevers. The Danmarks Akvarium in Charlottenlund, Denmark, has had Dr. Arne Schiotz as its director for the last twenty-five years. Arne's researches have been mainly directed towards the study of West African frogs. In North America, the private oceanariums had scientific curators, starting with Arthur McBride and F. G. Wood, Jr., at Marine Studios, then Ken Norris and John Prescott at Marineland of the Pacific. In the 1960s, with the opening of Sea World in San Diego, Carl Hubbs, a distinguished senior ichthyologist, became involved. Both the T. Wayland Vaughan Aquarium at Scripps and the Waikiki Aquarium in Honolulu were part of universities and had commitments to research.

The Vancouver Aquarium has had scientists working with it since before it was built, and scientists working in it since the opening months when my professor Bill Hoar moved into our small lab to pursue his salmon research. It was always a policy of the aquarium to make its facilities available to scientists, and this aspect became increasingly important as the aquarium became better equipped.

Some of the research was directly important to the economic life of the province, since in British Columbia only forestry and mining make larger economic contributions than the fishing industry. I've just dug up an aquarium newsletter from 1960, for instance, which tells me of three research projects going on at the time. In one, Ken Jackson and Richard Webster of the Fish Culture Development Branch of the Department of Fisheries spent several months with us doing a series of bioassay experiments with salmon fry to determine the toxicity of various chemicals, a matter of great concern as pulp mills and industries developed along the Fraser River. In another, Dave Idler of the Fisheries Research Board Technological Station was busy doing biochemical analysis of the blood of sockeye salmon smolts. Finally, two more researchers from the technological station, Bob McLeod and Richard Jonas, were continuing their studies on the biochemistry of steelhead trout. Adequate aquatic facilities were lacking at UBC and the tech station, and the aquarium had ample fresh and salt water that could be used for research.

A few years later, a team of Department of Fisheries biologists moved in to study the growth and condition of oysters collected from polluted waters. Another group used our facilities to study the effect of a new insecticide on salmon fry. We made a great effort to be as useful as possible to outside researchers. I think it could be said that not nearly as many marine and freshwater studies would have taken place had the aquarium not been available with its unique facilities.

During the 1960s Dr. David Randall of UBC maintained our principal lab for his fish physiology research. It was during this period that the present Department of Fisheries/Oceans Director of Science, Dr. John Davis, did his doctoral studies in the aquarium under Dr. Randall.

By 1968, after our first great expansion, the aquarium's research section at the rear of the building consisted of a row of saltwater and dry laboratories, an outdoor training and research pool, and various holding tanks in the work spaces. It was one of the busiest parts of the aquarium even though it operated largely out of the public eye. Sometimes we rented entire laboratory suites to university or government scientists requiring saltwater facilities for research into topics like the physiology of respiration in fish or the nature of respiratory control in seals.

The holding facilities were also in demand. The Department of Fisheries frequently used our freshwater reserves for some of their experimental fish. I remember a period during which a graduate student from UBC's Zoology Department used the tanks to hold many hundreds of purple sea urchins for a research program. There was so much demand for the aquarium's facilities and services that I was constantly turning down requests for their use. The aquarium itself was becoming an increasingly complex institution, and it became apparent that our own scientific requirements would have to be accommodated.

Nineteen seventy-six was the first year we were able to fund a full-time position for a scientist. Ichthyologist Dr. Jeff Marliave joined the staff shortly after receiving his Ph.D. from UBC. He began an extensive examination of larval fish and invertebrates of local waters, which continued into the 1990s as our major scientific program.

Despite all the activity at the aquarium in science and education, we still lacked good professional quarters for this work. I began thinking about an aquatic science centre for the north end of the building. At the same time, Sharon Proctor advocated that an office wing for the education staff be constructed alongside the "wet lab" on the west side of the building.

In September of 1976 the Park Board gave its approval in principle to our proposal to build both an education centre and a science centre on a parcel of land stretching across the north end of the building. The project included a ninety-five-seat theatre, a library specializing in publications on aquatic life, a docent lounge, a laboratory wing with running seawater, a design studio, professional offices and a research pool for marine mammals. It would provide much better quarters for our professional staff and more opportunities for working with classes, docents and special groups.

The holding pool was a major feature of the science centre. It would be double the size of the existing pool, holding 160,000 gallons of rapidly recirculating cold seawater. We wanted it to be a quiet and controlled space where sick marine mammals could be cared for, and we also planned to use it for quarantining new animals and to separate breeding groups.

It wasn't enough to plan, of course: we had to start fund raising. The Vancouver Foundation provided $350,000, the B.C. Telephone Company gave $140,000 specifically for the pool, and we got pledges from both the municipal and federal governments.

Perhaps the happiest day in all of 1979 was the day that Grace McCarthy brought us a cheque for $550,000 from the provincial government. Our young Vancouver florist of the 1960s was now the powerful deputy premier of the province, and she was still a friend ready to come to our rescue. Fortunately the H. R. MacMillan Family Fund, the Mr. & Mrs. P. A. Woodward Foundation and the Vancouver Aquarium Volunteers also contributed substantial amounts of money.

We decided to name the new facility the Van Dusen Aquatic Science Centre after W. J. Van Dusen, one of the principal founders of the Vancouver Foundation and H. R. MacMillan's long-time business associate. It was

Dinny, the water monitor, out for his morning constitutional.
MURRAY NEWMAN PHOTO

Our scientist, Jeff Marliave, looking at the fish in Fiji in 1979. Jeff specialized in the biology of the larval stages of fish. MURRAY NEWMAN PHOTO

Pure animal charm: Cuddles the crocodile. DON HANNA PHOTO

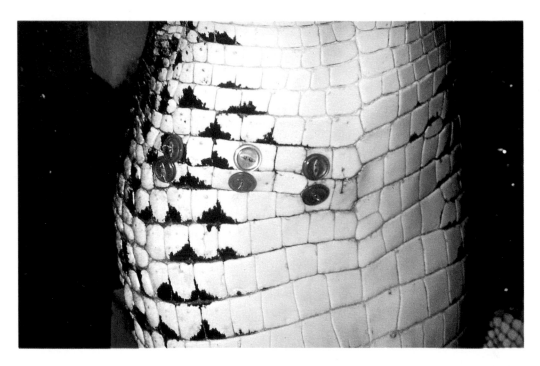

After an operation to remove objects Cuddles had swallowed, Dr. Roberta Hartman stitched the crocodile back together again with buttons to anchor the sutures. PIERRE DOW PHOTO

Chief trainer Klaus Michaelis with Samson, a Steller sea lion. Murray Newman photo

"Is the coast clear?" Josie, the female Steller sea lion, was much shyer than Samson.
Murray Newman photo

Robin Best, seen here with a manatee in Brazil, brought a joyous enthusiam to his research. We named our library for him when he died tragically young in 1986. MURRAY NEWMAN PHOTO

Robin Best organized our 1979 cruise down the Rio Negro and up the Amazon in the *Pyata*. MURRAY NEWMAN PHOTO

Kyak, skipper of the *Bylot*, was a Companion
of the Order of Canada. TONY WESTMAN PHOTO

Vancouver Zoo curator Alan Best brought back two snowy owls from our first Arctic expedition in 1968. MURRAY NEWMAN PHOTO

Ralph Shaw, Jr., and Robin Best guide a narwhal in the shallow waters of Koluktoo Bay in 1970. MURRAY NEWMAN PHOTO

Maury Young proudly displaying an Arctic char in Koluktoo Bay in 1975.  Murray Newman photo

David Lam and his Arctic char, the first fish he ever caught. David was later my diving
partner in Truk Lagoon.  Murray Newman photo

Inuit stone carver Bunnee Katchok, with the magnificent cliffs of Koluktoo Bay in the background. MURRAY NEWMAN PHOTO

Narwhals with their tusks out of the water at Koluktoo Bay. JOHN FORD PHOTO

The rocks of Admiralty Inlet...   Murray Newman photo

...inspired the simulated rock work of our beluga habitat.   Finn Larsen photo

"I'm going *where*?" An Alaska sea otter on his way to his new home in Vancouver.
MURRAY NEWMAN PHOTO

The B.C. Sugar Seal Pool seen from below, through the acrylic windows.   MURRAY NEWMAN PHOTO

Susan Gabe Hoffer carried out meticulous observation of octopus behaviour at the aquarium during the early 1970s. BILL CUNNINGHAM/VANCOUVER PROVINCE PHOTO

Dr. Sharon Proctor bathing her iguanas in 1971. Sharon was a leader in aquarium education work.

Four directors in a boat in 1979: (*Left to right*) Bill Braker of the
Shedd Aquarium, Leighton Taylor of Waikiki, me and John
McCosker of the Steinhart. The occasion was the opening of the
Roundabout Exhibit at the Steinhart. JEFF MEYER PHOTO

My profession now has a number of eminent women directors. Seen here at the 1989
opening of Toyko Sea Life Park are Yukiko Hori of Enohima (*third from left*) and Julie
Packard (*third from right*) of the Monteray Bay Aquarium. With them, from left to
right, are Takamasa Ikeda, Ikeda Zoo; Dr. Itaru Uchida, Port of Nagoya Public
Aquarium; Svend Tougaard, Eshjerg Aquarium (Denmark); Chuck Farwell,
Monteray Bay Aquarium; Dr. Tadasi Tujii, Shima Marineland Foundation; me,
and John Racanelli, now with the Florida Aquarium. PHOTOGRAPHER UNKNOWN

"Oh, look, there's the sloth!" Jim and Isobelle Graham and I accompany the queen through the newly opened Amazon Gallery in 1983. TONY WESTMAN PHOTO

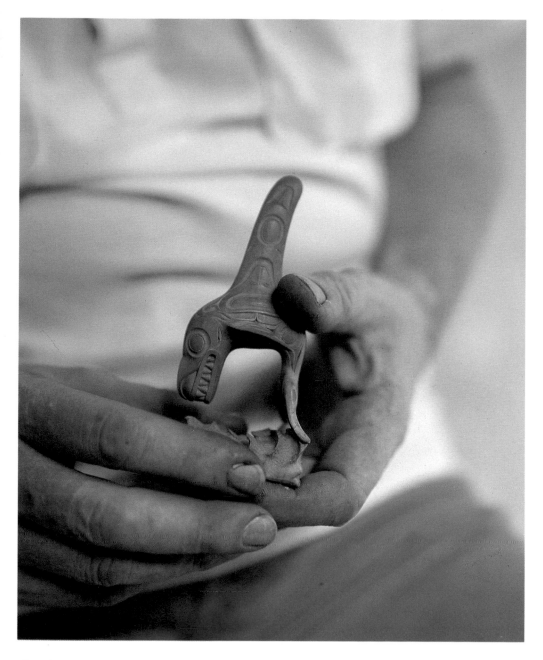

Creating a masterpiece: Bill Reid first carved "The Chief of the Undersea World" in boxwood.
TONY WESTMAN PHOTO

The Grahams flank Bill Reid on the day the bronze sculpture was unveiled in 1984.
TONY WESTMAN PHOTO

officially opened on September 27, 1980, by Phae Collins, W. J. Van Dusen's daughter, who had gone to Africa with us ten years earlier.

The new facilities, combined with the comprehensive changes brought about during the great expansion of the mid-1960s, gave the Vancouver Aquarium the best science and education facilities of any aquarium in North America. Since then, our greatest contributions in research have been Jeff Marliave's larval fish publications, John Ford's publications on killer whale acoustics and Mark Graham's publications on fish physiology. Our work in education, serving tens of thousands of students every year and involving hundreds of docents, has been greatly enhanced by these original studies.

One of the new professional fields to have emerged with the development of modern aquariums is that of aquatic animal medicine. Before the 1950s there was little appreciation of the health problems of dolphins or whales. David Huff, the current consulting vet at the Vancouver Aquarium, learned a great deal from Dr. Jim McBain, a superb veterinarian who worked at the aquarium and then moved to Sea World in San Diego.

Dave had never worked on whales or any other marine life before he came to the aquarium as a volunteer in the Amazon Gallery. Through his work there, he gradually became more and more interested in marine mammals. As he says, it's an area that offers unique challenges:

> It's an interesting field because all the knowledge comes from your colleagues. There's the odd book around but as with all textbooks, and even more so in this field, by the time the textbook comes out it's hopelessly out of date. So it's an interesting exercise in networking. You have to know all these people. They have to know you. And that's how you really get educated, by taking each case.
>
> I think I learned just from the volume of cases. See, that's the other problem with marine mammals. You can make a commitment to learn from everything you do, but if you're only seeing two or three, it takes a long time to get experience. In San Diego they have fifty or sixty cetaceans, so I learned a lot more. And what I learned from Jim really was a commonsense approach to what's important and what's not.
>
> People often say, "It must be a lot different, treating whales." But in many ways it isn't. Medicine is medicine. You have to look at the particular physiology. There are some physiological quirks and environmental things, but basically they're all the same. There are two disciplines you have to really know. One is

pharmacology, because you're always extrapolating, taking drugs from human or veterinary medicine and putting them into whales in massive amounts. And the other is clinical pathology, because taking blood samples is one of the only windows you have into the animal. Marine mammals are like other wild animals; they have all these instincts to hide illness.

We take blood from the killer whales once a month because we must build a backlog of "normals." We have to know what the normals are for each animal. It's not good enough to take Sea World's normals, because they're for different animals and they're from a different lab.

We have a wonderful system here on the computer where we can print blood samples for an animal's entire life up to the time of the last testing. That might give thirty-five tests on each killer whale. I can follow through on Bjossa by looking at her hemoglobins for years and years, and I can look at whether they're changing as she gets older and more mature. And I can look at any disease processes.

I asked Dave how an animal's blood might change as a disease develops. If she got a bacterial infection in her gums, for example, what would happen then? He replied:

We start to see the white blood count go up. But that's interesting too, because cetaceans don't have a very responsive immune system even at the best of times. Whereas in a dog the white blood cell count would go from a normal of ten or fifteen thousand up to thirty-five thousand, Bjossa is usually six thousand. And a really big rise is eight or nine. You see the white blood count going up and you see the differential; the portions of different white blood cells will change and you'll usually see the haemoglobin start to slide. The other thing that goes down is iron.

There's an enzyme called alkalinephosphatase that we watch as an indicator of health. It's used by growing bones. Killer whales grow for such a long period of time that they always have a high alkalinephosphatase. Dogs and cats and people just have it during the growing phase, but killer whales are growing all the time. When a killer whale gets sick, the alkalinephosphatase falls. People didn't understand this for a long time. Now we think that when these whales get sick at a physiological level, the bone cells stop dividing. They divert everything to fighting the infection

and they stop growing for a while. So we rely on that blood test
to look at deterioration and coming back.

Science and aquariums can also meet on big political questions, particularly those involving conservation. An interesting example concerns some
findings on sea otters, once an endangered species but now making a come-
back after a very careful transplanting program. In 1988 Dr. Michael
Waldichuk, chairman of the aquarium's research and conservation committee, wrote an article about the ecology of kelp forests in southern California
in which he noted the apparent decline of kelp in the presence of abundant
sea urchins. He pointed out that since sea otters devour sea urchins, their
presence may favour kelp forests through the reduction of sea urchin populations.

The following year, Jane Watson became a Vancouver Aquarium Research Associate and set to work studying the effects of sea otter foraging
along the west coast of Vancouver Island. By laying out quadrants on
shallow water bottoms, she studied the growth of kelp in relation to the
presence or absence of sea urchins and sea otters. Her preliminary conclu-
sions supported the idea that sea otters, by reducing the numbers of sea
urchins, cause kelp forests to proliferate as habitats for all kinds of marine
animals. Since kelp beds become nurseries for many fish species, it may be
possible that by promoting sea otter populations we can increase fish populations.

In co-operation with Parks Canada and the federal Department of Fisheries, several members of the aquarium staff examined a few sites in the
Queen Charlotte Islands as possible places for the reintroduction of sea
otters. In an important contribution to the project, Doug Pemberton from
our marine mammal staff dove off the southern tip of Moresby Island and
photographed "sea urchin barren" areas with large populations of red sea
urchins and very little kelp.

There is much fascinating work to be done in many areas of the marine
sciences. Surrounded by three oceans and possessing a large proportion of
the world's fresh water in its lakes and rivers, Canada is one of the great
wildlife areas of the world, both above and below water. I hope that governments will increase their support of marine research. And I hope that schools
will hire research biologists as biology teachers; these people have the passion
that will inspire the next generation to investigate and appreciate Canada's
magnificent natural history.

# 16

# Bringing the
# Amazon to Vancouver

*Wed. Jan. 10, 1940* I decided to fix up all the aquariums that were going to waste at school so I appointed Dave Meltzer as my assistant and we went around trying to find material and finally left or rather were kicked out at five.

*Fri. Jan. 12, 1940* Dave Lyttle brought some sand for the aquarium at school today and we (Dave Meltzer too) fixed it up as well as we could. Miss Peebles gave me a dollar to buy some materials for it. I decided I really needed a new aquarium so I asked Dad how about it and he finally gave me 3 dollars "for my birthday present" and I think Mother will give me one buck. Dave got some angelfish for 35 cents a piece and they're gorgeous.

I cite my grade 10 diary entries as a tribute to Miss Peebles of Hyde Park High School in Chicago. I suspect that almost every aquarium director has, somewhere in his or her past, an equivalent to Miss Peebles, a teacher who provided encouragement and a chance to exercise a talent.

Miss Peebles, my zoology teacher, had a great effect on my life. When she found out that I kept tropical fish at home, she not only encouraged my interest but trusted me with a few dollars to buy fish and equipment for her class. Among the first fish I maintained were sparkling little tetras of various kinds, armoured catfish and angelfish—all from the Amazon basin of South America. Amazon fish are the mainstay of many an amateur aquarist's collection, but they also provide some of the most fascinating displays in the world of public aquariums. Certainly, the Amazon has been very important to the Vancouver Aquarium and continues to provide inspiration for some of our most innovative and impressive exhibits.

The Amazon basin contains the largest range of freshwater fish in the world. At least 1300 species have been identified, of which about 80 per cent are related to the characin or catfish families. The Amazon cannot claim the record for length, but for sheer volume it is the greatest river in the world, diluting the salty ocean water for two hundred miles out to sea. It is so deep that oceangoing ships can travel 2300 miles up its course to Iquitos, Peru, at the base of the Andes Mountains.

In the Amazon, you will find some of the world's most fascinating fish. I would include in that group the gigantic catfish and arapaimas, freshwater sharks and stingrays, electric eels, little hatchet fish that fly over the surface like flying fish, characins with large canine teeth, characins with heavy teeth for cracking nuts, and four-eyed fish called *Anableps* that can see above and below the water at the same time. The richest parts of the basin in terms of diversity are the headwaters of the small tributaries, where the characins have undergone extensive speciation. With its muddy water, swift currents and broad expanse, the Amazon River is a barrier across which many species cannot pass, thus isolating them from each other in numerous tributaries.

When we first opened the Vancouver Aquarium, most of our tropical freshwater fish came from the Amazon. These included piranhas and large cichlids as well as the colourful tetras that Billy Wong looked after so lovingly. We also acquired some South American amphibians and reptiles, including several giant toads (*Bufo marinus*) that arrived in 1958. These toads are similar to common toads but of unusually large size. They originate in South America, but they have been introduced into many sugar-cane producing areas in order to keep down pests. They have become exceedingly common in Hawaii and in Fiji. In Australia, they have been introduced to keep insects down in the plantations of Queensland. But their toxic glands and omnivorous appetites make these toads less than perfect immigrants.

In 1959 Billy Wong was given two young electric eels to care for in his section of the aquarium. They were only about fifteen inches in length at the time but were still capable of making Billy jump when they discharged some voltage into the water while he was working in their tank. He started using rubber gloves and avoiding direct contact with the fish. Electric eels are not the only electric fish known, but they are certainly the most powerful, capable of discharging up to six hundred volts.

We got the majority of our early Amazon specimens from dealers or in exchanges with other aquariums, but I was always interested in going down there and seeing the habitats first-hand. In 1961 I succeeded in obtaining a small grant for an Amazon expedition from the Leon and Thea Koerner Foundation. Alan Best of the Stanley Park Zoo and I had many meetings to discuss the details. An experienced animal collector from his days with the London Zoo, Alan was familiar with the Columbian part of the Amazon, and he was very keen to get involved. I started making contacts, among them a well-known collector in the Colombian city of Leticia who transported himself and his specimens in a vintage World War II aircraft. Alan and I had pretty much planned the entire trip when it ran afoul of several members of the board of governors.

"Why pay for such an expensive trip when you can buy Amazonian fish in Vancouver?" was the argument put forward by one particularly intransigent board member, an accountant if I remember correctly. I was still having to defend my trips to Ichs and Herps conferences at the time, so I decided discretion was the better part of valour. The idea of putting together a full Amazon exhibit was shelved until Jim and Isabelle Graham appeared at the aquarium in 1969.

Jim and Isabelle had recently visited the bird-filled jungles of Malaysia, and they had been fascinated by the Jurong Bird Park in Singapore. Isabelle in particular had been captivated by the diversity of colour and shape in the birds she had seen. By 1971, Jim and Isabelle had enjoyed our Arctic trip and the coelacanth expedition; now they were ready to help build something lasting for the people of Vancouver.

Their first impulse was to sponsor an aviary. At that time, a number of high-profile aquarium members were interested in developing a major zoological garden at Tynehead Park in Surrey on the outskirts of Vancouver. Jim and Isabelle worked very hard to establish Tynehead and build the aviary there, but it never got off the ground because we were unable to capture the approval of the provincial government and therefore generate the necessary capital.

As Tynehead seemed less and less likely, I began looking for a way to reconcile the aquarium's mission with the Grahams' interest in birds. To my mind, the separation between zoos and aquariums has always seemed artificial. I thought we could combine animals of the air, water and land in one outstanding exhibit, and I was very interested in improving the Stanley Park Zoo, particularly the lower portion surrounding the aquarium. I talked a lot to the Grahams and others about it, and we decided to tour zoos, aquariums and bird exhibits in eastern North America and Europe to see what we could learn as a first step. Over the next two years, we saw the best the world had to offer.

We went first to the Metropolitan Toronto Zoo, which was just opening at Scarborough, northeast of the city. Gunter Voss, the dynamic first director who had much to do with the planning of this 710-acre, new-style zoological garden, escorted us through the fascinating zoogeographical pavilions, each of which thematically presented the plants and animals of a particular region. I was deeply moved and greatly influenced by these exhibits, which emphasized the interrelationships, the web of life, within a region, while at the same time exhibiting the animals in attractive, sunlit, green surroundings.

Our first U.S. visit was to New York, where we met with William Conway, the executive director of the New York Zoological Society. Bill Conway was then, and is still, probably the leading zoo director in North America. A protégé of William Beebe, he has become a leader in world conservation efforts and has a special interest in birds.

The Bronx Zoo is one of the great zoos of the world, and on the Sunday before we arrived, some 47,000 visitors had been through the turnstiles. As Bill toured us through the magnificent World of Birds pavilion that had opened in 1972, he was generous in sharing many of the technical details that made it such an outstanding facility. One of the crucial aspects was lighting, which was carefully regulated in the displays. "If the duration of night is too long," he said, "the small birds will starve."

He was very interested in special reproductive technologies such as embryo transplantation for breeding endangered mammal species. He was proud of his success with birds and said that over 1400 eggs had been laid that year in the bird pavilion.

The World of Birds was an excellent beginning to our quest for information, but another impressive facility was waiting for us at our next stop, the Philadelphia Zoo. Ronald Reuther was the director at that time, and he had a number of successes to his and his staff's credit. One was to have bred both Chilean and Caribbean flamingoes; tragically, vandalism had resulted in the cessation of breeding. The most interesting sight for us was the zoo's small and beautiful tropical house, which featured a rustic boardwalk through a thicket of tropical vegetation (a detail that strongly influenced our future plans). As Ronald walked us through the exhibit, he talked about the desirability of lateral lighting as well as sky light, high humidity and the importance of the preheating and filtration of water before spraying. Ron strongly supported our going to Britain and Europe to study the zoos and bird exhibits over there, and he rattled off a list of a dozen must-sees. By the time he'd finished with us, we were reeling with information, but our plans for the next stage of visits had begun to take shape.

In October of 1974, my wife and I flew to Basel, Switzerland, to attend the annual conference of the International Union of Directors of Zoological Gardens. I had been a member for two years, having attended meetings in Amsterdam and Antwerp. Through this organization, I was becoming acquainted with the world's most distinguished zoo and aquarium directors. Towards the end of the meetings, Jim and Isabelle Graham arrived in a Volkswagen van with Bob McLaren, his wife, Eve, and a German-born associate of the aquarium named Claus Mueller. Bob had just stepped down for the second time as president of the association. Since we were in Basel, we began our investigations at the Basel Zoo.

Ernst Lang, then the director, was a smart, articulate man who was a veterinarian by training. His zoo was richly endowed, for it had the patronage of the Geigys, a famous Swiss industrial family. Swiss zoologists are known worldwide for their practical understanding of the requirements of captive animals, and in the Basel Zoo Dr. Lang showed us many rare and endangered animals that were being successfully bred. They had bred over fifty pygmy hippos, but he was especially proud of their record for breeding thirteen rare Indian rhinos. The zoo was small and perfect, and I could see it as a kind of model for a renovated Stanley Park Zoo, although with different species.

Dr. Lang's newest building was a combination reptile terrarium and aquarium. It was spiral in shape, with the reptiles in the higher parts and the fish below. We were fascinated by both by the Indonesian Komodo dragons (giant monitor lizards, the largest land reptiles in the world) and by the beautiful European pond that could be viewed underwater through glass from inside the aquarium. Also new was the Basel Zoo's ape house, in which Lang's staff had tried to help along their gorilla breeding program by designing the spaces to allow for different degrees of privacy. Lang said they were showing the animals "blue movies" taken of breeding gorillas in other zoos.

With visions of ape pornography fresh in our minds, the Vancouver group drove to Zurich and Munich and then north to Nuremberg. At each zoological garden we were given tours by the respective director, and we took many notes about these well-run zoos. Then we went on towards the Czech border. The elevation was greater and the fields were covered with a light sprinkling of snow. At the border we were stopped by armed guards who carefully examined everything in our luggage.

The director of the Prague Zoo, Dr. Zdenek Veselovsky, was proudest of his breeding cheetahs and showed us the long outside run in which they got their exercise. The actual facilities were old and in poor repair, and we got the sense that Dr. Veselovsky was frustrated by the inefficiency of his country's political system. He told us a strange story about a private importer who operated in Czechoslovakia, near the Polish border, and had a major collection of East African animals.

It was too good a chance to pass up. After taking leave of Dr. Veselovsky, we piled into our van and headed north towards the Polish border, where we found that the improbable-sounding story was true. The wildlife farm was owned and operated by a Mr. Wagner, a worldly character who told us he frequently travelled to East Africa to collect wild animals. While most citizens of communist Czechoslovakia were not permitted to travel outside of the country or own private businesses, Wagner had found a lucrative market for his animals in the United Kingdom and other capitalist countries. The government actually encouraged him in this business because of the hard currency he brought into the country. He took us on a tour of his barns, which we found to be filled with rare Grevy's zebras, reticulated giraffes and other East African mammals from northern Kenya. It was very impressive but not a little strange.

We returned across East Germany, visiting the Dresden, Leipzig and East Berlin zoos along the way. The Leipzig Zoo, directed by Prof. Dr. Siegfried Seifert, was fascinating for its huge and highly odorous cat collection. It had an extraordinary number of species of large felids, not only typical lions, tigers, leopards and jaguars but rare subspecies. The level of husbandry in the East German zoos was clearly very high, and they had some notable breeding successes. At the same time, we were aware that they had less to work with than the zoos in West Germany.

Finally it was time to leave East Germany. We drove the van through Checkpoint Charlie, the main gateway through the famous wall that divided East and West Berlin. It was night and rather eerie as we zigzagged among the concrete barriers designed to stop tanks. We parked near some offices from which armed guards emerged to examine our vehicle. A mirror was held under the van to determine if we might be taking someone across the border illegally. We gave up our passports to an official and stood among groups of dispossessed-looking individuals waiting patiently to cross over to the West.

After visiting Hamburg, we flew to Jersey to visit the Jersey Wildlife Trust. This small zoo was founded by Gerald Durrell, who had originally been an animal collector. Concerned about the rapid decline in the populations of many animal species, he decided to establish a trust for the purpose of breeding these endangered birds and mammals in his own small zoological park. An excellent writer (and the brother of author Lawrence Durrell) Gerald became famous for his amusing and sensitive books on his collecting activities in remote parts of the world. We found the attractively landscaped Wildlife Trust to contain simple enclosures for rare pheasants, lemurs and other animals. Almost all of the animals were small, but he also had a family of gorillas.

In Jersey we were told that the finest bird exhibit in all of Europe was near Hanover—and we had left it out of our itinerary. Jim Graham felt that if it was the best we must see it, so we flew back to Germany. Vogelpark Walsrode was devoted solely to the exhibition of birds, and it was astonishingly innovative. We were fascinated by the great diversity of species and the various ways of exhibiting them. One of the ponds for waterfowl even had waves created artificially by a wave-making machine. It was the first time I had seen such a device.

All told, we visited thirty-five different zoos and aviaries in our quest, and we accumulated a tremendous amount of information. What emerged from our planning was a concept: a modern aviary to be located in the Stanley Park Zoo adjacent to the aquarium. We engaged designer Rudy Kovach to paint some renderings of the zoo area and the new aviary, and we got the aquarium's education director Sharon Proctor to write an eloquent description of the project. To root the dream in reality, Jim and Isabelle made a substantial funding offer to the aquarium association. Jim was adamant that the aquarium association should plan and operate the project, not the Park Board. He felt the Park Board neglected the zoo and would not properly maintain the new aviary.

When the concept came before the Park Board in October 1975, it was clear from the start that some of the commissioners were circling their wagons against any chance that the aquarium association might extend its territories in Stanley Park. In the end, the Park Board avoided making a decision and moved that a long-range plan be developed for the Stanley Park Zoo area. The dejected aquarium supporters repaired to the Grahams' home for a "wake."

There was no way around it: we would have to develop our new project as part of the existing aquarium building. During another round of thorough planning, the idea arose of recreating a whole ecosystem, one that presented the birds in their ecological context of plants, fish, reptiles and even some mammals and insects. The region we settled on representing was the Amazon, both for its astonishing natural diversity and because of the importance of making people care about the danger it faced from the encroachments of cattle farming and industry.

By the end of the decade the design for the outer shell of the Amazon project was in hand. However, to guarantee a high quality of exhibit, it was clear that aquarium staff would have to go to the Amazon itself. I talked to Jim and Isabelle about a trip and suggested we ask Mervin Larson of the Arizona Sonora Desert Museum to join us. Merv had done impressive work in creating realistic backgrounds and was an expert on smaller animals of the jungle, particularly insects, spiders and other arthropods. Ever interested in excellence, the Grahams agreed to include Mervin in the trip.

In November 1979, the four of us departed Vancouver for Lima and a three-and-a-half week trip to the Amazon basin. After visiting Machu Picchu high in the Andes, we headed to the tropical Amazon areas, beginning with the hot, dusty Peruvian town of Puerto Maldonado. This is a port town located at the juncture of several rivers that join to form the Madre de Dios in the headwaters of the great Madeira river, which in turn flows into the Amazonas just downstream from Manaus.

Those Peruvian riverbanks were teeming with life both on land and in the air. Probably the most charming things we saw as we explored the river with our guide were the butterflies, particularly the brilliant blue morphos that flew slowly over the trails, stopping occasionally, then flying farther along. Hundreds of yellow butterflies resembling the cabbage butterflies of North America congregated on the banks of streams and river.

At night we slept under mosquito netting with a mosquito coil exuding its insecticidal smoke from the floor. It was hot and humid as we listened to the sounds of the tree frogs and the many unidentifiable noises. One evening, near a Yagua Indian village, Jim and Isabelle and I walked down a trail with our flashlights and were followed by a small, playful house cat. Suddenly the cat encountered a fer-de-lance, a poisonous pit viper, near the path. The snake repeatedly struck at the cat but always missed due to the cat's extraordinary reflexes. With less impressive reflexes at our command, we beat a hasty retreat.

On another night we were taken out on a boat along some side waters, and with strong beams of light we spotted the glowing eyes of caimans. The animals lurked in the water, submerged with just their bulging eyes above the surface reflecting light like rubies. Our guide captured several of them for me to photograph, then we let them go. Our purpose was to photograph and gather ideas, not to collect.

After we had returned to Puerto Maldonado, Mervin became ill. None of us felt very well, but he was positively blue as he lay on a bench in the rest house. Only Isabelle and I felt well enough to go out for dinner. When we returned to the lodge, Jim and Merv were running temperatures of a hundred and two. In the end, I too got sick, leaving Isabelle the only healthy member of the expedition.

We flew back to Lima to have a medical checkup and were seen together by a doctor who prescribed a fantastic array of medicines. The drugs made such an impressive pile when we finished purchasing them all that we couldn't resist photographing them. Mervin left us there and the Grahams and I flew eastward over that portion of the Amazon the Brazilians call Solimões, finally arriving at the large city of Manaus. We were met by our research associate Robin Best, then a scientist with INPA, the Brazilian organization for research on Amazon fish.

Robin was tall and remarkably handsome with an air of innocence. Since his father had been curator of the Stanley Park Zoo, Robin had grown up with animals. Now he was studying manatees in Brazil with his Brazilian wife, Vera da Silva, who was engaged in her own research on freshwater dolphins. Robin was particularly interested in the feeding behaviour of manatees and was working with the Brazilian government on a plan to place manatees in hydroelectric reservoirs so that they might devour floating hyacinth vegetation that clogged the machinery.

Robin drove us over to the house where he and Vera lived with half a dozen other young scientists, all sleeping in hammocks. Then he took us over to the research station and enthusiastically showed us his manatees, which were maintained in pools. The manatees, great blubbery animals, loved to be rubbed and were very tame. We also saw a pair of giant otters that Robin and Vera were observing.

Robin had worked hard to learn Portuguese quickly, and he was extremely good with the local population. He was mixing with them all the time, up and down the river, looking for areas that could be set aside as national parks. With him as guide our short expedition along the Amazon on the venerable double-decked riverboat *Pyata* was a joy as well as a rich source of information. There were so many interesting forms of animal life above and below the surface as the shore slipped past: Surinam toads, caimans, piranhas, white plumed egrets and the river dolphins that Vera was studying.

At night we slept in hammocks strung across the deck in the open air. Each of us was draped in our own mosquito nets and the whole area was covered by a roof to keep us dry in case it rained. In the daytime we set our nets in the side water of the Amazon and caught armoured catfish, silvery arawanas and colourful peacock cichlids. We photographed and took note of everything, particularly the riverbank and its vegetation. All too soon it was time to leave.

Barely six years later, Robin would die of leukemia while working on his doctor's degree in Cambridge, England. He and Vera had just returned from China, where they had attended a scientific conference on freshwater dolphins. In recognition of Robin's great services to the aquarium and in remembrance of our friendship, the aquarium's research library was named the Robin Best Library at a ceremony in early 1987.

The project was finally coming together. All the designs were carefully reviewed with Park Board staff ahead of time, and in January 1980 the Park Board approved the construction of the Graham Amazon Gallery. That meant that serious fund raising could commence, and ultimately over 375 donors contributed $3.25 million to the project.

Creating a great exhibit involves a lot of teamwork as well as consultation and conceptual borrowing across both geographical and professional borders. For example, Gil and Stefani Hewlett took members of the project team to visit the Denver Zoological Gardens, the Topeka Zoological Gardens and the Sedgwick County Zoo in Wichita, Kansas. In each they studied the tropical exhibits and developed many ideas relevant to creating the Amazon Gallery.

We decided to create the artificial rockwork ourselves, based on photographs taken in Brazil while aboard the *Pyata*. In their pursuit of authenticity, Gil and Stefani talked to Ewald Lemke, an outstanding exhibit designer at the provincial museum in Victoria, about obtaining a mould of a kapok tree and producing realistic casts. Mr. Lemke went to Florida where he found a magnificent, buttressed kapok in a botanical garden and created replicas of the base of the trunk for us.

The detailed design and development of the gallery involved much discussion. The conservation and ecological aspects would make it different from the standard tropical exhibits of other zoos and aquariums; it would have a central theme and it would be regional.

Sharon Proctor, our curator of education, was greatly involved in expanding and defining this theme. I remember her giving an excellent talk once to staff on the intricacies of the exhibit. For plant maintenance and to promote reproduction in the bird species, she explained, we required a twelve-hour photoperiod in the pavilion. In summer, this would require a darkening effect to mask out a portion of the sunlight of long days, and in the winter high-intensity artificial illumination would be needed to lengthen the northern day inside. Any insecticide to be used had to be harmless to the birds and other exhibit animals. Liquid fertilizer would be fine, but some kinds would leave green stains that we might or might not want. Concrete can hurt the feet of birds and red-lead paint can be toxic: these had to be avoided.

Behind the scenes, we planned a quarantine room of about 270 square feet in area, with cages for new or ill birds, and a food preparation room of 550 square feet. It had to contain refrigerators, sinks, closets for food storage, a cutting table, blenders and a three-burner stove. The menu was to include mealworms, crickets, fruit flies, mice, rats and gerbils—unappetizing to you and me, but a banquet to our expected guests.

As the shell was constructed and we counted down towards the opening date, our staff began to assemble the animals for the exhibit. An outside consultant, Geoff Webb, created a magnificent rainstorm exhibit over the caiman tank. It was operated hourly by an automatic timer. As the sound of thunder built in volume, the sky darkened and lightning flashed. Rainfall began as a gentle shower and quickly developed into a deluge. As the storm moved on, the sun sparkled once again on the glistening jungle pool.

It was shaping up to be a terrific exhibit, and clearly it deserved an equally terrific opening ceremony. And we got it, largely through the efforts of Ron Basford, formerly minister of justice and attorney general for Canada, who happened to be the president of the aquarium association in 1983. The Honourable Ron knew that the queen would be in Vancouver in March of that year and used his connections to send an invitation to Buckingham

Palace. We all held our breath until it was confirmed: the monarch would attend the grand opening on March 9. The impending visit led to a crash course on protocol for everyone who might have contact with the queen. "Do not initiate conversations," we were instructed, "and do not point."

By the beginning of March the gallery was complete, a giant terrarium with a mix of animals, some in cages and others running free. The plants were in place, the soil perfectly landscaped, the interpretive graphics and water systems all shiny and ready for action. In the main glass-domed area, a plank pathway enabled visitors to weave their way through the jungle under the shadows of a giant buttressed tree trunk. The bird population consisted of thirty-eight individuals representing twenty-one species. Overhead, South American cardinals and toucans were warily getting used to each other. In a corner tank, a twelve-foot-long anaconda coiled itself lazily around the submerged tree roots in its tank. A pair of two-toed sloths moved slowwwwwly along the branches of the various tree species. In the largest fish tank, a giant arapaima swam gracefully while the caimans waited quietly for the tropical rainstorm to burst upon them.

The sun came out for the 5000 enthusiastic people around the front of the aquarium on the afternoon of March 9, 1983. As we waited for Her Majesty's arrival, I gave some kind of impromptu speech to fill in the time. No one listened; everyone was too excited waiting for the queen. I gave up, and Jim Graham started a more formal speech. Again, no one listened but it didn't matter, for soon after he began the royal cavalcade announced itself with the roar and flashing lights of the police motorcycle escort. Ron Basford and I walked out to the queen's limousine where Ron shook hands with her, then introduced her to me. We then walked up the ramp of the aquarium with RCMP officers in red tunics keeping the friendly crowd back. Flags flew and a band played as the queen, wearing a light yellow top coat and straw hat, officially opened the Amazon Gallery.

The formalities over, Jim and Isabelle and I toured the aquarium with the queen, while various members of the aquarium peeked out at the procession from corners, like jungle animals observing some new intruders into their habitat. Security was heavy but discreet. I concentrated on the instructions I had received from the protocol officer and kept repeating to myself, "Don't point, don't initiate conversation!" The aquarium was immaculate as we strolled through the MacMillan Tropical Gallery and then into the new exhibit. Her Majesty looked first at the giant arapaima, then at the caimans lounging on the manmade bank of the Amazon. Suddenly, Geoff Webb bounded out to turn on the tropical rainstorm, with its burst of thunder and lightning.

So far everything was going like clockwork. We passed the videotape screen that warned that the Amazon rainforest was being destroyed, the mounted blue morpho butterflies and the giant anaconda, then looked upwards in a search for the birds in the walk-through aviary. There I forgot my instructions and showed very bad form by pointing and blurting out, "Oh, look! There's the sloth!"

Then the schedule began to unravel. As we approached the marmoset exhibit, the queen took in the beautifully created scene. Marmosets are small monkeys, and they are arguably the cutest creatures in all creation. Tree branches extended along the side of the exhibit, enabling the animals to come to the glass. This our two perfectly matched marmosets did, leaping up to perch side by side and peer at the queen, who peered back. Isabelle Graham later commented that it was a pity no one was able to take a picture at that moment; it would surely have been one of the most wonderful pictures of this regal woman, lost in the world of nature for a few fleeting seconds. Then she remembered where she was and moved on.

The gallery had been closed all day, and the animals seemed particularly primed and receptive as we walked through. As we departed the Amazon Gallery, I forgot myself again and pointed down the MacMillan Tropical Gallery at the sharks. The queen marched over to them, an unplanned excursion that caused great confusion for the security people.

The schedule was now in tatters as the aquarium worked its magic. "This is the most animated and delighted she has looked through the entire visit," commented a British photographer as we walked outside to the B.C. Tel Pool, where the belugas began chirping as if they anticipated the royal arrival. The queen gave them a good look over, then walked on to the killer whale pool where Hyak, Finna and Bjossa gave a lively performance. After that, another unscheduled move occurred when Her Majesty went over to the Finning Sea Otter Pool to see the new baby that had been born two months before.

It may have bothered the protocol people, but for me the schedule stretching was a tribute to the new gallery and indeed to the whole aquarium. The public evidently agreed with the queen, for the Amazon Gallery has been a strong attraction ever since.

Miss Peebles would have been proud.

# 17

# How to
# Blow-Dry an Otter

The good news about the Vitus Bering expedition of 1741 was that it revealed the existence of many animal species in the North Pacific that were previously unknown to European naturalists. The bad news (and it was very bad news) was that the expedition triggered a relentless, mindless slaughter that resulted in the extinction and near extinction of some of the world's most interesting sea mammals. One of these was the sea otter (*Enhydra lutris*), which was identified by Georg Steller, the German biologist with the expedition.

For 170 years after the Bering expedition, exploitation of the sea otter went unregulated. Prior to commercial exploitation, they could be found all along the North American coast from Baja California to Alaska, along the Aleutians to Kamchatka in Siberia and as far south as Hokkaido, Japan. By 1911, there were none left in the coastal waters of Oregon, Washington and British Columbia; all had been killed. A small population survived along the central Californian coast, which under protection grew to perhaps 2000 in the mid-1970s. You now can often see them from shore near Monterey as they swim among the kelp beds or among the boats in the marinas.

The main surviving population, however, was in Alaska. After more than fifty years of careful management by the U.S. Fish and Wildlife Service and the Alaska Department of Fish and Game, northern colonies reached the size where recolonizations could be attempted. The first transplantations along the coast of Alaska in the 1950s were unsuccessful because people did not understand that they must be done quickly by air, keeping the animals cool and clean. Similarly, the first transplants to B.C. from Alaska in the late 1960s were failures. But the 1970s brought success when some of these Alaskan otters were reintroduced to areas along the British Columbia, Washington and Oregon coasts.

Every year of my tenure at the aquarium I would get a few phone calls from people reporting that they'd seen a sea otter somewhere along the B.C. coast. We usually established that what they had seen was in fact a river otter (*Lutra canadensis*), quite a different animal though common around coastal marinas. I had a set speech for most of these callers: "If you see an otter in

Puget Sound or the Strait of Georgia, it is almost certainly a river otter. Sea otters live on the outer coasts, not the inland waters."

If the caller was more persistent, I would add Part Two: "Of course, rules are meant to be broken, and as sea otter populations recover they *may* occupy certain inland waters too. You can check by the way it rests at the surface. The sea otter always rests at the surface with its belly up while a river otter's back is up and its belly is down."

Related to river otters, weasels, skunks and badgers in the family *Mustelidae*, sea otters are among the few animals that use "tools." After diving as deep as 120 feet for their invertebrate or fish dinners, they return to the surface and use their forepaws to manipulate the food while floating on their backs. Otters can often be seen pounding hard-shelled mollusks against a stone or shell held on the chest. This tool-using behaviour doesn't reflect foresight or intelligence in the human sense; it is probably derived from frustration behaviour, which also involves pounding the chest. Sea otters have been observed in captivity going through a learning process beginning with frustration (at not getting a clam open) and leading to the pounding of two objects together (the clam against another clam or a rock).

The sea otter's thick fur—ironically, the prize that led to its near extinction—protects it from the cold by maintaining a layer of air among the hairs so that the skin is never touched by cold water.

The aquarium's first sea otter came to us on loan from the Alaska Department of Fish and Game, and the U.S. Bureau of Sport Fisheries and Wildlife. "John" was three years old when he came to us in 1969, and he lived a healthy life in the Vancouver Aquarium for the next eighteen years. He lived first in the holding area and then in an exhibit tank in the B.C. Hall of Fishes. At this point only the Point Defiance Zoo and our aquarium had been successful in keeping this species, but successful breeding had not been achieved. It was one of my dreams to create a larger facility in which we could establish a breeding colony. As always, the major preoccupation was how to fund the dream.

Help arrived in the form of Finning Tractor's Vancouver dealership, whose president and CEO Maury Young had noticed John's solitary existence. Finning had first come to the aid of the aquarium in 1962 when it lent us a large generator after a hurricane knocked out electrical power in Stanley Park. In 1966 they sponsored a tropical fish exhibit in honour of Earl Finning, the company founder. This time Maury got the support of his board of directors to finance a first-class sea otter pool at the aquarium.

Through the assistance of John Vania, the head of Marine Mammal Studies for the Alaska Department of Fish and Game, we got permission from the appropriate agencies in Alaska and Washington, D.C., to obtain three female otters from Cordova, Alaska. This was the centre for otters captured for translocation down the coast, and at that moment there were thirty-nine otters being held in a floating cage on a lake near the town. Maury Young generously offered his company's aircraft to bring the new otters down to Vancouver, and so it was that on an overcast day in July 1972 I found myself aboard a twin-engine Cessna bound for Alaska.

The cabin of the plane was completely filled with two large plastic garbage cans, a dip net, luggage, a camera and other equipment. With me were Klaus Michaelis and Maury himself, who as an experienced pilot acted as navigator. (I also confess to assigning him less technical jobs such as loading otter cages and maintaining their water levels for long hours, all of which he did without complaint. As aquarium donors know from their years of experience with me, he or she who pays the piper sometimes has to carry the pipe.) After a long trip involving several delays due to rough weather and an overnight stop in Anchorage, we finally landed in Cordova, a town of about 1500 people with a splendid backdrop of snow-covered mountains. The Prince William Hotel had no room for us so we went to a smaller inn called The Reluctant Fisherman overlooking the fish docks. It too was full, but the manager, recognizing us as paying customers, evicted several men who had not paid their rent. And so we ended up with four cots in one room.

Next morning John Vania woke us at 6:30 to tell us that a Canadian military Hercules aircraft was coming in at nine for a major transplant of sea otters to Vancouver Island's west coast. It was important that we pick out our three otters as soon as possible or we wouldn't get any. When we drove down to the lake, we found a big crew already there to move the otters into cages for transport to the airport, where John Vania was injecting the animals with a tranquillizer called Azium. With John's help, Klaus selected three female otters for the aquarium. We worked fast to load up, and by 10:45 we were on our way back to Vancouver, flying southeast along the Alaska Panhandle at 15,000 feet with a tailwind of 258 miles per hour.

It was a long trip. Even with the cabin heating system turned off, it was difficult to keep the cabin temperature down to the 30-35° F that was necessary for the animals' health and comfort. Our problem was the clear Alaskan sunlight that shone through the cabin windows. Finally, by climbing to 19,000 feet, where the air temperature was -14° F, we managed to reduce the cabin temperature to the desired range.

As we flew along the St. Elias range of mountains we had a spectacular view of the Malaspina Icefields. But we hardly looked at the view, for the sea otters were very quiet, mainly resting on their backs in the half inch of water on the bottom of their cages. The largest otter in particular seemed to be very slow. As the hours passed, we gradually left the clouds behind us, and when we landed in Vancouver seven hours and two time zones later, we were greeted by a sunny summer evening.

By the time we reached the aquarium the otters had been out of the water for eleven hours. Two of them appeared to be rather groggy from Azium, but all swam and groomed actively when put in the water. Better yet, they began feeding as soon as Klaus put fish fillets into the tank.

Next day we were dismayed to find that one of the otters had died. The autopsy revealed that its kidneys, intestines, stomach, liver and heart were normal. There was no indication of infection or injury but there was pulmonary congestion in the lungs, which were engorged with blood. As was the case in so many of the government transplants of sea otters, we had lost this animal from the stress and overheating that accompanies transport. We were very disappointed to lose this otter, but with John and the two new females we now had the basis of a breeding colony.

We named the two females Attu and Kiska. Initially they and John were housed in an open air pen in the aquarium's research area. There, Susan Hoffer spent the daylight hours of an entire month observing their activities. The otters' two wood-and-wire cages were connected to one another, with John residing in the smaller cage and the females in the other. Both cages were filled with water one-and-a-half feet deep. Otters are extremely sensitive to the presence of humans, so Susan made her observations from the window of a laboratory overlooking the cages. She even went so far as to cover the window glass with paper, peering at the animals through peepholes as she recorded their activities on a twenty-channel event recorder, a special computer used by scientists in this kind of work.

The most fascinating thing was to watch the otters using "tools" to eat sea urchins, their favourite food. Unlike other foods, the hard-shelled sea urchins had to be broken open. The otters usually tried to crack urchins open first with their forepaws; if unsuccessful, they would resort to the use of a rock, which they would hold in both paws and hammer against the sea urchin. Sometimes they would crack two urchins together to open them, scooping out the meat with their tongues or forepaws.

When John was first allowed into the females' cage, he immediately attempted to mate with both of them. Later he settled down to mating only (but frequently!) with Kiska. He would approach her either from below or from the side, grabbing her around the neck or chest with his forepaws and often biting her. If she was on a platform, he would generally try to drag her back into the water, tugging at her tail or neck with his forepaws. Susan observed, "He was usually the aggressor, but she occasionally initiated the play, either by sniffing his genital region or (less subtly) by leaping on him.

There would be much splashing and rolling about in the water, and it would continue for as long as twenty minutes. However, they did not remain together for this period of time, but frequently broke away from each other to groom or look around, returning to each other shortly thereafter."

In designing the Finning Pool, our architects and engineers had to consider the problems and needs specific to the maintenance of healthy sea otters and at the same time accommodate the visiting public. The planning and construction went very quickly.

The finished sea otter complex was actually a group of three pools, with one large display pool and two smaller holding pools. The main pool was thirty-eight feet long and twenty-nine feet wide, with a capacity of about 20,000 U.S. gallons, while the smaller pools held a total of 8000 U.S. gallons. The smallest pool was shut off from public viewing to permit complete isolation of an animal under veterinary care or to serve as a nursery for a mother and pup. All three pools had a maximum depth of four and a half feet. The largest pool had an artificial "beach" so that the otters could climb out of the water and dry off. To keep the water surface free of debris or uneaten food, a continuous scum gutter was built into this simulated beach. All the gutter water returned to the pool's filter for cleaning.

Visitors to the aquarium always remark on the fact that, although the otter pools are enclosed, they lack a roof. I always hasten to explain that this isn't because we ran out of money; rather, exposure to the elements provides the air and temperature conditions that sea otters normally experience in nature. Visitors are protected from the elements by an extended roof over the public corridor at the perimeter of the pool. This roof also darkens the corridor, making the public less visible to the otters and therefore less disturbing to them.

The sensitivity of otters to the presence of people was carefully considered in the design and construction of the new Finning Sea Otter Pool. Visitors could observe the otters from a lower level through glass and see them both above and below water, but they were not allowed to view the otters from a higher level at the other end of the pool. The architects introduced a colouring agent into the cement to give it a warm buff tone and contoured the building to provide a flowing design that reflects the movements of the animals themselves. Microphone jacks in the viewing areas enabled our guides to give explanatory comments on the behaviour and life story of the sea otters.

While the Finning Pool was both attractive and functional, its plumbing was also a thing of beauty—at least to an aquarium professional. Sea otters have an extremely high metabolic rate and consequently release large amounts of body wastes into their pool water. This creates a problem: a sea otter can die if its fur gets soiled and the air layer next to the skin is penetrated by the cold water, so it is imperative that the pool water be as clean and pure as possible. As we had in our other marine mammal pools, we used a diatomaceous filter to remove wastes from the water.

The Finning Sea Otter Pool was opened by Maury Young and Vancouver's popular mayor Arthur Phillips, in 1973. The trio of sea otters prospered and we learned, without much trial and error, about caring for them. At first, despite our installation of a state-of-the-art filtration apparatus, there were some problems with the water system. After an exhaustive investigation, we finally discovered that chlorination (to get rid of potential toxins) had a damaging effect on the animals' fur. After this, chlorination was followed by dechlorination and the problem was solved.

Our work with the otters in the 1970s and 1980s resulted in the aquarium's having a group of experienced veterinarians, biologists, handlers and volunteers who knew more about sea otter care than anyone else in Canada. With a custom-built habitat and the excellent skills of our staff, the aquarium's breeding program was very successful. By the late 1980s ten healthy offspring had been raised, and we ultimately sent several to Japan, where they are breeding successfully. Another recipient was the Oregon Coast Aquarium, which received four otters when it opened in 1992 in Newport under its new director, Phyllis Bell.

We learned a lot about breeding during those years. For instance, although adult males can be housed together, they fight if a female is added to the group. On the other hand, a group of females can coexist with one male.

Males, being larger than females, are very rough in their mating behaviour. They often bite the upper part of the female's nose during copulation, causing bleeding. The birth of furry little baby sea otters partly mollified staff sensitivities about this behaviour, but there was a lingering impression that some male otters were unduly brutal.

However, a far crueller situation was developing on the northwest coast of the Pacific Ocean. With the development of the pipeline across Alaska from the oil fields at Prudoe Bay to Valdez, and the transportation of oil in great ships down the coast, the potential for an ecological disaster from an oil spill was increasingly great. In order to work out techniques for cleaning and rehabilitating oiled otters, Dr. Randall Davis and Terrie Williams of the Sea World Research Institute in San Diego conducted a controversial experiment—they deliberately put oil on sea otters. What they learned turned out to be of great importance.

Shortly after midnight on March 24, 1989, the tanker *Exxon Valdez* ran aground on Bligh Reef in Prince William Sound, Alaska. Within half an hour the tanker had lost 150,000 barrels of oil, already too much for local crews to control. It disgorged the oil into the clear waters of a wilderness area rich in marine life, including thousands of sea otters.

The U.S. government reacted quickly, asking Randall Davis to set up and operate a service for cleaning sea otters at Valdez, twenty-five miles from the centre of the spill. In a very short time he found himself in charge of twenty-eight fishing boats, sixty onshore pools, ten cleaning stations and a staff of about two hundred. The first sea otter rehabilitation centre opened at the Prince William Sound Community College in Valdez on March 27 and oiled otters began arriving on March 30. Dr. Judy McBain was put in charge of veterinary care in Valdez, and it was she who asked the Vancouver Aquarium to assist in the rehabilitation program.

Within several days of the spill Jeremy FitzGibbon, who had replaced Klaus Michaelis as the Vancouver Aquarium's chief mammal trainer, was in Valdez to help in the rescue effort. As he tells it, "At the very beginning, I was the only aquarium person in Valdez, and then Sea World sent up some people, which really helped. It was a classic example of why we need aquariums or zoos, because nothing would be known about sea otter husbandry if it wasn't for our having these animals. They are extremely difficult to deal with. They have sensitive fur and they are difficult to house. If we hadn't had the experience of sea otters in captivity, we couldn't have saved a single one. Without that experiment in San Diego in which a few otters were purposely oiled, a hundred would have died before we figured out how to clean the fur.

"When we arrived in Alaska, it was chaos. We had no facilities. There were half a dozen otters in already. The next day they started coming in by the planeload. These otters looked as though they had been dunked in a barrel of crude oil. We learned later there was no hope for these. We might as well have euthanized them. The big thing was the toxicity of the oil. They licked themselves to clean the fur and it destroyed their livers. Their livers were complete mush when you did the autopsy. And toxic gases killed many otters immediately.

"We were set up in two one-bedroom apartments, part of a college or something. We ripped the wall out to house the otters so we could clean them up as they came in. Each otter would take four to six hours to clean by five or six people.

"Since I was the only person with hands-on experience, I was the one who organized the whole husbandry part of it. We had great volunteers, local people, super people, but they had no idea how to handle an otter. After a few days, the Sea World people arrived, then people from Tacoma, Monterey and Chicago. One lady who was over sixty drove her car from Florida to Valdez, stayed in her car for two weeks because there were no rooms anywhere. She volunteered for us twelve hours a day for two weeks, then drove back.

"We had forty-five otters in a matter of a few days, so we moved to a school gymnasium where sixty or seventy otter pens were being built. We had the pups, too, which was really the last straw. I hadn't slept for about three days and someone brought in this little two-week-old pup, this little ball of fur. I didn't know what to do so I phoned Monterey, because of their experience with sea otter pups, and asked them to send someone right away. I had this pup all night and I didn't know what to do, it was screaming. I mixed up fish in a blender to try to get him to drink. I could get a little bit of food into him but not much. I couldn't sleep with this pup because he was screaming the whole time, so I went into the communications centre where all the telephones were. It was about four in the morning and there was a night guard there. As soon as I put the pup on the cold tile floor, he fell fast asleep. It was just too warm all the time. Then I wouldn't let anybody use the phones, and everyone had to use the phones. I said, If anyone comes in and wakes this otter, you're going to have to answer to me.

"The gymnasium was better than the previous quarters, but we found out in moving the otters from one place to another that they were much better outside. Within three minutes one would change from an otter that was comatose, not interested in food and just looking like it was going to die, to one that was jumping up and wanting food. They just couldn't stand being indoors. We thought the gymnasium would be all right, because it was so big, but it wasn't, it was the same thing. They had spent many millions of dollars on this gymnasium and the piping work alone was incredible. I just told them that we had to move all the otters outside. You guys have to build the whole thing outside, I said, so we started to do that and the transformation in the otters was incredible.

"We got very good at removing the oil, that's an easy thing to do. Dawn detergent seemed to cut the crude oil best, so that's what we used. Getting the otter back after that is a tougher problem, because each otter is a little different. The natural body oils would have to return to the fur but, more than that, we destroyed the fur in the cleaning operation. When you look at otter fur under a microscope it is basically all split ends, which trap the air bubbles. When you shampoo them, you get rid of the split ends and there is no way of trapping air in the fur. The otters can't insulate themselves. Their own oils come back in a couple of days, but some otters would still soak through up to two weeks later because of the fur.

"It wasn't just a question of taking the oil out and then keeping the otters dry for two weeks. We had to return them to the water as soon as possible, otherwise their fur would get worse and worse because they didn't get to groom it. Each otter would have to be put in the water and left as long as possible. It had to be cold water, since warm water wrecks their fur. The colder the better. Left to its own devices, the otter would stay in until it died, so you had to wait until it was shivering and then take it out and blow-dry it. Then you just kept gradually increasing the time you kept it in the cold water.

"The *Exxon Valdez* oil spill may have killed anywhere from 3000 to 10,000 otters. About 500 were brought in, of which 350 survived. The first ones were hopeless, but in the Vancouver Aquarium we have Annie, the earliest survivor. We thought for sure she was going to die. When otters get the liver infection in the belly, it just swells right up. You can't miss it. Whenever that happened the otter died, you couldn't help it. When I was bringing otters back to the aquarium I purposely brought some of the hard cases to see if we could do a better job down here, and I picked her. We kept draining her belly and everything down here and she survived, which really surprised us."

Jeremy and his colleagues brought back eight otters. We had a specially built rehabilitation facility waiting for them and we had organized an army of volunteers to provide round-the-clock care. After a few days we sent two of the otters temporarily to the Monterey Bay Aquarium because the staff there was expert at hand rearing and we were overwhelmed with work.

All of this cost money, of course. The aquarium was able to recover expenses of around $55,000 from Exxon, including travel expenses to Alaska, extraordinary veterinary costs and the expenses involved in setting up the rehabilitation centre at the aquarium. Eventually, we sent three of the otters to new homes in the Seattle and Point Defiance aquariums.

On March 15, 1990, the aquarium's newly renovated and enlarged Finning Sea Otter Habitat was officially opened. The Youngs and the Barkers were in attendance as honoured guests, but without a doubt the most honoured guests were the five rescued Valdez otters.

# 18
# The Reykjavik Affair

By and large, the Vancouver Aquarium's relations with the press have been excellent. The local media were very helpful to us in the early years when we were small and poor, and in return we provided (and still provide) a steady stream of stories to fill their pages and airtime. Everything had a positive tone: unusual creatures arriving for the first time, heroic measures to keep some animal alive, an exhibit opening and so on. You'd be hard put to find a negative story about us until the mid-1960s. That, of course, was when killer whales became part of the equation.

You can't remain small and keep killer whales, at least not in a responsible way. The major reason is a physical one: they need as much space as you can give them, and we were always trying to find ways to extend our killer whale habitat. Another reason is financial: they cost a lot to house and to feed, and you need a larger organization to do it. And finally, killer whales attract crowds of people, and you need an infrastructure to deal with them.

The arrival of Skana and the others was far from the only reason the aquarium expanded over the course of the past three decades, but they were certainly the biggest part of it. Our earlier preoccupation with finding a thousand dollars here and ten thousand dollars there grew into a three-fold monster: to find millions of dollars, to win the approval of the Park Board and to keep the opposition down enough so it would not turn off donors or Park Board commissioners.

For, as our reputation and influence grew, opposition developed to balance it. We were big enough to be cast as Bad Guys occasionally, and the whales—beautiful, majestic and inscrutable—made perfect Victims. A host of groups arose, each with its own issue and each busily promoting itself as a Good Guy. Sometimes, the Victim was not an animal but the verdant spaces of Stanley Park itself, which the wicked aquarium was accused of wishing to cover with concrete and asphalt in its never-ending quest for expansion. Similarly, anyone opposed to our raising our admission fees could say the entire population of the Lower Mainland were Victims.

I'm not saying the issues—some of them— weren't valid. Stanley Park is a treasure that should be protected; admission fees are a concern, especially to young families; keeping killer whales in captivity is most certainly a moral issue. Nor am I saying that most of the reporters weren't doing the best job they knew how to do. It's just that most of the issues were and remain very complex and are not easily reduced to a three-hundred-word newspaper article or a two-minute television item. In such a reduced information environment, it is the simple story and the stirring phrase that catch the attention.

Throughout the 1970s Skana and Hyak were the stars at the aquarium, and their shows entertained millions of visitors. On September 18, 1980, Skana became listless and could not finish a show. Very quickly, the entire staff became very worried, and a gloomy pall spread over the aquarium. The press reflected the extreme concern of the staff very sympathetically.

The marine mammal staff took daily blood samples and bacterial cultures in order to diagnose her illness. We soon discovered that she had an infection in her reproductive tract, and we tried to treat it with antibiotics. However, she continued to be listless and wouldn't eat. She died on October 5, just as her handlers were preparing for her daily medical checkup. The autopsy told us that she had an internal fungus infection caused by an organism named *Mucor*. Skana had been thirteen years at the aquarium, a record at that time, and had never been seriously ill before. Her demise left Hyak all alone but for the presence of White Wings, the white-sided dolphin. Killer whales are social animals and we felt it important to find a companion for Hyak.

By this time the people of British Columbia and particularly those of the Victoria-Vancouver region had become familiar with killer whales through the aquarium and the media. I knew it would be unpopular for us to try to capture a live killer whale locally and felt a little frustrated about it: to my mind the entire awareness of the killer whales' right to live was brought about by aquariums exhibiting these animals and by the high level of media attention that followed. Of course, Greenpeace and others who opposed the collection and exhibition of these animals had generated lively debate in the press and contributed to the high level of awareness that developed. But without aquariums, the plight of killer whales would be as ignored as that of moose in the forests of British Columbia, large numbers of which are killed each year by sport hunters.

If local waters were out, the only other place to go at the time was Iceland. Three years before, my colleague Dr. W. H. Dudok van Heel of the Dolphinarium Harderwijk Holland in the Netherlands had captured a live killer whale in Iceland with the help of local fishermen. He had been followed by Don Goldsberry, who was then working with Sea World, and then by the Hunt brothers of the International Animal Exchange in Michigan, who had developed business arrangements with fishermen in Reykjavik. The Hunt brothers, Tom and Brian, were very well known after years of work in Africa, and they had a good reputation regarding Icelandic killer whales.

Trying to cover all the bases, I contacted the federal government to see how the Department of Fisheries would react to the aquarium's importing two juvenile orcas. Fisheries replied that it had no objection. That left us with one remaining challenge—the usual one of financing the project.

At the next board meeting, I described my understanding of the whale collecting situation in Iceland. Up until the collecting began, killer whales were usually shot on sight by fishermen in the North Atlantic. I argued that if the fishermen could make some money by capturing a few specimens every once in a while and selling them, they might stop shooting so many.

Moreover, we had an opportunity to acquire some orcas right then: my information was that six had recently been captured and the fishermen had not been able to sell them to anybody. The whales were swimming around and around and the ice was closing in. If somebody didn't hurry up and buy them, they would be in danger of freezing and serious injury, maybe death.

As I looked around the boardroom table, my eyes stopped frequently on a new member. Jean Southam, my companion on so many cruises on the *Marijean* with her father, H. R. MacMillan, sat next to Ralph Shaw listening to the discussion. As I continued with my argument for buying the whales, she wrote a note and passed it to Ralph, who read it and leaned over to her for a brief, sotto voce exchange. Ralph then passed me the note as Jean kept her gaze on the table. The other governors became aware that something important was happening, and all eyes were on me as I opened that little piece of paper and announced that we had just found a way to pay for the whales. Jean said later that she couldn't stand the idea of the whales freezing in the ice and that was what had moved her to offer to buy them for the aquarium.

The news of our plans got out, and in early December the Canadian division of Greenpeace announced it would oppose any attempt by the aquarium to bring killer whales from Iceland. It claimed that of sixteen killer whales captured in Icelandic waters since 1978 for sale to aquariums, two had died of frostbite, three had been released after suffering extreme frostbite and one had drowned after being run down by a boat. Greenpeace Director Patrick Moore released photographs to the press that showed killer whales that had apparently died of frostbite. The accusations may have been true. The fishermen had little interest or experience in handling live marine life up until that time. Anyone who has been on a commercial fish boat will remember the rough treatment that all dying marine animals are given. To the fishermen, the killer whales were just big fish.

On the morning of December 12, Jeremy FitzGibbon and I took off for New York, where we met our new veterinarian, Dr. Tag Gornall, and Brian Hunt of International Animal Exchange. Our group then flew to Iceland, where we were met at the Keflovik airport by the exchange's British veterinarian, Dr. David Taylor.

This was my first time in Iceland, a small country that I admire very much. Like so many northern countries it is highly dependent upon its fisheries. Physically, it is an extraordinary place to visit. We drove in darkness from the airport down the icy highway, which crosses vast snow-covered lava beds totally bare of trees or shrubs. Before reaching Reykjavik we stopped at the small zoo and aquarium where the fishermen had taken the whales to be looked after while they waited for buyers. There we met director Jon Gunnarsson, a fine-looking man in a Finnish fur hat. He showed us his small zoo, which exhibited seals, Arctic fox, a pair of African lions, a pair of chimps, geese, snowy owls, ravens and sheep. We were surprised to learn that the sheep were fed dried herring.

By 11:00 A.M. it was starting to become dimly daylight. There was a howling gale and, although it was only a few degrees below freezing, it felt terribly cold. The whale pool was a fifteen-foot-high concrete structure constructed on a petrified lava flow at the edge of the sea. About sixty feet by forty feet, and perhaps twelve feet deep, it contained salt water pumped in from the ocean. As we walked up the steps to the pool deck we were almost blown away by the fierce winds. In the pool were five little whales swimming vigorously. I could see that they had received a few abrasions during capture and transport, but otherwise they seemed healthy. In any case, our vet and the Hunts' vet were there to confirm their overall health. Blood samples taken by the Hunts' veterinarian were sent to London as well as to the local hospital for analysis.

Next morning we returned to the whale pool to examine the whales more closely. Ranging in length from five to eleven feet, they appeared to be very hungry despite the three feedings they received per day. For some reason I turned my gaze from the whales to a ridge that sloped towards the sea in the distance and caught a strange vision of Icelanders strolling along, swinging slender canes. As I stared at them, it dawned on me that today was Sunday and these strange people were golfers hitting balls into the snow!

Later we went to visit the country's chief fisheries officer, Dr. Thordur Asgeirsson, in order to obtain permits to take killer whales out of Iceland. The current quota had been set at six, since more could not be handled in the limited facilities available for holding them. Each animal had to be given the best possible care, he said, and if more whales were caught the quality of care would be decreased.

When I asked how many killer whales were known to inhabit local waters, Asgeirsson said there were schools of hundreds, perhaps thousands, but that no effort had been made to determine the exact number. Killer whales had no commercial value and had always been looked at as enemies since they ate herring out of the fishing fleets' nets.

Nonetheless, the anti-whaling controversy had not passed Iceland by, and the government was rethinking the situation. The Ministry of Commerce was interested in the new live whale industry, but the Ministry of Fisheries had mixed feelings about it. Part of this was due to campaigns by groups such as the Whale Protection Society, Save the Whales and Greenpeace; Greenpeace had placed the blame on the Icelandic government for the two killer whales that had died of frostbite two years before.

In any case, Asgeirsson said, the killing of big whales was a large industry in Iceland and far more important than the live killer whale industry. Iceland killed about four hundred whales a year, mostly fin, sei and sperm and a few pilot whales. Much was known about the local stocks, and whaling had stayed at the same intensity around Iceland for thirty-two years. This was the best evidence for the stability of the stocks. Foreign scientists were unanimous, Asgeirsson said, that Iceland was the only whaling nation not reducing stocks through overfishing.

I later heard from another fisheries official that fishermen were refraining from shooting the orcas because of the aquariums' interest in collecting them. When killer whales were caught in purse nets by seine boats, the larger ones were released. The whales were generally unhurt in the capture, but as they were transported on the decks of small boats back to Reykjavik they were subject to abrasion and chapping from windburn.

It occurred to me that Iceland's estimates of wild killer whale abundance were similar to the overestimates in British Columbia prior to systematic counts. Before the great orca census efforts of the early 1970s, everyone thought there were thousands along the B.C. coast instead of the 650 that are now known to live in the area. In Iceland there may have been only a couple of dozen hungry whales feeding on herring in the drift nets. Who knew? But I was intrigued by the realization that aquariums were responsible for a new attitude among Icelanders about killer whales.

The results of the blood tests finally came in, confirming that all of the whales were in good health. It was fortunate that we had arrived before any frostbite had occurred. We determined that the frostbite problem stemmed from the fact that in a holding pool the whales remained at the surface longer than they would in the ocean.

The deal we eventually worked out with the International Animal Exchange was that we would buy two whales but would take four of them back to Vancouver. After they had rested in our holding pool, one would be sent to Japan and another to California. I phoned Gil Hewlett in Vancouver to tell him we were buying the two largest females and arriving in Vancouver with four whales. While the flight would be twelve hours long, the elapsed time for the whales to be out of water would be twenty hours.

Gil reported that while the newspapers were being gentle with us, our activities had become national news. "Patrick Moore told the newspapers that Greenpeace will fight our acquiring another whale," he said. Soon after, the Vancouver television station BCTV warned me that Greenpeace people in Iceland were going to block us. If we did succeed in taking off with the whales, he said, Greenpeace would prevent our refuelling en route to Vancouver.

It was turning into a cloak-and-dagger operation. I decided I would fly back to Vancouver on my own and leave Jeremy FitzGibbon and Tag Gornall to return with the whales on a chartered 737 Nordair plane.

When I got back, I learned that Greenpeace was seeking an injunction in the B.C. Supreme Court to prevent the importation of killer whales. Patrick Moore was reported to have said that the aquarium wanted to import whales to perform circus tricks and that the whales were worth $250,000 each. When I was interviewed by the press I declared that Greenpeace had put so much pressure on our charter aviation company that the plane was several hours late leaving Canada to go to Iceland. This could imperil the whales, I said.

The B.C. Supreme Court ruled that Greenpeace had no status to oppose the import of the killer whales. Justice Callaghan said that in his opinion the balance was clearly in favour of the Vancouver Aquarium.

The four whales arrived in Vancouver shortly before noon on Saturday, December 20. Security was tight as the whales, suspended in canvas slings, were transported by cranes to our trucks. Motorcycle police accompanied us in a dramatic parade through city streets to the aquarium, where the whales were transferred to the research pool at the back of the building. I had invited a Greenpeace official to see them in order to verify that the whales were in good condition. That visit went very well; I remember explaining the arrangements we had made while transporting whales, such as covering them in white lanolin ointment to protect their skins.

Several weeks later the two smaller whales were sent to California and Japan respectively. The other two stayed with us, and we named them Finna and Bjossa. Although we had thought they were both females, it turned out that Finna was a male. A few weeks later we moved them into the holding pool adjoining the killer whale exhibit pool, the residence of Hyak and White Wings. For several days, Hyak frequently lifted his head from the water to stare over the gate into the pool at the young whales. He spent all night keeping vigil outside the closed door.

Finally the gate was lifted and Hyak came into the small pool, crowding the young ones. We were not at all sure what would happen and were worried about Hyak having a territorial reaction. This did not happen, although Finna and Bjossa splashed water at him with their flukes. Before long all of them, including the dolphin, were getting along amicably.

As usual, the new whales would not swim voluntarily into the big pool and finally had to be coaxed nearly a week later. Training started immediately, and by mid-April both Finna and Bjossa were clearing the water completely with their high jumps. Both whales were fully integrated into the format of the whale shows by the summer.

Now that we had three whales, it was clearly desirable to give them more room to swim in. Our dream was to build a totally new, six-million-litre killer whale habitat at the north end of the aquarium. With a backdrop of Burrard Inlet and the North Shore Mountains, it would have beautiful landscaping with a native Indian motif of totem poles and a longhouse. The idea was to allow visitors to observe the whales in an environment that closely reflected wild conditions. To build it, of course, we had to find more capital.

We got an early grant of $200,000 from Edgar Kaiser, Jr., the grandson of Henry J. Kaiser, the American industrialist who had built the famous Liberty Ships during World War II. Soon after, I submitted a proposal to the Max Bell Foundation, asking them to become the overall sponsor of a marine mammal centre. The foundation responded with the largest single pledge in our history: $1.5 million.

But even the huge Max Bell donation was just a beginning. A powerful fund-raising campaign had to be mounted, and I thought I knew just the person for it: Gordon MacFarlane, head of the B.C. Telephone Company. There was a tradition of support for the aquarium at B.C. Tel. Gordon Farrell—who had been head of the company before it had been sold to eastern interests—and his family had been great supporters from the very beginning. In 1966 Ralph Shaw enlisted B.C. Tel's then chairman Cyrus McLean to be a major contributor, and Cyrus remained an enthusiastic patron. The telephone company's next chairman, Ernest Richardson, had generously backed our B.C. Tel Pool during the great expansion of 1967.

Now Gordon MacFarlane was B.C. Tel's top man. Not your typical executive, he had risen through the ranks as an engineer rather than as a businessman, and he had a longstanding interest in community service.

Gordon became our white knight, and with him chairing our Marine Mammal Centre committee, we got preliminary approvals from the Park Board and started our public fund-raising campaign. He held breakfast committee meetings downtown every week and launched each member into the community to contact potential donors. Pledges came in rapidly and our funds grew accordingly, but our goals were very high.

While aquarium supporters gave enthusiastic support to the project, many strong opponents appeared at Park Board meetings to attack it (needless to say, the newspapers loved the battles and gave them a lot of coverage). First we were scolded for using too much park land for whale pools. Park Superintendent Stuart Lefeaux placed markers on the grass behind the aquarium to indicate the large size of the proposed killer whale habitat. We countered that, explaining that at less than one and a third acres, the project would take up a fraction of 1 per cent of Stanley Park's one thousand acres.

Then local native people made accusations that we would be destroying an ancient burial ground with our project. We countered that, too, when Sharon Proctor commissioned an archaeologist to drill core samples in the area and proved there were no ancient middens in our development zone.

There were three lively public meetings during 1984. Each one inspired a great deal of passionate debate, but the consensus of the Park Board remained with us.

We weren't so lucky on the federal level. Nineteen eighty-four was the year that the Liberal government in Ottawa was in its death throes. We'd had assurances from friends in Ottawa that several million dollars would be granted to us, but with the change in government those funds did not materialize. This, the recession and the negative impact on our donors of the acrimonious public debate caused us to rethink the project, but we realized that by changing the location and design of the facility, we would lose a further half million dollars in architectural fees.

It was staff scientist Jeff Marliave who came up with the idea of enlarging the existing whale pool by building a new pool alongside it, then connecting the two. That would allow the whales to remain in their pool while the new one was built, double the volume of their existing habitat and cost much less money. For those concerned about our encroachments on Stanley Park, the new plan would take only a tenth of an acre out of the duck pond west of the aquarium. Though less impressive than the original plan, the habitat would still reflect the shapes and colours of the coastal Gulf Islands, complete with native plants.

This new plan was quickly approved by the Park Board, and we were able to begin construction. Our sculptors worked long hours in the aquarium laboratories perfecting the rock design on a scale model. Aquarium background designer Peter Heiss had gone to Campbell Bay on Mayne Island to photograph the natural sandstone cliffs. Working with these photos in the lab he produced a model in sections, each section of which would be used on site to develop the final version on a much larger scale. The final production would make a dramatic background for the habitat.

Hyak, Finna and Bjossa watched the whole process of creating their new residence with great curiosity. As the excavation commenced alongside their pool they frequently lifted their heads high out of the water to see what was going on. Hoarding was constructed between the old pool and the new works but the whales appeared to be frustrated by this, so a large window was made in the plywood fence to allow the whales to watch the progress.

While the construction was going on, the aquarium hosted the Sixth Biennial Conference of the Society for Marine Mammalogy. During the four days of meetings, nearly eight hundred men and women from all over the world heard the latest scientific findings related to seals, sea otters, manatees, whales and dolphins.

A schism had developed among marine mammal scientists, and it was very visible at that conference. The split was over the issue of aquariums and captive cetaceans. My old friend Ken Norris, now a revered senior scientist and founder of the Society for Marine Mammalogy, represented the faction in the society that appreciated the value of captive cetaceans to the acquisition of scientific knowledge. Drawing from years of experience beginning with his stint as first curator of Marineland of the Pacific thirty years earlier, Ken presented a paper on the use of captive marine mammals in behaviour studies. He argued that "A full understanding of the behaviour of marine mammals requires studies both at sea and in captivity. Each provides a different view of behaviour, and by working in both ways one may check and correct interpretation made in each."

There was considerable debate over this idea. I found it interesting that many of those who were unsympathetic to aquariums had little or no experience with them. It also seemed to me ironic that some of the scientists who studied population dynamics in relation to whaling (again, people with little experience of captive animals) sometimes were negative about aquariums. They apparently belonged to the "better to kill them than cage them" school of thinking.

As construction neared completion, the killer whales found themselves playing musical chairs between pools. When the new pool was completed, we flooded it with water and opened the gate for the first time. As usual, the whales were reluctant to enter a new space. When coaxed with a net, however, they moved. The gate closed and we then drained the old pool to permit its expansion and renovation. Among other changes, the old jump tower was demolished to make way for the new sandstone cliffs and environmental presentations.

Big changes were also underway in the underwater viewing area, which became an interpretive museum, the H. R. MacMillan Gallery of Whales. Sharon Proctor and her staff created three-dimensional exhibits to explain the evolution, biology and behaviour of whales, with emphasis on the research of Michael Bigg and John Ford on the killer whales in our coastal waters. Greg Davies did all the internal design work, establishing the colour schemes, selecting the carpets and designing all the exhibits.

Stefani Hewlett took charge of opening ceremonies as well as publicity and truly outdid herself with a spectacular coup: a musical joint production of the Canadian Broadcasting Corporation and the Vancouver Bach Choir called "In Celebration of Whales." Backed by members of the Vancouver Symphony Orchestra, the choir and soloists Judith Forst and Mark Pedrotti rehearsed a program that included the newly commissioned "Fanfare-Overture" by Jean Coulthard, "And God Created Great Whales" by Alan Hovhaness and "The Whale" by John Tavener. Stefani planned the event to take place in the stands around the new killer whale habitat.

Everyone prayed that it wouldn't rain, and it didn't. It was perfect. The music was wonderful, the new habitat looked marvellous and the whole event was narrated by Knowlton Nash, CBC's national news anchor.

The climax of the event was the appearance of our whale trainers Klaus Michaelis, Jeremy FitzGibbon and Doug Pemberton, each dressed formally in white tie, tails and magnificent top hats. They conducted themselves with an air of blasé sophistication, as though this were standard dress for whale presentations. Finna, Bjossa and Hyak, also dressed in black and white, were a little more boisterous, and they soaked a few front row visitors with their tremendous leaps.

In so many aspects, from conceptualization to construction, the Max Bell Marine Mammal Centre was a significant departure from all previous whale and dolphin exhibits. For the first time emphasis was placed on the environment and biology of the orca rather than its show performance. Since then, the centre has become a model whose influence can be seen in various parts of the aquarium community.

# 19

# Chief of the
# Undersea World

There is much one can say about a great work of art, but in the end, it's pointless. The bronze sculpture that graces the plaza in front of the aquarium is without question a great work of art. No words or photo can do it justice.

I had always wanted something special to mark the entrance of the Vancouver Aquarium. In my travels to Europe I had been impressed with the sculptures found in the zoological gardens in places like Antwerp and Amsterdam. But there were always other priorities for any money we could get together, things that had to do with the care of the animals or the maintenance of the building. It took the interest and vision of two import-ant donors to make it happen.

Jim and Isabelle Graham were travelling in New Zealand in 1980 when they visited the small aquarium on the east coast at Napier. Outside at the entrance was a sculpture of a fisherman hauling in a net. The Grahams liked it, and they started thinking about offering something to the Vancouver Aquarium in the same manner. Back in Vancouver they talked to the board about it, and board member Jane Lawson van Roggen became involved with the project.

We began by reviewing the works of the top Canadian sculptors of the time, most of them from eastern Canada. I was unenthusiastic about what I saw because I thought it was not sufficiently relevant to the aquarium. For his part, Jim was adamant that the sculpture couldn't be too abstract; it had to relate to the aquarium in a way that people could understand and appreciate. Eventually we found our way to Bill Reid, the foremost artist in the Haida tradition of the Pacific Northwest, and we talked to him about sculpting a killer whale for our entrance. The killer whale is an important motif in Haida art and mythology, and Bill had created some superb carvings of them in wood and precious metals.

We were well aware when we spoke to Bill that he was one of the guiding lights in the renaissance of Haida art and culture. The traditional Haida cosmology takes in all of nature and almost everything has spiritual meaning. For instance, among the minerals, copper is considered a "noble" metal. Birds and mammals of the forest represent the heavens, and sea animals represent the underworld. The killer whale is the chief of the sea, while the bear is lord of the land and the eagle rules the sky.

Bill was sixty-four years old at the time, a tall, dignified man with a wonderful sense of humour. He suffered from Parkinson's disease and often seemed very frail. Still, he loved the idea, and after some thought he said he would like to work with a black granite that was mined in Africa. It would be powerful like the whale, he said, and it would be huge.

All of this sounded very good to us. Jim and I agreed that something of imposing size would be perfect for the space. But as Bill thought more about the immense amount of labour required to carve such a project, he lost hope. He felt his health would make it impossible. Finally, he wrote us a sad letter saying he could not do it after all, and we would have to find someone else.

We went next to Robert Davidson, Bill's brilliant protégé, who proposed a circle of killer whales to be carved out of wood. It sounded perfect, but then a complication developed. Bill Reid got back to us, saying he had found the solution to the problem: he would create the sculpture in bronze rather than granite. That appealed to Jim Graham, who had built his fortune in the foundry business. Long discussions followed, including some debate about the appropriateness of cast bronze as a material for a Haida motif. Since bronze is an alloy that usually contains copper, it seemed to work as a concept. Finally, we asked Bill Reid to go ahead.

The sculpture began as a small piece that Bill carved in boxwood, adapting it from a Haida speaker's staff he had seen in the Smithsonian Institution a few years before. From there, Bill assembled a team to help him create first a four-foot maquette, then the full-size sculpture. Working in Reid's studio on Granville Island, they took six months to produce an eighteen-foot plaster cast that was sent to the Tallix Foundry in New York for casting.

The choice of the Tallix Foundry earned Jim criticism from some of his foundry friends in B.C., but he has never regretted the extra expense this involved. He wanted the best, and Tallix produced the best finish and patina in bronze that he had seen. The giant plaster model was designed to be cut up into ten different pieces, all cast individually. Finishing the sculpture would involve a delicate process of welding the different pieces together again so that the weld was invisible. It had to be done very well indeed, and Jim was taking no chances.

The completed sculpture came back to Vancouver on a flatbed truck from New York. Because of its height, it would not fit under the bridge at the entrance to Stanley Park. It had to be delivered at four in the morning so the truck could go against the one-way traffic and avoid the bridge. Finally, the sculpture was set into a round reflecting pool designed after one that Jim and Isabelle Graham had seen in San Francisco.

*The Chief of the Undersea World* was unveiled in a ceremony on Saturday morning, June 2, 1984. Bill recited the legend of the killer whale in English, while Guujaaw (Gary Edenshaw from Haida Gwaii, otherwise known as the Queen Charlotte Islands) repeated the story in Haida. Haida songs and dances culminated in a dancer taking Isabelle Graham's hand and walking with her to the front of the sculpture. Isabelle pulled the cords at the base of the huge form and the large white drape fell away. Everyone in attendance gazed upon the magnificent sculpture.

*The Chief of the Undersea World* bears a great deal of gazing. Even now, almost ten years after the opening, I am drawn to it every time I approach the front entrance of the aquarium. At first you simply take in the overall form of the leaping killer whale, with its huge eyes, fierce mouth and exaggerated dorsal fin. Then you begin to see the other elements in the sculpture. There are trout in the tail flukes. Human faces stare out of its flanks, and the pectoral flippers have embroidered-looking ornamentation where they meet the body. Finally, a human head can be seen in the blowhole. The soft finish of the bronze is not cold and metallic but warm and somehow alive. In a way few other works of art can match, it straddles the worlds of the natural and the supernatural.

If you come back to visit the Vancouver Aquarium in a hundred years, chances are you won't recognize the place. Our building is flexible and adaptive, but it's not like the Shedd Aquarium, which is a marvellous piece of Chicago's architectural heritage, or the strikingly modern but rigid aquarium buildings designed by Peter Chermayeff in Baltimore and Osaka. The Vancouver Aquarium has been expanded and added to many times in its past, and it may be expanded more or changed altogether. I can't predict that.

What I can predict is that a hundred years from now Bill Reid's sculpture will still be there, and still holding the eye with its powerful grace.

# 20
# Birth and Death

Bjossa swam by the underwater viewing windows of the killer whale habitat, a small tail fluke protruding from her swollen belly. Her body arched itself in a contraction, and John Ford peered intently at the little body that was beginning to be revealed.

"It's a girl!" our curator of marine mammals exclaimed, and the crowd of staff pressed closer in expectation of the full birth. Instead, Bjossa swam off around the pool once more, the small fluke hanging listlessly beneath her.

"Let's all breathe with her," joked veterinarian Dave Huff. Soon Bjossa returned to the window and there were several more contractions, each moving the fluke a little farther out. Cameras clicked, and there was a great deal of groaning from the humans in sympathy with the killer whale.

Finally, Bjossa arched her body in another effort, and a black and yellow form shot out of her in a swirling cloud of blood and milk. It was September 1991, and a new killer whale had been born at the aquarium. She would soon be known to thousands of people as K'yosha.

There are few things so exciting as the birth of a whale, and few so sad as one's death. This birth came only six months after the death of Hyak, our senior killer whale. Hyak had been with us for twenty-three years, a record time for orcas in aquariums.

The death of a whale in an aquarium is an event that causes serious moral questioning, but it also brings out a great deal of reaction based on sentimentality. Death is disturbing, but it is also part of the natural cycle.

Maintaining whales in good health is difficult, for you need excellent facilities, an experienced and dedicated staff, high-quality food and a lot of luck. These animals live a long time in nature, perhaps as long as humans do, and the chances are that they will live a long time in an aquarium. However, like human beings, they become ill occasionally and sometimes die prematurely from disease. Often it is difficult to determine from the appearance of the animal whether it is sick or well. A blood sample is the best diagnostic tool, and blood samples are analyzed regularly to monitor the health of each marine mammal in a modern aquarium.

Hyak had been close to death once before. In 1983, he almost died from what we thought was an infection somewhere in his bowels. It was a terrible moment, as he was clearly weak and those who knew him best suspected he was in pain. We were so sure he was dying that we had actually ordered a crane to remove the huge body.

Then veterinarian Jim McBain had the idea of putting the orca on Banamine, a painkiller many times more potent than morphine. He also prescribed a low dose of tetracycline over a period of time. Amazingly, Hyak did a complete turnaround and got better.

Over the years, Hyak had a lot of transient illnesses that we never could identify. Typically, he would go a little bit off his food, his white blood count would go up and his hemoglobin would drop slightly. David Huff, who replaced Jim McBain, would put the whale on antibiotics and he would get better. The vets never had a definitive diagnosis, but they assumed that Hyak had some kind of low-level infection.

Then in January 1991 Hyak got very ill with what appeared to be a respiratory problem. He became inactive, and there was a discharge from his blowhole. David Huff was visiting Sea World at the time, but he flew up to Vancouver and went into action, treating the whale with antibiotics, Banamine, antifungals and vitamin K. After about a week Hyak seemed to have returned to 80 per cent of his normal health, and David felt confident enough in the situation to return to Sea World.

The next day, poor old Hyak died. The autopsy revealed abscesses the size of grapefruits in the lung. Some of these cysts were new, but many were clearly chronic and had been there for years. One had ruptured, apparently spontaneously, and that had killed our whale. The story was covered vividly in the press and on television, and there was an outpouring of emotion among the Vancouver public. Hyak had been with the community for over a generation; many adults had fond memories of seeing him during school trips to the aquarium when they were children. I don't think it hyperbolic to say that there was a period of mourning in Vancouver for Hyak, and this was even more intense among aquarium staff.

Death of aquarium animals is inevitable, no matter how well run an operation is. In contrast, the birth of a marine mammal can only come about through excellent facilities, hard work and luck.

The first baby whale at the aquarium was not an orca but a beluga. It had always been difficult to keep our first belugas, Lugosi and Bela, in good health because of the harsh treatment they had received in Alaska before we acquired them. We finally lost Bela in 1976. In August of that year, we acquired two females from Churchill, Manitoba. Unlike Bela and Lugosi, who had been caught accidentally in a fisherman's net and held for days in the hold of his boat, Kavna and Sanaq were caught by John Hicks and his crew and were carefully handled.

In the spring of 1977 we noticed that Kavna, the larger female, frequently rested on the bottom of the pool at the base of one wall. Here she would lie upside down for a few minutes as though sleeping and then rise to the surface for a few breaths only to return to the bottom again. She was getting larger, and we began to believe she might be pregnant. We established a regular watch so we could record changes in her behaviour. Little was known about whale reproduction. At that time only one beluga calf had been born in captivity, at the New York Aquarium, and sadly it had not survived very long.

We knew that the peak calving period for Hudson Bay belugas was mid-July, so as summer approached our biologist Stefani Hewlett established a daily routine of observing Kavna. At a little after six o'clock on the evening of July 13, Kavna circled slowly around her pool and then moved to its centre, where the water flow was least evident. Suddenly she expelled a great cloud of pale, mustard-coloured fluid. This was it; the expulsion of amniotic fluid signalled the beginning of labour. Phone calls were made, people came running, cameras were set up. Tony Westman of the National Film Board was on hand to film a special production that was later distributed worldwide. The event we'd waited and hoped for was underway.

Except that nothing happened, at least not immediately. Kavna wolfed down the regular 6:30 P.M. meal of herring with her usual enthusiasm. Her vent was opening a few inches occasionally as she swam slowly around the pool, but that was all. The next major development wasn't until about nine, when it became clear that the calf was being delivered head first.

All of a sudden the joy changed to anguish. Dolphin births are normally flukes-first. We feared this baby would be stillborn. Stefani's notes, later published in the magazine *Animal Kingdom* (April 1978) tell what happened next: "At 9:47 P.M., baby delivered past the blowhole, up to the pectoral fins, limp and hanging half born! The baby, half born, opened its mouth and wagged its head. My God, it's ALIVE! Then with one violent thrust and a burst of blood and fluid, the umbilical snapped and the baby swam free. Brown, with limp little flukes, it swam vigorously and unaided to the surface, popping straight out of the water to part its pectoral fins at least three times. . . . We could see nothing through the windows now: fluid, milk and blood clouded the water."

The calf, a male just short of five feet long, attracted great attention from people across Canada and the United States. This was all new to us. Although we were in communication with our colleagues in other aquariums and received a great deal of advice, there was no manual on the care of these animals. Our main concern was not to get Kavna unnecessarily excited, for we feared any interruption in her nursing. We considered removing Lugosi but finally decided we would leave all the belugas together. For all we knew, Lugosi's aggressiveness might be a natural, beneficial stimulus that motivated the other animals at an appropriate time.

The public was fascinated. Daily attendance increased from about 4500 per day to over 6500.

Nonetheless, we were cautious and still feared we might lose the baby, so we resisted giving him a name. My friend Norman Louie, a Vancouver physician of Chinese origin, told me that in China a baby is not publicly acknowledged until it is one month old. By this time it has a better chance, and a "red egg party" is given for friends and family to celebrate. We decided to hold a party like this, and aquarium members David and Dorothy Lam helped organize it. As well as inviting our immediate aquarium friends and family, we decided to invite members of Vancouver's large and important Chinese community. The party was a great success, filling the entire aquarium. Our long-serving aquarist Billy Wong was part of the receiving line, standing shoulder to shoulder with the Lams. A "Name the Baby" contest was announced on August 16, and within a month we had over 10,000 entries. The name finally chosen by a VIP panel was Tuaq, meaning "the only one" in the Inuit language.

Tuaq grew rapidly. When he was two months old and had doubled his weight, we were dismayed to see his thick skin cracking and breaking away in clumps. This made us very anxious about his health, but it wasn't accompanied by any other symptoms. Many years later, when the New York Aquarium was successful in keeping alive two beluga calves, we learned that they also had shed their skins in this rather alarming fashion.

Towards the end of October, Tuaq started losing his equilibrium, listing to one side as he swam. He appeared to be too weak even to nurse from his mother. Our veterinarian, Allan MacNeill, removed him from the B.C. Tel Pool for treatment. During the night of November 2, Tuaq died of a massive infection. The autopsy determined that the infection had been caused by soil bacteria called *nocardia*, which is known to cause death in domestic animals. How Tuaq got the infection was a mystery, and it remains so. The staff and public were greatly saddened by his death. For me, his death was both a disappointment and a challenge to acquire more knowledge and better facilities.

We still hoped that we would be able to establish a breeding colony of killer whales in the aquarium. The first time we got a chance at this was in November of 1988, when Bjossa, the female killer whale acquired in Iceland, gave birth to her first calf. This was the first killer whale birth ever in a Canadian aquarium (the first in the world was in the early 1980s at Marineland of the Pacific).

Nursing for newborn cetaceans isn't quite as easy as it is for most land mammals, and the calf's early attempts at suckling made this very obvious. First, a newborn whale suckles from a moving target, since the mother whale swims constantly. In addition, it must dive down underneath its mother and locate the mammary glands, which unlike the underslung udder of a cow are quite inconspicuous on a whale's streamlined form. Add to all this a very definite time limit, equal to the time the calf can hold its breath.

We don't know why or at what point Bjossa's calf stopped receiving adequate sustenance. All we know is that it died a little over three weeks after its birth. Marineland of the Pacific in Los Angeles had had the same problem when a series of young were born to a female killer whale. That particular female had several young, none of which survived since they were not nursed properly.

I refused to give up on the dream of breeding killer whales. The fact that Bjossa was a healthy and fertile female, sharing her space with two thriving males, seemed to bode well for our future hopes. At the time, of course, this was cold comfort. The sense of loss in the aquarium was profound.

The birth of Bjossa's second calf in 1991 brought us once more into the emotion-charged atmosphere of high hopes and expectations. We scoured all the available research on killer whale reproduction in an attempt to get as much solid information as possible and keep expectations realistic. The research indicated that killer whale calves suffer a high mortality rate in the first year, a phenomenon found in other species such as bottlenosed dolphins and several species of ungulates (hoofed animals, which are distantly related to whales). By the beginning of the 1990s, the survival rate for captive-bred killer whales was comparable to that in the wild. Of the thirteen pregnancies conceived in North American aquariums that had reached full-term prior to September 1991, seven had resulted in calves that were still alive. The fact that this was Bjossa's second calf also seemed hopeful.

As before, mother and calf were watched closely by a team of staff and experienced volunteers. They recorded nursing behaviour and respiration as well as interactions among all the animals in the pool. We carried out DNA tests on the placenta to determine paternity and took some comfort in the fact that the father was Hyak—it was as if something of him would live on in the aquarium.

During October, the public watched the proceedings either from behind the railings at the back of the stands or on video monitors set up on the marine mammal deck. The underwater viewing area was kept closed to the public in order to provide a quiet nursery. Although it was impossible to know exactly how much milk she was getting, the calf appeared to be nursing well for the first month of her life.

By the end of October, however, we could see that the calf was not getting enough nutrition, and we decided to separate her from her mother. We moved her to a holding tank and brought along the dolphin White Wings to give her some company.

We decided we needed help to keep the calf alive. Gil consulted with Brad Andrews of Sea World. Brad was optimistic, saying he was hopeful that the pattern of calving in Vancouver would follow that of his oceanariums. Eight killer whale calves had been born at Sea World, he said, of which the second and third, both of them first-time births, had died. The last five calves had survived, including three that were first-time births. This pattern of increasing success rates was similar to the earlier history for bottlenosed dolphins, which showed poor calving success in the late 1950s and early 1960s compared to very high success rates at aquariums today.

Brad went further than supplying information: he sent us Andy Johnson and Robin Friday to work with our marine mammal staff and our veterinarian. Andy Johnson was supervisor of animal care at Sea World of San Diego and Robin Friday was assistant curator of animal training at Sea World of Florida. The two brought experience not only with formula feeding but also with handling techniques. (Andy eventually became our curator of marine mammals.)

Tube feeding was initiated immediately on a round-the-clock basis with a special cetacean formula fine-tuned to fit the calf's needs. A veterinary milk substitute, the formula mixed bottled water, salmon oil and essential nutrient supplements. Although only about twice the weight of an adult man, the calf consumed about ten times a man's caloric intake. She took in about 24,000 calories a day in six feedings.

The huge team effort involved not only the staff of the marine mammal department but many volunteers who worked with K'yosha through the rain, wind and darkness of Vancouver's autumn. The rescue of the calf showed great promise from the beginning. K'yosha readily accepted tube feeding, and in early November we were able to verify weight gain.

Holding the calf during feeding required five divers at first, but as she got used to the experience, and realized that it was always followed by the satisfying sensation of a full, warm stomach, fewer and fewer were needed. From mid-November on, only two divers were required, one to hold her and one to assist with the feeding tube. K'yosha began to swim right into the divers' arms and started to gain an average of three pounds a day. An additional positive sign was the progressive development of her immune system through the month of November.

The plan was to gradually replace the formula feedings with blenderized fish. Once the calf was entirely onto a diet of that, we would provide her with whole fish to play with, which is how weaning occurs naturally in killer whales.

By mid-November, John Ford was able to identify the calf's unique, personal call as well as one that mimicked Bjossa. K'yosha was very tactile and playful with her poolmate White Wings and with the divers.

As typically occurs in the wild, Bjossa rapidly recovered from the separation from her calf, and she showed no signs of any stress in terms of behaviour, feeding or blood values. We hoped that she and Finna would enjoy a reunion with K'yosha and White Wings when weaning and training were well established.

Then, early in January 1992, veterinarian David Huff got a call at his clinic asking him to come down because K'yosha was acting "a little funny" and had perhaps bumped into a wall. Unalarmed by the symptoms, David nonetheless went to have a look, describing it as follows: "Everything essentially looked okay. I came down at five o'clock and I remember very clearly standing out on the pool deck, looking at her and saying, 'There's nothing wrong. She's just fine.' She was swimming normally in circles. Virtually as soon as I said that she just took off and did a speed swim—a very fast swim right into the wall. She hit her head almost like she had knocked herself out. And from then on, she was swimming with no co-ordination at all in the pool."

The staff moved her into the small holding pool, took blood samples and administered all the drugs that might help. Nothing worked, and they watched helplessly for the next three or four hours as her condition deteriorated. K'yosha started listing as she swam, getting worse and worse until she rolled over on her back and couldn't right herself. Dave sent in divers to hold her up, but eventually she died.

The diagnosis showed an acute brain infection, possibly brought on by low immunity in conjunction with the absence of mother's milk. The staff were stunned. Everyone had worked so hard, and it seemed inconceivable that the little whale should die after gaining so much weight, the best indicator of health.

Public reaction was even stronger than after the death of Hyak. K'yosha had so appealed to the public in British Columbia that many people reacted the way they would to the loss of a family member. Many felt that somehow the orca should have been saved. The whole thing set off another debate over whether the aquarium—or any aquarium—should keep whales in captivity.

We were already deeply into that debate ourselves, largely because of the loss of Hyak but also due to the drowning death of a killer whale trainer in Victoria earlier that year (the trainer had slipped into the pool and the whale had prevented her from coming up for air). These incidents had brought criticism down on the Vancouver Aquarium, and pressure was exerted on the Vancouver Park Board to prevent the aquarium from obtaining a whale to replace Hyak. But the pressure was unnecessary: the aquarium's board of governors informed the Park Board that we were declaring a one-year voluntary moratorium on the acquisition of cetaceans. During that year we would undertake an extensive public examination of our policies and future directions.

Among the components of this process were a public opinion survey and an economic impact analysis. The survey found that 70 per cent of Vancouver's residents supported the continued presence of cetaceans at the aquarium and that cetaceans were the institution's most important feature. The economic analysis concluded that if the orcas and belugas were removed from the aquarium attendance might drop by as much as half.

Other research, including a review of four hundred articles, reports and documents, was conducted to examine as fully as possible the different issues attached to the debate. The review revealed that the different positions on captive cetaceans leave little room for compromise. Articles in favour of maintaining cetacean collections were prepared predominantly by scientific and technical specialists. They deal with issues such as scientific research, conservation, educational values and biological needs, and they make a direct link between aquarium visits and public awareness about the need for protection in the wild. Articles opposing cetacean collections question the humaneness of confining large, intelligent animals. They tend to be based on nonscientific sources and centre on concern for the well-being and treatment of animals in display environments. Other issues addressed include stress and psychological problems, longevity and ethical arguments based on "speciesism."

We also examined some practical issues. One was that the acquisition of animals and the construction of facilities was becoming more and more difficult. So many proposals ended up in public hearings, where even a small number of opponents could dominate proceedings and create a great deal of adverse publicity. This publicity not only touched the general public but could make it difficult for high-profile donors to support aquariums.

Our final report was released in March 1992 under the title *Values and Visions*. The main provisions were:

> The Vancouver Aquarium will continue to exhibit and study cetaceans for the purposes of public education and scientific research. Public awareness programs, breeding programs, and scientific and husbandry research beneficial to the well-being and conservation of cetaceans will continue to be counted among the primary objectives of the institution.
>
> The practice of collecting killer whales from wild stocks will be discontinued. The practice of collecting belugas will be suspended, subject to successful breeding programs. Breeding loans between institutions will be pursued to maintain genetic variability.
>
> Acquisition of other cetaceans is not currently contemplated but could be considered in the future on a case-by-case basis.
>
> Rescue and rehabilitation of sick, stranded or injured animals, or those exposed to environmental threats or impacts, would constitute an exception to the general policy outlined above. Intervention and short-term husbandry will be considered when it is judged that lack of action will result in further injury or death. Whenever feasible, where wild stocks will not be harmed, rehabilitated animals will be reintroduced to wild populations in the area from which they were rescued. The disposition of animals judged unreleasable will be adjudicated by appropriate regulatory authorities. The aquarium, upon request, may also provide accommodation and care for animals from other facilities, for medical or humanitarian reasons.

The report reflected current thinking on the role of aquariums. Virtually all modern coastal institutions are active in the rescue and rehabilitation of stranded and injured marine mammals. Along the Pacific coast these activities have mainly been directed towards seals, sea lions and sea otters, but occasional cetaceans are rescued as well. The Point Defiance Aquarium in Tacoma has recently been successful in rescuing and rearing a young harbour porpoise, a relatively difficult species to maintain in an aquarium.

On the east coast, where the continental shelf slopes more gradually, dolphins and whales often become stranded. The New England Aquarium in Boston has been particularly active in rescuing pilot whales and dolphins, devoting considerable time and effort to the study of the health problems of these animals in nature.

Obviously, saving a few animals here and there doesn't address the greater question of mortality on the high seas. Some of it is entirely natural, of course. Any zoologist can tell you that animal population levels are cyclical; as populations reach a certain point, animals die of disease, often in epidemics. What we *can* do something about is large-scale mortality caused by human beings. Historically marine mammals have been the most abused animals in the world's oceans. Seals, sea lions, sea otters, sea cows, dolphins and whales have been slaughtered relentlessly because they were important resources or because they were perceived to be undesirable (or even useless). Many of these animals have been hunted and killed to the brink of extinction and, in the case of at least one, the Steller sea cow in the North Pacific, extinction did take place.

It has been heartening to see the outcry against indiscriminate slaughter of marine mammals by industrial fisheries, particularly with the use of tuna purse seines and drift nets. Due to international opposition, the United Nations passed resolutions banning high seas drift nets after 1992.

But sustaining effective conservation programs over large areas is not easy, however strong the international outcry. It takes compassion and a strong commitment to animals and natural environments. City people, particularly young ones without possessions or vested interests, can easily consider themselves to be "conservationists," but farmers, fisherfolk and rural folk tend to see environmentalism as something imposed on them by unrealistic outsiders. There is also a strong North/South division at work, since the people in poor countries often see environmentalism as a luxury they can't afford.

Zoos and aquariums have a crucial role to play. They are institutions that generate a love of living animals in children and a sense of appreciation in adults that does lead to commitment. The births of belugas and killer whales move people as few other events can. Aquariums can take credit for first bringing dolphins and whales to the world's attention as remarkable mammals that have family life and social behaviour analogous to other mammals. Before this these animals were seen merely as sources of meat, oil and leather products.

The killing of dolphins and whales continues at a steady pace in many places in the world. I have seen how Inuit visitors to the aquarium, who know orcas only as the fiercest predators in Arctic waters, struggle with that image when they see how friendly and playful our whales seem to be. I sometimes think it might be possible to reduce the killing of whales and dolphins by constructing cetacean exhibits in appropriate communities. Our main challenge in the aquarium, however, is to fully understand the needs of our own whales in terms of their social, medical and nursery requirements so that they can reproduce satisfactorily and live long, contented lives.

# 21
# Orphan Seals

The harbour seal, *Phoca vitulina,* is the most common true seal along the Pacific Northwest coast. It belongs to the pinniped order of placental (higher) mammals, along with the so-called eared seals or sea lions. Harbour seals mate in the autumn; the young are born in spring and early summer out of water on a beach. They weigh about twenty pounds at birth and are very well developed, covered with short fur and already able to swim. The nursing period is short and babies quickly learn to catch and eat fish. They grow rapidly, ultimately reaching a length of six feet and a weight in excess of two hundred pounds.

Seals of any species were not common in local waters when the aquarium first opened. Fishermen did not tolerate them because seals and sea lions regularly removed and ate fish that were caught in nets or on lines. In response to the concerns of fishermen, the Department of Fisheries paid out bounties to people who brought in the snouts of dead seals. In addition, Fisheries patrol boats regularly machine-gunned sea lions in their rookeries.

Baby harbour seals were brought to us occasionally in the early days, but we had great trouble feeding them because we didn't realize they could not digest cow's milk. My wife, Kathy, helped to get them started on a liquid diet. They snapped with their sharp little teeth, and one particularly energetic little fellow left a permanent scar on her elbow. Bill Duncan, a colourful aquarist originally from Aberdeen, Scotland, worked with the baby seals in the late 1950s and fed them an improved formula of blenderized herring, fish oil, water and vitamins. We lacked suitable pool or exhibit facilities for them, though, and could not handle very many. There was also a seal pool in the Stanley Park Zoo where several harbour seals and the occasional sea lion lived.

In the 1970s an elderly businessman named Gordon Russell approached us and suggested that he would be interested in sponsoring a project at the aquarium. Ralph Shaw and I discussed various possibilities with him and grew to like Gordon very much. He was a small, spritely man who had over his life developed a very successful sales agency for heavy equipment. As a youth, he had played hockey and was known as Ginger Russell for his red hair. He had travelled all over the west in his business, knew many people and wanted to contribute something to the community. Ralph nominated him to the board of governors, where he served for several years.

We needed a seal pool, a habitat in which we would be able to exhibit harbour seals and show them both above the surface and through glass below water level. We also needed a nursery pool and an attractive outside tide or touch pool. Our plans evolved, and we visualized a complex of exhibits in association with the Finning Sea Otter Pool on the plaza just north of the killer whale pool. Two much-loved past presidents, David Lawson and Mye Wright, had recently died and we were looking for ways to keep their names alive in our institution. We decided that the new construction would include the David Lawson Nursery Pool for harbour seal pups and the Mye Wright Touch Pool, a shallow seawater pool where children could actually touch starfish and other intertidal animals.

When it opened in May 1977, the 40,000-gallon Gordon and Mary Russell Pool contained six harbour seals. Orphaned harbour seals arrived during the summer and were carefully tended by marine mammal staff with good results, since by this time we understood their feeding requirements much better than before. Most encouraging of all, at the end of June a four-year-old female harbour seal successfully gave birth to a male pup. Sonja proved to be a good mother, playing swimming games with her pup and responding quickly to his cry.

As the years went by, a great change in people's attitude towards marine mammals took place. The government ceased to pay bounties for seal noses, patrol boats no longer fired their guns on sea lion rookeries and marine mammals became protected. Harbour seal populations increased greatly along the coast, and orphan pups were brought to us in ever increasing numbers. By 1987 the aquarium's Stranded Marine Mammal Team was caring for ten to fifteen orphaned pups a year, then releasing them when they were sufficiently mature to fend for themselves.

In the negotiations with Park Board concerning the planning of the aquarium's Arctic Canada exhibits, there developed the idea of a new seal habitat to be constructed between the killer whale habitat and the proposed beluga habitat. This new seal facility would replace the old seal pool in the Stanley Park Zoo and could be easily viewed by visitors to the park outside the aquarium. Unlike the old zoo seal pool, the new one would have a modern filtration system that would give it very clear water. Visitors to the aquarium would be able to observe the seals swimming beneath the surface through inside windows. All of these ideas were excellent, but we had to find a way of paying for them.

Fortunately, B.C. Sugar was about to celebrate its 100th anniversary and was looking for a centennial project. That it turned out to be our seal pool is owed to Jane van Roggen, who was the aquarium president at the time. She represented us in a public meeting with the Park Board that had been organized to seek approval of our Arctic Gallery. Jane spoke about her hopes for the aquarium and vividly described our work in rescuing orphaned seals.

In the audience that night was Peter Cherniavsky, whose wife, Ann, is a close friend of Jane's. At that time, Peter was B.C. Sugar's chief executive officer. Peter phoned Jane the next day and told her that B.C. Sugar would like to sponsor the seal pool. Elated, she phoned me immediately and we rejoiced in the aquarium's good fortune. It was a substantial donation of $500,000. That was enough for the seal habitat, but it didn't leave anything over for the free viewing areas we'd promised the city. MacMillan Bloedel again came through for us, sponsoring the bridge and promenade area from which Stanley Park visitors could view the seals and belugas.

The B.C. Sugar Seal Pool was officially opened by Peter Cherniavsky at a B.C. Sugar Centennial banquet held in the aquarium. The pool was particularly notable for its beautifully designed and constructed rockwork above and below the surface. From below you can watch the seals glide by in their effortless way, nonchalantly swimming upside down or right side up as their fancy takes them.

With the completion of the new Seal Pool, the Russell Pool was integrated with the Finning Pool to provide more space for the sea otter collection. We now had a much better series of exhibit tanks for marine mammals. The B.C. Tel Research Pool at the back of the building provided good holding facilities, but with the growing harbour seal population along the coast we were getting more and more orphaned pups each year.

One of the key people in our seal projects was Michelle McKay, a slender dark-haired young woman who volunteered for several years at the aquarium guiding behind-the-scenes tours. She then worked with the seals, learning a great deal from our veterinarian David Huff and trainer Jeremy FitzGibbon. Michelle is a persuasive advocate of the seal program, and she argues that it is an important window into what is happening in nature. As the seal population expands in local waters, more and more of the pups that are brought to us are sick. We are not sure why this is; perhaps an over-population naturally produces epidemic conditions. In any case, the danger of introducing disease from sick, orphaned seal pups to our healthy marine mammals has become an increasing concern.

In co-operation with the Stanley Park Zoo staff, Michelle set up a seal pup nursery in the summer of 1991 as part of the old zoo facility. It was a good place to show our seal rehabilitation program to the public. There were about thirty pups that year, of which 60 per cent were sick when they arrived. The sick ones were housed in individual fibreglass tubs until they were well enough to be put into a pool with the others.

The program is now fully developed. When a new pup arrives, it is immediately taken to the holding facility at the back of the aquarium, where it receives a full body check. A blood sample is taken and sent to a laboratory for evaluation. On the basis of the blood results, antibiotics or other treatment can be given. The pup is weighed and started on a formula or herring, depending upon its stage of development. Most of the pups arrive dehydrated, so they are put on fluids administered through a stomach tube by gravity rather than with a plunger. The formula is a simple one using water, fish oil and a veterinary milk substitute that is high in fat and low in carbohydrates.

By 1992 we were maintaining the pups for only five or six months. They gained weight faster on the new formula, and once they could eat with the other seals there was no point in keeping them, other than to exhibit them as needed in the new Seal Pool. Michelle observed that the pups learned quickly from older seals.

The young seals are released into the ocean in co-operation with the Department of Fisheries and Oceans. Some of them are released in Howe Sound around Popham Island, Bowen Island or Porteau; others are taken across the Strait of Georgia and released in the Gulf Islands. Animal lovers are very pleased about this, but fishermen scratch their heads in wonder.

All of the young seals have orange tags attached to their hind flippers. These tags, provided by the Department of Fisheries and Oceans, have identifying numbers. But although the tags are occasionally observed on wild seals, we seldom get a report on them. Sometimes a seal is accidentally caught in a fisherman's net and information about it is given us. One day we hope to be able to radio tag the young seals and keep track of them this way. In the meantime, we are learning a great deal about animal rescue and rehabilitation and about animal medicine.

# 22

# From the Land
# of the Midnight Sun

One day, Charlie Invarak said to me, "Let's you and me go up the hill and shoot a caribou. I shoot and dress and carry. You take pictures. Any problem?"

I thought about it. "No problem," I replied. Charlie grinned and disappeared from the opening flap of my small, conical tent.

It was the summer of 1989, and I was back in the High Arctic, somewhere on Admiralty Inlet south of the village of Arctic Bay. And despite my affirmation of "no problem," forty-two-year-old Charlie Invarak and I were still working out the details of a somewhat complicated arrangement involving two sets of needs: his family's need for meat and my need to collect information and take photos in order to make our upcoming Artic Canada exhibit as realistic as possible.

Negotiations, at least from the aquarium's point of view, were somewhat less than hardball, for the fact was that I liked Charlie a lot. He had an outgoing nature and despite his limited vocabulary had no fear whatever of the English language. "No problem" and "Any problem?" were two of his favourite expressions. Charlie and his wife (who, he told me, spoke only Inuktitut) had nine children, ten if you included the one they had lost. His fourteen-year-old son Namen was with us on this trip. I too had a companion, my friend Dr. Aki Horii.

As the four of us walked up the hill, Charlie and I continued our negotiations. It took some doing, but we finally understood each other. I would photograph the caribou, then he would shoot it, not the other way around. Nor would we split up, letting him go hunting by himself. I said, "We are paying. We came here to see live animals, not dead ones." He replied, "I need meat. Okay, we stick together. You shoot. I shoot. No problem."

Our little party continued hiking up the rocky hill to a tundra-filled plateau where the rolling green contours seemed to go on forever in the crystal-clear air. There were no animals in sight, so Charlie climbed a small mountain for a better look. I scouted around a bit with Aki and Namen, who led me through a bog where I lost my boot in the icy water. By the time I had retrieved my boot and dried my foot off, Charlie was waving his arms from the top of the mountain to signal he had seen a caribou. Regrouping, we walked silently for a while over the treeless hills to a rise where Charlie pointed at a fine buck about five hundred yards away. I could barely see it.

"Shoot!" he hissed. "Let's get closer," I whined. "Shoot! Shoot!" Reluctantly, I snapped several photos with my telephoto lens. Yes, I was paying; yes, we could probably have got a lot closer. But this was Charlie's world. While I only had an aquarium board to face if I didn't do a good job, Charlie would have to face a hungry family.

The caribou began to move as Charlie lay prone and aimed carefully through his telescopic sights. Namen crouched next to him as did Aki and I. Charlie missed on the first shot but dropped the animal on the second. It was an amazing shot with a .223 calibre rifle, which fires a small projectile with a powerful charge. We hiked to within fifty yards or so, and the animal rose to its feet and stood still. Charlie gave the rifle to his son, who brought the caribou down for a second and final time.

The caribou was a big buck with a mighty, velvet-covered set of antlers. Charlie cut its throat with a quick slash of his knife, then skinned the animal and dressed the meat, leaving most of the meat and the head under a pile of rocks. He said he would return by snowmobile in October or November when the meat would be well aged and full of flavour. He cut the hind quarters free and tied the dissected tendons together so he could heave the bloody, fifty-pound haunch over his shoulders for the long trek back to the rocky shore of the inlet.

Ever since my first visit to Pond Inlet in 1968, I had been fascinated with the Canadian Arctic, so vast, so beautiful and so challenging. It is an important part not only of Canada's geography but of its identity, yet few southerners have any clear idea of what it is or what it means. The aquarium had mounted expeditions and extremely popular members' trips to the Arctic over the years, and our staff had participated in a great deal of research there. These activities were useful, but they touched only a few people. I had always wanted to create an exhibit that would offer the greater public the sights and sounds of the Arctic and a sense of how its plants and animals interrelate with the harsh environment.

In early 1985, we presented a proposal to the Donner Canadian Foundation and won a significant grant to create a special exhibit called "IMAQ, the Arctic Sea." Public response was excellent once the exhibit opened, and all in all we were extremely pleased with "IMAQ, the Arctic Sea." However, it had always been conceived as a temporary exhibit in a space that we planned to use eventually for local marine life. We wanted to create a permanent pavilion on the Canadian Arctic but knew that it wasn't going to be easy. As well as the usual challenge to our fund-raising abilities, we would once again have to ask the Vancouver Park Board for permission to expand.

The Park Board supported the Arctic Canada concept but on the basis of a quid pro quo. If they were going to give consent to this project, the aquarium would have to give something extra to Stanley Park. This "something extra" would be free viewing of the animals from outside, preferably both above water and under the surface, enhanced landscaping and new public washrooms. Somehow we had to design our new exhibits to fit into these criteria while at the same time reserving enough inside display to induce people to buy admission and keep up the economics of our self-supporting institution.

Of course, the Park Board requirements increased the cost of our project, and funds were already difficult to raise. A very generous donation from the Molson Family Foundation turned things around. Negotiations were undertaken with the federal and provincial governments, and the principal funding from them was a low-interest loan. In 1988 we finally managed to put together enough funds to go ahead with the project. Government input totalled $3.25 million, with participation from the provincial Ministry of Regional Development and three federal departments: Fisheries and Oceans, Western Diversification, and Indian and Northern Affairs.

We decided that the Arctic Canada project would be centred on a new beluga habitat, a major undertaking that would have to be developed in conjunction with the B.C. Sugar Seal Pool and the enlarged Finning Sea Otter habitat. The new, two-million-litre beluga habitat would be four times the size of the previous pool and would be a more stimulating environment for the white whales.

The next question was theme. I discussed it at length with Gil and Stefani Hewlett and with Sharon Proctor, whose department was responsible for programming new exhibits. We all agreed that the biology of Lancaster Sound would be our primary focus, despite our interest in presenting other themes such as the relationship of the native peoples to the natural world.

Lancaster Sound, which separates Baffin and Devon islands, is the entrance to the fabled Northwest Passage. The sound and its adjacent waters are the summer home of Canada's narwhals. There are large numbers in and around Pond Inlet and Eclipse Sound and in Admiralty Inlet. There are also thousands of belugas, a few bowhead whales, some killer whales, many walruses and thousands of seals. It is an extraordinary region with great mystique. A strong, adaptive culture has allowed the native peoples there to survive the long, harsh winters for thousands of years. Over these lands and waters of scenic beauty floats the haunting memory of the explorers searching for the Northwest Passage.

The region holds a surprising abundance of wildlife, migratory waterfowl and migratory whales. In the water there are colourful invertebrates, masses of krill, large sharks and billions of small codfish. Indeed, it is one of the greatest wildlife areas still intact in the world. It is also an area of oil and mineral exploration and a possible avenue of movement of oil ships from one side of the Arctic to the other.

Mindful of the need to keep our association members informed and interested in the project, we organized a group tour to Arctic Bay for the summer of 1989. It proved to be so popular that two trips were organized back to back. Aquarium staff researchers and scientists joined these trips to obtain information that would be useful in planning the Arctic Canada exhibits. A bonus of the expedition was the opportunity for them to experience the way of life and culture of the Inuit. The travellers crossed the ice of Admiralty Inlet to camp at Cape Crauford at the northwest point of the inlet on Lancaster Sound. Here they were under the supervision of the Inuit hunter/guides of the Ikajutit Hunters and Trappers Association in Arctic Bay, including our friend Charlie Invarak.

My own trip to the region took place at the end of that summer. Aki Horii and I flew north from Montreal to Arctic Bay with Peter Heiss, the talented aquarium staff artist who designed and constructed artificial rock backgrounds for exhibits. His job was to obtain latex moulds of cliffs that could be reconstructed in our new exhibit.

On the flight north I was surprised to see Brad Andrews sitting near us. Brad had been the curator of marine mammals at Marineland when I had first met him some years earlier. When Marineland was absorbed by Sea World, Brad had moved to San Diego and rose to become a Sea World vice-president. It turned out that he too was en route to Arctic Bay, for the purpose of studying narwhals.

Arctic Bay is a community of 550 people living in prefabricated, insulated homes along the shore of a fiord that connects with Admiralty Inlet, an immense north-south slash in the northern contour of Baffin Island to the west of the Eclipse Sound region. Over half of Arctic Bay's residents are under sixteen years old.

We stopped in at the home of the government wildlife officer, Glen Williams, and his wife, Rebecca. Glen had first come to the region years before as a young RCMP officer, while Rebecca was from Arctic Bay. Glen had recently taken up scuba diving, and he showed us videos that revealed a surprising diversity of marine life in beautifully clear water: starfish, anemones, sculpins, eelpouts, comb jellies and coralline algae. When I remarked on the clarity of the water, Glen said it varied with plankton quantity. Sometimes there were clouds of krill and it was impossible to see very far.

There was also some business Glen wanted to discuss. The people of Arctic Bay had a quota for a hundred narwhals a year, he said. The local hunters were interested in using part of that quota to collect live narwhals for aquariums. This would bring them not only much more money per animal but also employment. Glen wanted us to see a particular bay where he felt the capture might be possible; if it seemed feasible to us he wanted to set up an operation for narwhals similar to the Hicks brothers' beluga collecting operation in Churchill, Manitoba. He hoped that the Vancouver Aquarium and Sea World would set up a holding tank on the shore and provide the expertise for keeping the narwhals alive until they could be airlifted out to the nearest jet plane airport for transhipment. I agreed to have a look at the site.

Just up the coast from Arctic Bay, Peter Heiss found an outcropping of rock that he decided was perfect as a model for his artificial rockwork. Aki and I left him there and joined Glen for a cruise across Admiralty Inlet to look at the whale collection site before setting off on our expedition. Glen went in one boat with several children, while Aki and I went with Charlie and Namen in another. Brad Andrews came along in a third boat accompanied by his guide.

At first we sped beneath gigantic cliffs, golden in the low sunlight. On the other side of the inlet, however, there were icebergs among the pan ice and the weather was colder. Narwhals moved quietly in small groups along the leads in the ice. We tied up to some pan ice, and I got off to observe and photograph the whales. It is sometimes difficult to see narwhals because they have no dorsal fins. This time, though, two of them were easily seen as they "jousted" at the surface about fifty metres away; their ivory tusks projected into the air and gleamed in the sun.

When we arrived at the shore I examined the area Glen thought would make a good collecting site. It was exceedingly bleak and barren; I thought it would be very difficult to work there. We camped overnight, not very restfully since we were visited by a howling gale that collapsed Aki's tent. My reservations about the site increased. It was extremely exposed and an ice barrier formed overnight along the shore under the force of the winds.

Next morning when we were breaking camp, Charlie spotted two large bearded seals asleep on sections of the floe ice, hundreds of yards from the beach. We sped out in our boat and Charlie shot and killed one of them with one shot at about fifty yards. The second got away.

This was my first inkling that our trip was really a hunting and fishing opportunity for Charlie. I explained to our guides that I was in the live animal business and particularly wanted to observe and photograph live, unharassed animals in nature. I hadn't come to the Arctic to see animals shot and killed. They didn't appreciate this idea very much, but they understood and agreed to make it as easy as possible for me to observe live animals.

We continued our cruise southward on the west side of Admiralty Inlet. I wanted to know how far south the narwhals ranged in the inlet. The scenery was spectacular as we proceeded along the base of an enormous red escarpment with vertical columns and eroded formations resembling statues and flying buttresses. After carefully manoeuvring through an ice-filled bay, we beached the boat in the mouth of a stream and hiked up a hill to find strange sandstone formations towering above us like the ruins of ancient temples. At this point, Glen and his party separated from us so they could hunt without disturbing our observations.

Later, as we cruised southeast across the inlet towards Yeoman Island, we encountered floating fields of ice, then a magnificent iceberg that towered above our small boat. Ever mindful of necessity, Charlie broke off some ice from the berg to melt for drinking water. It is always a surprise to southeners when they hear that the Arctic is actually a very dry desert where fresh water is often hard to obtain.

On the eastern side of the inlet we found signs of an ancient settlement. One house ring was larger than any I had ever seen, perhaps twenty feet in diameter. Once upon a time it had been a sod-covered hut consisting of a ring of stones and a roof supported by whale bones and animal skins. Charlie said it would have accommodated a man, his three wives and their children. Later, when we visited Glen's camp, we saw more evidence of the earlier people. Glen was already cutting and dressing a caribou that had been shot, but he led the way over a rocky hill to show us several beehive-shaped rocky structures. These were ancient fox traps, he said. The fox would climb into the top of the structure to get a piece of meat, then be unable to escape.

We got back in the boat and set out for a cove near the mouth of the Kuk River. There we pitched our tents in a drizzling, cold rain. With dinner in mind, Aki and I got out our fishing rods and cast out, but we did not catch any char. Charlie, however, put out a net and brought in an enormous char weighing almost twenty pounds. Its stomach was filled with tiny amphipod shrimps, which we could see swimming in great numbers near the shore. These and the enormous clouds of krill that coloured entire sections of the inlet red were yet more evidence of the richness of the waters.

We were now a long way south and had clearly passed beyond the southward migration of the narwhals. But we had begun to see evidence of the caribou herds that are of such importance to the meat-eating Inuit.

Charlie was obliged to hunt every month of the year if he and his family wanted to eat, and theirs was primarily a meat diet. It seemed like a dreadfully difficult and precarious life to me, but Charlie was used to it and saw no reason to complain. Once, feeling philosophical, he said, "Caribou, lotsa work." Then he added, "Die, big problem. Big troubles. If I die ten people without food."

Our diet on this trip, though supplemented by food Aki and I had bought at the Hudson's Bay store in Arctic Bay, was almost entirely the product of our guide's hunting. Seal liver with bacon was tender, tasty and very fresh. Caribou steaks were as good as, or better than, any other steaks in the world. The red meat of the char we caught was excellent but very rich and hard to eat in great quantity. Seal meat, our staple during that trip, was fishy-tasting and greasy. Seal blubber, raw or cooked, was too exotic for Aki and me. Charlie of course had his own ideas about what was exotic: he could not be induced to eat apples or canned peaches.

Soon it was time to return to Arctic Bay. We set out but were obliged to make camp as the weather turned rough. Aki and I began to worry about our return flight home. Charlie, however, kept tuned in to the radio for weather information and when evening came announced, "Getting better. Maybe morning we go."

We went, but the weather wasn't much better. Our boat often seemed ready to take off into the wind. Up, up, up we'd go, then slam back down into the trough, everyone getting sprayed with salt water. Finally, we came around the point of an island against treacherous, curling waves that pitched us in all directions. Ahead of us was a long, exposed stretch of sea we had still to cross. I was glad when Charlie decided to turn into a quiet cove where he said his brother had set up camp.

There in the cove we found two tents belonging to Charlie's relatives. It was a lively scene, with dogs, children and small boats. A woman was flensing a seal skin as we arrived.

My spirits rose somewhat when one of Charlie's nephews put his head in the tent and invited Aki and me to a tasty lunch of caribou stew and bannock. It was already late in the day, for we were now following the normal summertime cycle of the area, rising from night sleep around 10:00 A.M. and having "breakfast" at noon, "lunch" at 6:00 P.M. and "dinner" at midnight.

We decided to spend the night in Charlie's tent in order to speed up our departure next day, so caribou hides were laid down along the back and one side of the floor. A burning gasoline stove provided warmth for the chorus of snores. Around the stove lay dirty dishes, a side of raw caribou meat, pilot biscuits and various refuse.

By early morning the wind was down and a light rain was falling. Charlie decided we would go—"Three hours calm, six hours rough," he said. It was true. In the beginning the water was smooth, but suddenly it changed to giant, frightening waves with icy spray that drenched us. However, during the early part of the trip we encountered a fascinating scene: thousands of fulmar petrels feeding frenziedly on masses of planktonic krill so dense the waters of the inlet were red. The fulmars were so stuffed with krill that they had difficulty rising off the surface of the water as we approached. Many of them vomited streams of red krill in their efforts to avoid the boat.

We arrived at Arctic Bay just in time to meet Peter Heiss, take showers in the little hotel and then board the aircraft for Vancouver. Aki and I were both quiet on the way down as we mulled over our strong impressions of the trip. I now knew more about the migration of the narwhals in Admiralty Inlet and had a sense of the difficulties of collecting them there should we ever want to do so. While I had been impressed and delighted with the flora and fauna of the inlet, I had never seen so clearly the tough life the local people led nor the cheerfulness with which they faced the rugged conditions. Charlie had taken good care of us in the manner of the Inuit people and had got us safely through the hazardous waters. I was very grateful to him.

What a change it was to be back in Vancouver. The construction of the Southam Arctic Gallery was proceeding on schedule, with 23,000 cubic yards of earth and rock to excavate, 3200 cubic yards of concrete to pour into the forms, and over 200 tons of reinforcing rods to bind the concrete. Most impressive was the installment of the largest acrylic window yet used in the aquarium, over seven metres in length and two and a half metres high. In the beluga habitat, refrigeration would maintain the water temperature at 10° C.

We had a festive opening ceremony for the exhibit, which included the participation of the Honourable Titus Allooloo, a minister from the government of the Northwest Territories. We already knew Mr. Allooloo from an expedition to Pond Inlet in 1981 and were very pleased to have him there. Like other Inuit people who have visited our aquarium, Mr. Allooloo was fascinated by the new perspective he gained on the whales, particularly as seen through the acrylic windows, swimming gracefully in their tanks. He liked our new Arctic Canada Pavilion but was amazed by the performances of the killer whales. He knew the orca of Lancaster Sound as a ruthless predator of narwhals and belugas, and he had difficulty getting his mind around the idea of killer whales as friendly performers—exactly the same conceptual difficulty I had had with Moby Doll twenty-five years before.

We were also happy to tell him that we were giving something practical back to the Arctic as well as educating southerners about it. That same summer, our curator Mark Graham had taken some time out from his research on the physiology of Arctic cod in Resolute Bay and, in co-operation with his Fisheries colleagues and backed by federal funding, created a small public aquarium there. The aquarium consisted of three tanks, each devoted to a different aspect of local marine habitats and featuring the spectacular marine organisms that have adapted so perfectly to the frigid waters of the Arctic. Among the creatures exhibited were Arctic cod, eelpouts, sculpins, anemones, starfish and sea cucumbers. Mark also collected these species for the Vancouver Aquarium, where they live in a specially refrigerated fish tank.

Soon after the opening, one of the aquarium's three belugas died, leaving us with only two females, one mature and one immature. Since we had great hopes that the new habitat would allow us to breed belugas, we decided to make another visit to the Hicks brothers in Churchill, Manitoba. This time we wanted to obtain three belugas, preferably an adult male, an immature male and an immature female. These would be placed together with our existing females and, we thought, create an optimum social grouping for breeding.

Our decision was not made lightly, knowing the opposition that automatically arose whenever we talked about acquiring cetaceans from the wild. Once again we had to run the gantlet at open Park Board meetings for permission to obtain the necessary permits from the federal Fisheries department and to raise the required funds. We prepared for action and went ahead.

In addition to mounting the predictable opposition in Vancouver, the people from the animal rights movement showed ever-increasing sophistication in their tactics. Their first tactic was to mount a sort of counterexpedition in which some activists followed our team to Canada. They chartered a boat and shadowed the collectors, who were not happy with the interference. Their actions of course generated the sought-after media coverage and helped focus the spotlight on the efforts of the Lifeforce Foundation and the International Wildlife Coalition to challenge the federal Fisheries permit.

When the press called to get my views, I explained my hopes that with five belugas we would be able to establish a breeding colony that would make any further capture from the wild unnecessary. Most of the reporters understood that, but they were more interested in asking whether it was moral to take the three new animals in question from their natural environment. I put it to them this way: "The native people in Canada get about eight hundred permits annually to kill belugas. The three new whales are each covered by one of these permits; in effect, we are saving them from being shot by bringing them to the aquarium."

As things shook down, the Federal Court in Vancouver threw out the animal rights groups' court challenge, and three belugas were duly captured and sent by air to Vancouver. A police escort met the whales at the airport and accompanied them to the aquarium. Despite the threat of some kind of action by militant animal rights activists, there were no incidents, and the three belugas took up residence in the new habitat.

In the end, Arctic Canada turned out to be one of the most successful exhibits we've ever tackled at the aquarium. From above, on the Molson Family Foundation Arctic Plaza, visitors look across the bright blue waters of the beluga habitat to the rocky shore that Peter Heiss and his associates constructed. This natural-looking background extends down into the water. Within the carpeted Southam Gallery, magnificent acrylic windows look into an underwater view of Lancaster Sound, with varying depths and contoured, rocky walls. The belugas swim happily in the water, which is chilled to exactly the temperature at which they are most comfortable.

Once you tear your eyes away from the windows, a walk through the gallery gives you the story of this wonderful region both visually and in sound. We had always intended to highlight the marine mammal sounds collected during John Ford's research, and Sharon had come across a novel idea at the Boulogne Aquarium in France when we toured European aquariums some years earlier. In order to hear the sounds of the arctic sea, visitors put their heads under acrylic hemispheres that shut out the ambient sounds of the other visitors. The sounds vary from shrill whistles and explosive chattering to musical-sounding warbles.

As always, we tried to leave the visitors with a lasting message about conservation. The final section of the exhibit discusses the consumption of petroleum products on the level of the average citizen faced with the question of driving a car or taking the bus to work. It gently suggests that greater usage of Vancouver's public bus system is one of many ways to reduce the use of gasoline and thus reduce the need for developing oil resources in Lancaster Sound.

Even those who don't want to enter the aquarium can enjoy some of the exhibit. The plaza sponsored by MacMillan Bloedel near the duck pond in Stanley Park provides free viewing of both the belugas in Arctic Canada and the harbour seals in the new B.C. Sugar Seal Pool.

As Charlie Invarak would say, "Any problem?"

# 23

# Return to
# the South Pacific

The South Pacific is an ichthyologist's dream. I love going there and have done so many times. It is a delight to collect specimens in those sparklingly clear waters, so full of wonderful fish and beautiful underwater scenery. The area is part of the vast Indo-Pacific faunal region that stretches from the tropical coast of East Africa across the Indian Ocean eastward into the Pacific as far as Hawaii.

At the same time, for me and many men of my generation, the South Pacific is full of the ghosts of the Second World War. Even now, almost fifty years later, the landscape still bears countless reminders of great battles and the waters are full of sunken warships.

The war caught up to me on my nineteenth birthday, March 6, 1943. I had almost one year of credits at the University of Chicago, but being too skinny to meet officer requirements I entered the U.S. Naval Training Station at Great Lakes, Illinois. When I completed basic training I entered Hospital Corps School and eventually found myself on the island of Guadalcanal, attached to "I" Company of the Third Battalion, Third Marines of the United States Fleet Marine Force. I remained in the region for the rest of the war and for a year afterwards as a hospital corpsman on a destroyer escort.

Two decades or so later, I spent a kind of sabbatical in the South Pacific. The year was 1969, an odd time to leave the aquarium considering all that was happening there. The education and research departments were going full blast, belugas and killer whales were drawing unprecedented crowds, and new exhibits and expeditions were being planned. It was exhilarating, but at the same time I was tired of the endless committee meetings, correspondence and telephone calls.

Sometimes I found myself sitting moodily at my desk and chewing over a vague dissatisfaction. I was a marine biologist with a doctoral degree, I told myself. Why couldn't I have a sabbatical year to spend in the tropical Pacific observing coral fish behaviour and collecting specimens for the aquarium? After all, if I were teaching in the university I would have a year for academic pursuits every four or five years. Besides, I would improve my contribution to the aquarium by becoming an expert on the fishes and invertebrates in the region. Anyway, there was a capable staff, a strong board of governors and president Ralph Shaw to look after things while I was away.

I finally brought the question before the board and after some discussion got my answer: the board felt one year was too long, but they would give me three months, all expenses paid, to travel across the Pacific to Australia. I was determined to take Kathy along, and my long history of good relations with the Vancouver press allowed this to happen. I talked to the editor of the *Vancouver Sun* and proposed that I write a series of articles for the travel section of the paper. The money from this was just enough to pay for Kathy's expenses. Soon we were flying west over the Pacific Ocean.

We stopped off in Hawaii at the Waikiki Aquarium to see the director, my old friend Spencer Tinker. Dropping in at Waikiki was something of a ritual for me, a chance to check up on the Vancouver harbour seals we had traded him for some sea turtles and—I confess—drool at his fish collection. The glass tanks in the Waikiki Aquarium are always filled with colourful or structurally peculiar fishes that live in the coastal waters of Hawaii. There were long-nosed butterfly fish, saddle wrasses, yellow surgeonfish, red squirrel fish, gorgeous moorish idols, spiny scorpion fish . . . I could go on and on until I worked my way through the 336 species he had at the time. After some firm intervention from my wife, I tore myself away from Spencer's collection, but not before negotiating some more trades of specimens.

A few days later Kathy and I stood on the banks of the Balesuma River on Guadalcanal. As we looked across a field of saw grass, I could almost see the olive-coloured tents beneath the palm trees in the distance. The scene brought back the memory of my battalion bivouacked within that same coconut grove, along with ten thousand other men of the Third Marine Division. This was a staging area in 1944 where we prepared for the invasion of Guam.

Those days of preparation had mostly been spent hiking day after day across the fields and through the jungles and digging foxholes in the ground. Even in wartime, I was fascinated by the natural history of this tropical island. On our marches through the Guadalcanal jungle I had always kept my eyes open for the small, arboreal marsupial mammals called cuscuses, the great forked-tongued monitors and prehensile tailed skinks, and the red and green parrots and flashing white cockatoos.

As I walked those forests so many years later with my wife, I could see Indian mynah birds and South American toads—immigrants, like ourselves, from foreign habitats. I was pleased and reassured to see that the cockatoos and parrots were still there, too.

Our sabbatical trip took in many islands and a number of zoos and aquariums. We collected a variety of specimens for the aquarium, including saltwater crocodiles from New Guinea, serpent neck turtles from Australia and a beautiful green python.

The sabbatical was a great success, both from a personal point of view and for the aquarium and its holdings. When Kathy and I returned to Vancouver, board members Jane Lawson (later van Roggen) and Mye Wright arranged an evening for me—a fund-raising event, of course—in the Playhouse Theatre to show my slides and tell people about our adventures.

Starting in 1978 Kathy and I organized a series of study trips for aquarium members and staff to the islands of Micronesia, the equatorial region west of Hawaii that extends almost to the Philippines. The idea was to take slides for use in lectures and publications and to learn more about the environment from which so many of our specimens came. Our long-term ambition was to redesign the aquarium's Tropical Gallery to present some of the marine habitats of the tropical Pacific, perhaps even to redevelop the entire gallery around the theme of the coral ecology of the region.

Our itinerary wasn't a simple proposition from a logistical point of view. Our long-suffering travel agent Dick Craddock was hard-pressed to gather the information I required on remote islands such as Majuro, Ponape, Truk, Yap and Peleliu. Although ravaged by the war, these islands were left alone for some forty years and even now are seldom visited by North Americans. I had been on some of these islands beginning in 1944 when I sailed with the Marines to Peleliu after leaving Guadalcanal. Returning to them was always an odd experience, a mixture of the beautiful present and the ghosts of a strange and terrible time in my youth.

The ghosts were strongest for me on the small island of Peleliu, part of the Palau archipelago several hundred miles east of the Philippines. As we sped across the turquoise lagoon in two nineteen-foot speedboats during the 1978 trip, I remembered again my first view of Peleliu as a twenty-year-old hospital corpsman, watching from my troopship as the island burned under the flame throwers and napalm of the United States Marines' First Division. I was part of the 16th Field Depot, a group of black Marines that carried ammunition to the front lines.

It was September 15, 1944. The Imperial Japanese forces had removed the native Palauans from the island and, using Korean labourers, had fortified great caverns and caves in the limestone ridge that ran the length of the island. Heavy artillery guarded the entrances of the caves, and the surface of the island was covered with a network of carefully located gun emplacements and pillboxes. The 12,000 Japanese defenders were led by Colonel Kunio Nakagawa.

Two hundred and ten Marines died and more than nine hundred others were wounded on the first day of the landing. When my group landed a few days later, we set up our battalion aid station in a bombed-out building that had been a Japanese command post. As the stretcher bearers brought in the wounded, we could occasionally see the flame throwers at work in the distance as they burned out the caves on Bloody Nose Ridge. Night after night the ridge was illuminated with flares as the Japanese defenders were concentrated in an ever smaller area. Occasionally a few boatloads of Japanese troops tried to land from neighbouring islands during the night but bright star shells fired overhead would reveal them to the Marines and they would be eliminated.

Major General William H. Rupertus, commander of the First Marine Division, expected the operation to last only four days. It actually continued for two and a half months, and U.S. Army forces were sent in to relieve the Marines. In the end, most of the defenders died in their limestone caves and over 5000 Marines and Army troops were casualties.

I was pulled out of my gloomy reverie by our arrival at the dock, which featured a cheery sign saying "Welcome to Peleliu." Later we visited Bloody Nose Ridge and other scenes of war. Much had changed due to the encroachments of the fast-growing tropical vegetation. When I searched for my battalion aid station, I found a structure grown over by bush and great, serpentlike vines.

Despite the battles of the past, the area was full of marine life, as I found both on that trip and on others when I was able to dive in the surrounding waters. Palau had become an internationally famous diving destination. During my visits, I have often stayed on the central island of Koror at the Japanese-owned Palau Pacific Hotel, one of the great resort hotels in the world for people who like underwater adventure. Young members of diving clubs from Japan are frequent visitors there. These youths come for the joy of diving but you occasionally see older Japanese who come to visit Peleliu to pray for their dead at the shrine there.

One of the great dives of the world is the "blue hole" on the edge of the reef near Peleliu. One year we dove there with Count Enrico Dobrzensky and Countess Aline Dobrzensky from Vancouver. Enrico, a great adventurer, was on the aquarium board and wanted to experience this famous dive. We swam over a shallow reef, then descended through a hole and down a dark chimney. Below us we could see light, and as we went down we reached a ledge covered with white sand from which we looked out into the open ocean. Below us was a dark abyss along a vertical wall dropping several thousand feet to the ocean bottom. A slow current flowed past and the brilliant blue water was filled with small, brightly coloured fish feeding on the plankton. Farther out, schools of barracuda and jacks patrolled. It was a tremendously exciting scene as we swam along the wall and then finally back up to the surface where our boat waited for us.

Later we dove along the wall at Peleliu's landing beach and enjoyed the company of a school of friendly snappers with blue stripes on their yellow sides. It was all very peaceful.

The ghosts of the Second World War were present but less personal for me in Truk Lagoon. Truk is one of the largest island lagoons in the world, and its 140 miles of barrier reef enclose an area of 822 square miles. Forty miles in diameter, it has fifteen main islands and numerous small ones within the circle of its surrounding reef. The larger islands are the tips of mountains submerged in the lagoon and in the process of forming an atoll. Truk had been the Imperial Japanese Navy's most important central Pacific base, and it had been extensively mined to thwart any attack by sea. On February 17, 1944, the U.S. Navy launched an air attack codenamed Operation Hailstone. Many Japanese ships were sunk and the base was demolished.

I first visited Truk in October 1945, immediately after the end of the war, when my destroyer escort, the U.S.S. *Forster*, was among the first Allied ships to arrive at the lagoon. When we arrived, we were met by a Japanese destroyer outside the reef and led slowly through the minefields. Finally we found ourselves between two mountainous islands within the lagoon as Japanese boats filled with troops moved towards us. On the hillsides on both sides we could see Japanese artillery, and we felt very vulnerable. It was so soon after the official end of the war that our captain instructed our gunners to man the various guns on deck just in case. However, the Japanese troops were friendly and offered to help paint our ship. The war was truly over.

An aerial view of the Vancouver Aquarium in 1986. FINN LARSEN PHOTO

We named the original aquarium interior the H. R. MacMillan Tropical Gallery when it was transformed in 1967.    *Top*: DON HANNA PHOTO; *bottom*:  PHOTO COURTESY VANCOUVER AQUARIUM

The renovated Fred Brown Micronesia Exhibit of coral reef fish.  GREG DAVIES PHOTO

The Jean MacMillan Southam Arctic Canada Gallery, with its windows looking into the beluga habitat.  FINN LARSEN PHOTO

The P. R. Sandwell Gallery, presenting the marine waters of British Columbia.  Finn Larsen photo

An awesome experience—aquarium visitors marvel at a Pacific giant octopus. AL HARVEY PHOTO

The dorsal fins of killer whales are a common sight along the B.C. coast.   JOHN FORD PHOTO

Below the surface of the coastal waters are an astonishing number of fascinating invertebrates, such as these starfish. MURRAY NEWMAN PHOTO

The Pacific octopus is very strong, yet without a skeleton it is very flexible. This one tries to sneak out of the collecting basin towards the side of the boat. MURRAY NEWMAN PHOTO

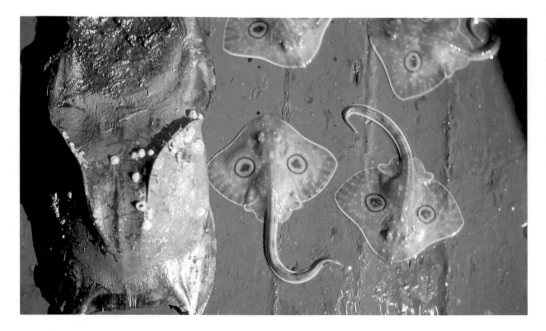

Among the fascinating fish of the Pacific Northwest are skates, seen here newly hatched along with their egg case. MURRAY NEWMAN PHOTO

The scary-looking wolf eel. PHIL EDGELL PHOTO

The handsomely coloured tiger rockfish.   PHIL EDGELL PHOTO

The odd-looking ratfish. MURRAY NEWMAN PHOTO

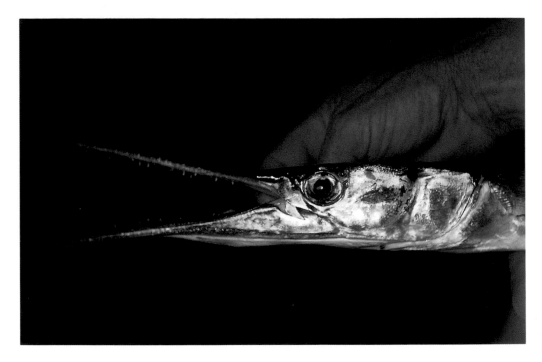

The aptly named needlefish, captured off Rio Balsas in the Pacific Ocean. MURRAY NEWMAN PHOTO

Our great supporter, industrialist H. R. MacMillan, on a beach in Mexico in the mid-1960s.

H.R.'s daughter, Jean MacMillan Southam, has continued her father's support for the aquarium. MURRAY NEWMAN PHOTO

The village of Bouni, on the island of Grande Comore, in 1971. The Grahams supervise the building of the bright blue cages designed for holding the coelacanth.  MURRAY NEWMAN PHOTO

The coelacanth, a "living fossil," mounted for display in the aquarium.

Aquarium patrons Count Enrico Dobrzensky and Countess Aline Dobrzensky near Peleliu in Palau with youngsters from a Japanese diving club. MURRAY NEWMAN PHOTO

John Ford listening to the sounds of killer whales along the coast of B.C.
JEFF FOOTT PHOTO

"It's a girl!" The birth of K'yosha in 1991.  JOHN FORD PHOTOS

Kyosha, shown here nursing, was the spitting image of her mother.  BEV FORD PHOTO

Lugosi smiles for the camera. TONY WESTMAN PHOTO

Tuaq, the baby beluga, with his mother, Kavna. Baby belugas are dark brown at birth but change to grey and then finally to white when they are fully mature. MURRAY NEWMAN PHOTO

On the 1978 visit to Truk, the aquarium group stayed at a hotel located on the site of a former Japanese seaplane base. It still featured a concrete ramp, rusting metal machinery and old pillboxes made of chunks of coral and gun emplacements. Today magnificent coconut palms bend over the water's edge, softening the visual reminders of the war. The many sunken ships that lie on the lagoon bottom are habitats for tropical marine life, and we organized a diving trip out to the wreck of the *Sankisan Maru*, lying about four hundred yards west of the island of Uman. It was a 4770-ton cargo ship sunk on February 18, 1944, with no reported casualties, and its wreck lies upright in a hundred feet of water with the deck angling downward from forty to sixty feet below the surface.

David Lam was my dive partner on the excursion to the *Sankisan Maru*. One of Vancouver's best-known citizens, he was born in Hong Kong and made his fortune in the real estate business after he moved to Canada in the 1960s. He distinguished himself as a philanthropist and became so well known for his good works that he was appointed lieutenant governor of the province in 1988, a position he held with great distinction. David first became involved with the aquarium in the early 1970s, and he joined us on several trips to the South Pacific and to the Arctic.

We entered the water and spent the first few minutes practising buddy breathing (sharing each other's air supply in case of an accident). Then we swam over to the mast and descended slowly, observing the school of small colourful fish swarming over the encrusting sponges and corals on the ship's structures.

We reached the deck at forty feet where purple soft corals moved slowly in the current. Schools of blue and red fusiliers swam gracefully over the superstructure, much of it in ruins from the original bombing raid. The remains of trucks, guns and ammunition lay scattered across the deck. Everything was going well in our dive. David and I exchanged the "okay" sign with our hands and swam over the side of the hull down to the sand at a hundred feet. As we swam along the bottom we saw an opening under the keel with light coming from the other side, and we swam under the ship.

Just as we reached the other side, David suddenly signalled to me, beating his fist on his chest, which meant he was having trouble breathing. We were still hemmed in by the ship's bottom as I removed my regulator from my mouth and attempted to give him air, but I was on the wrong side and the air hose was not long enough. David slashed his hand across his throat indicating he was out of air, and he started rapidly for the surface with me following. It was a bad moment when we broke the surface to see that our dive boat was some distance away, but the boat man saw us and came as fast as he could.

As we waited, I was aware that we had come up too fast. David coughed up a little blood in the water and again once we were on the boat. We were both shaken up by this experience and worried that David might have sustained an internal injury, so we went to the local hospital, where David spent the night under the watchful eye of his wife, Dorothy. Fortunately, he felt fine the next day, but the doctor advised him to refrain from diving for a while. I don't believe he ever went diving again, but he remained a personal friend and a supporter of the aquarium.

The fact is that forests grow again after being battlegrounds, and sunken warships become excellent fish habitats, but these trips underscored for me another truth: nature seems to be able to deal with a single traumatic confla-gration better than it can with the ongoing depredations of industrialized society. A different kind of battle has to be waged to protect natural environ-ments, one in which public education and carefully planned and administered conservation efforts are the main arms. We saw one of these projects on Malakal Island when we visited the Micronesian Agriculture Demonstration Centre (MMDC), a fisheries research station near the town of Koror.

Most impressive were its programs for the culture and conservation of giant clams and hawksbill sea turtles. The numbers of these animals, once very common in Palau, have been reduced to a critical level because of their importance as food and artifacts, both there and throughout their entire range in Micronesia and the tropical Pacific. MMDC has bred and released thousands of turtles, and its giant clam program has become particularly successful, with the distribution of young clams back to their natural habitats.

Obviously, the Vancouver Aquarium is far from the only aquarium with an interest in the tropical Pacific. If you wait long enough in Palau you will likely cross paths with just about everybody in the aquarium world. I re-member running into Bruce Carlson and Leighton Taylor of the Waikiki Aquarium and Bill Flynn of the New York Aquarium one evening as I was going for one of the excellent Japanese meals served in the Carp Restaurant. We had an uncharacteristically gloomy chat about diving accidents, bad air tanks and the fact that Leighton had just changed hotels after a bomb scare.

After they left the restaurant, I looked up at the counter and saw the decals of the Waikiki Aquarium and the New York Aquarium newly applied to the wall behind. There are times when an aquarium director must be a man (or, increasingly, a woman) of thought, and others when he must be a man of action. This was a time for action. Like a wolf marking his territory, I whipped out a Vancouver Aquarium decal—the logo is a killer whale leaping over a wave—and fixed it to the best location on the wall.

My staff and I returned frequently to the region and collected more and more South Pacific specimens. Our collection of tropical fish flourished, marred only by a mysterious incident in 1986.

Late one night, somebody broke into the basement of the aquarium and poured a fifty-pound bag of copper sulphate into the tropical seawater system. The poisonous substance circulated among the tropical saltwater tanks and 675 fish died. Only the 106,000-litre shark tank and a much smaller tropical invertebrate tank were spared.

We were in despair over this wanton and crazy act. At the same time, it was heartening to see how a committed membership and well-connected board can save you in a crisis. The ball started rolling when board member and cardiologist Dr. Dick Hooper suggested that Vancouver doctors fund the replacement of the surgeonfish. Other groups and individuals wanted to do likewise and soon it seemed as though the whole world was helping us. In an unbelievably short time, our tanks were once again graced by the presence of moray eels, flashlight fish, butterflies, angelfish and all the other jewels of the tropical reefs.

Towards the end of the 1980s I started thinking about creating a full Micronesian exhibit based on the Truk Lagoon area. The actual design of the exhibition hadn't jelled in my mind, and in any case I would rely as usual on my talented staff for the details. What I knew for certain was *where* I wanted it to be in the aquarium: in the Fred Brown tank. Fred was the owner of Pacific Press in the mid-1960s when he helped us with the great expansion of the aquarium. The project to which he'd given his money and his name was the reconstruction of the old thirty-five-foot tank, which had been the largest tank in the original building.

Over the years that tank had served very well for the exhibition of tropical fish; by the 1980s, however, it was showing its age, most notably in its glass front, which was intersected by a number of concrete mullions. I was painfully aware that the technology existed to replace the glass with a single piece of clear acrylic. I had first seen it used in the aquarium section of Tokai University in Japan in 1979. I'd since seen some wonderful examples in places like the National Aquarium in Baltimore, and I could visualize a window that would sweep across the front and curve over your head at the ceiling. It would allow us to fill the tank with more water, and therefore more fish. I knew it could be marvellous—all we needed was the money to do it.

I checked with our architect, Nicolas Lozovsky, to see what he thought it might cost. Nick is a White Russian who escaped the Soviet Union and trained as an architect in Lebanon. I always liked to talk over my ideas with him because he could easily visualize what I was presenting and could, in his pragmatic way, analyze the various components and give me a realistic assessment. He listened patiently to my enthusiastic description of the project and splashed some cold reality on me. If I wanted to have a greater depth of water in the tank, the whole end of the old aquarium gallery would have to be rebuilt and strengthened. Furthermore, he said, a penthouse from which the fish could be serviced would have to be built on the roof. All this could be done, he added, but it would cost a lot of money.

This time the Park Board was not concerned since the project did not enlarge the "footprint" of the building. The family of Fred Brown (who had passed away many years before) agreed to help with the funding. The City voted half a million dollars after Jane van Roggen and I had appeared at City Hall several times, and the Van Dusen Foundation pledged $250,000. With the money in hand, I organized another expedition to Truk.

As usual, the trip had a dual function: the members got an excellent adventure with some safe but exciting diving and the aquarium was able to pay for some staff to both collect fish and photograph the area in preparation for the exhibit. In terms of staff participation it was one of the biggest expeditions we've ever mounted, since it included members of the curatorial, design and educational staff.

We did most of our collecting from an old whaling ship called the S.S. *Thorfinn*, the proud possession of a former B.C. tugboat and sportfishing boat skipper named Lance Higgs. He had sailed the *Thorfinn* under the Canadian flag to Truk where it was based and operated for parties of divers. It was about 270 feet long, and in its thirteen cabins it could carry twenty-six guests. It was a great ship to travel on because it had lots of space, was very seaworthy and carried many small boats.

Of all the places the *Thorfinn* took us, the most beautiful was the aptly named Paradise Island. Actually composed of several perimeter islets on the southeast sector of the Truk barrier reef, it had white coral sands, bright turquoise waters and exquisitely beautiful little islands shaded by pisonia trees and coconut palms.

Underwater it was even better. Coral formations like fairy castles rose above the white sand bottom of the lagoon. The base of these formations was a series of non-living coral boulders to which were attached delicate table corals, round brain corals and thickets of staghorn corals. Many of the coral heads had blue or pink tips. Some were cauliflower shaped, others more lettuce-like.

Small light-blue damselfish lived in some of the coral heads. They were spread out, feeding on the plankton, but as we approached they retreated into the corals. The entire coral castle was occupied by fish of many species, some solitary, some in schools or disorganized aggregations. I lay on the bottom for a moment, watching the blue chromises and other fish. Suddenly a sea turtle arrived and took a jellyfish into its mouth, only to regurgitate it and swim rapidly away when it saw me. A black-tipped shark, attracted by the turbidity, swam around us but never came within photo-taking distance. It was a small shark, several feet long, yellow-grey in colour with dark tips to its fins.

After the dive we went ashore, walking barefoot over the coarse, coral sand. The island was covered with a canopy of vines, making the bush remarkably dense. White-capped, dark grey noddies flew overhead, and there were small black-and-red birds in the trees. Tiny hermit crabs crawled over the beach in search of detritus. Later a group of us set a small gill net around coral heads in about twenty feet of water. I took a lot of pictures as the rest of the group chased small fish into the net and collected them in small dip nets. These were typical residents of coral formations—blue damsels, blue-green chromises, slender wrasses, moorish idols, small parrotfish and many more species. I left the area certain that this lagoon was a perfect model for our exhibit.

And so it turned out. We worked extremely quickly, and a little over a year later I watched Wilma Brown, the matriarch of the Brown family, staring with delight through the curved acrylic window into the brand-new exhibit. If her reaction and those of the other guests at this preview were any indication, we had added another crowd-pleaser to the aquarium. It was a marvel, she said, and kept me busy explaining the team effort that went into creating an exhibit. Chief among the marvels was the artificial coral created from the photographs we'd brought back. Over the bottom of the habitat were little castles of coral, just as we had seen near Paradise Island.

As well as being beautiful, it was an extremely practical exhibit from an aquarist's point of view. The walls and background suggest the ocean stretching off into infinity, but the aquarists, invisible to the public, have easy access from above. It was different from any of our other exhibits in that the great acrylic face of the habitat curved over the heads of the visitors, creating a feeling of actually being in the water.

As the Brown family and other friends and staff exclaimed delightedly over the tank, I stood back a little from the window and tried to figure out what was missing. One by one I looked at the details, the special touches that make a great fish exhibit. The black-tipped sharks patrolled ceaselessly around the tank, just as they had in Truk Lagoon. The small, brightly coloured reef fish darted into the coral heads at any approach from the sharks. The background disappeared into an infinite blue distance.

Then it struck me that all that was missing of the South Pacific were the ghosts. And that was just fine by me. My mind at rest, I rejoined the party.

# 24

# Above, Below
# and Beyond the Fishbowl

An old aquarium hand like me can walk around the Vancouver Aquarium and "read" it, not only as the story of one institution but as a history of the international aquarium movement. Unlike grand old buildings like the Shedd or Berlin aquariums, or some of the more recent aquariums, which suddenly appeared on the landscape in their final size and shape, we grew organically, shaped by the knowledge and necessities of the moment just as a coral reef grows and is shaped by the currents of the constantly changing ocean.

At one level, the story of the Vancouver Aquarium is easily read in the names of the donors, which are emblazoned on the various galleries, exhibits and facilities. But there is another story that takes more technical knowledge to fully appreciate. If you know what to look for, you can see it in the tank shapes as they change from gallery to gallery, in the educational interpretation, the windows and even the architecture of the various areas. At this level, the story is one of creative cross-pollination, of influences picked up from the network of aquariums and their architects, directors and curators. You can see these influences everywhere in our building, just as you will see traces of the Vancouver Aquarium in many aquariums around the world. That cross-pollination continues today in our staff's almost daily exchanges of information with colleagues throughout the world by phone or fax, in the visits made to other institutions and in the visitors we receive.

This type of exchange began for me with the Ichs and Herps in the 1950s and 1960s. When I look back on the trading of animals, personnel and information then, I am struck by memories of the extraordinary openness and generosity that characterized the budding aquarium community in those more innocent days. The community is far bigger now than forty years ago, and while it is harder to know everyone and keep track of what they're up to, those qualities still exist to a great degree. Yet much has definitely changed since those years.

It sometimes takes a gathering of the clan to see just what those changes are. I recently played host to two such gatherings, at an international symposium on aquariums and the environment in 1990 and the International Union of Directors of Zoological Gardens (IUDZG) conference in 1992.

Compared to the Ichs and Herps conferences three decades earlier, these were much more focussed and—thanks to my efficient assistant Pat Graffin—more tightly organized affairs. They were also a good deal more decorous; to my knowledge there were no poolside free-for-alls. But then, I go to bed earlier these days and might have missed something. . . .

Probably the most visible change on a human level is in the gender balance. In the 1950s, the face of the aquarium community was almost entirely male. At the 1990 and 1992 gatherings, however, it was striking how many women there were among the directors and curators. Eminent examples are Yukiko Hori of the Enoshima Aquarium in Japan, Rachel Leger of the Montreal Biodome and Julie Packard of California's Monterey Bay Aquarium.

Here in the Pacific Northwest, the Seattle Aquarium has had two women at the helm in recent years, Sherry Sheng (now director of the Washington Park Zoo in Portland, Oregon) and current director Cindi Shiota. The Seattle Aquarium also launched Laura Mumaw, who is now head of the Auckland Zoo in New Zealand.

The careers of these women also point to another trend. Sherry Sheng started out in Taiwan and is now in the United States; Laura Mumaw came from Hawaii, moved to Seattle and is now in New Zealand. This movement from one country to another is becoming increasingly frequent among aquarium professionals. Another good example is Erich Friese, who started in Hamburg, Germany, and then worked in the Seattle and New York aquariums before going to Sydney, Australia. I expect that the development of many new aquariums in Japan will make that country an important training ground for the next generation of curators and directors.

Another great change can be seen in the missions that serious aquariums have taken on. Lou Garibaldi, director of the New York Aquarium, likes to say that the older institutions were like stamp collections: the point was to exhibit as many fish as possible and to make sure the labels were correct in English and Latin. Now, however, aquariums all over the world are evolving into institutions that emphasize conservation and feature ecosystem-based exhibits and mixed displays involving both terrestrial and aquatic representations. Some of these developments were anticipated in the 1960s by institutions like the Bergen Aquarium in Norway and Bernhard Grzimek's Exotarium in Frankfurt.

Perhaps the best way to illustrate some of the most significant changes and trends is to tour the aquarium world as I've seen it in recent years. (Readers who would like more information about specific aquariums would do well to obtain Leighton Taylor's 1992 book *Aquariums: Windows to Nature*, which describes many of the significant North American and Japanese institutions and gives a more rigorous history of the community than I've attempted here.)

## Ecosystem-based exhibits

Many of the new trends in aquarium and zoo design come together in splendid new institutions like Montreal's Biodome. The Biodome, which opened in the summer of 1992, is a redevelopment of the gigantic velodrome building from the Montreal Olympics. In form, it is essentially a huge greenhouse. The greater part of its exhibits are based on separate ecosystems, largely aquatic but terrestrial as well.

Rachel Leger, the Biodome's able director of live collections, helped create four western hemisphere ecosystems on 7000 square metres in the middle of the dome: the tropical rainforest, the boreal forest of northern Quebec, the gulf and estuary of the St. Lawrence River and the polar world. I think of the Biodome as an aquarium because of its complex water systems and extensive aquatic exhibits. As well, it absorbed the staff and talent of the now closed Expo 67 Aquarium.

Some older institutions have also moved to accommodate the new thinking. One of these is the aquarium of the Berlin Zoological Gardens. The three-storey building opened in 1913 and by the 1920s was world famous for its comprehensive collection. During World War II it was destroyed by bombing, but it had been rebuilt in its original condition when I first saw it in 1960. By 1988, when I took an aquarium tour group there, it had been reconstructed again and modernized.

You can see both the traditional and the new streams of thinking in the Berlin Aquarium. It remains a great aquatic house with a very large collection of animals: fish and aquatic plants and invertebrates are on the main floor, reptiles and tropical vegetation on the second, and insects and other arthropods on the third. The ecosystem-based orientation is strongly featured in a new building with five spacious, landscaped aquariums. Erected under the supervision of director Jurgen Lange, two of these represent coral habitats, one a South American river, one an African lake and one the waters of Southeast Asia. The healthy condition of all the fish in these displays reflects the careful attention to nutrition and husbandry that has always been characteristic of the Berlin Aquarium.

## The rise of the regional aquarium

In her presentation to the Vancouver 1992 IUDZG conference, Julie Packard said, "We are a strictly regional aquarium, and with the exception of special exhibits, we exhibit only plants and animals from Monterey Bay." In our increasingly television-fed culture, which expects to be offered everything at once, Monterey Bay represents a different orientation: it celebrates the local rather than the exotic, and the particular rather than the general. The Monterey Bay Aquarium's emphasis on stewardship and building appreciation of the natural world is another theme that has taken on increasing force in the profession.

Despite its size, the Monterey Bay Aquarium is in many ways a family affair. During the late 1970s David and Lucile Packard, through their family foundation, decided to develop a public aquarium in Monterey. Their daughters, Julie Packard and Nancy Burnett, are both professional biologists who are keenly interested in the project, so there was an unusual mixture of commitment and knowledge behind it from the start. One of the first and wisest things they did was to entice Dave Powell away from the Steinhart Aquarium to work with them. Ken Norris, by this time a professor at the University of California (Santa Cruz), joined the board of this new aquarium. And in 1978 I was invited to assist briefly as a consultant, an experience I greatly enjoyed. I flew down to Palo Alto to have dinner with the Packard family and discuss the project. The concept they had developed was extremely ambitious: to use the site of the largest abandoned sardine cannery on John Steinbeck's Cannery Row to exhibit and interpret the marine life of Monterey Bay.

Next day we drove down to the cannery site where we—architects Charles Davis and Linda Rhodes were also part of the group—had intensive meetings all day long. The old cannery seemed immense to me, much too large for an aquarium. As I looked over the desolation of the abandoned cannery area, its decrepit buildings falling into decay, I wondered if this project could possibly work.

But then I examined the kelp bed just offshore, a sea otter at the surface and a line of pelicans gliding above. Impressed and moved by the biological richness of this marine environment, I looked again at Chuck Davis's preliminary plans. It struck me that they were backwards: instead of looking out on the street, the aquarium should look out on the ocean. We discussed this for a time, with a great deal of note-taking, for it implied a drastic modification to the existing design concept.

A great deal of discussion was devoted to the feature tank, which was intended to be the aquarium's centrepiece. As an algologist, Julie wanted a living kelp ecosystem to be developed in a huge vertical tank. This had never been done before, and I urged caution. Fortunately, a cautious approach didn't fit with the Packard vision. The Monterey Bay Aquarium was built full size and the kelp tank was constructed as planned. What made the tank work was the exposure to open sunlight above and the construction of a surge-generating machine to provide water movement. They did reorient the building in the final design, making the aquarium a marine observatory with the sea itself as a main focus.

Monterey Bay was not my first consulting job; one of the nice things about surviving in a demanding job is that eventually people figure you must be doing something right and begin to ask for your help. Starting in 1977, I worked for almost a decade with the Corpus Christi Aquarium Association in Texas to establish a site and a concept for a public aquarium. I worked closely with Arthur Zeitler and Lillian Murray on the conceptualization and helped select the aquarium's first director, Quenton Dokken, who was then a doctoral student in marine biology.

The exhibits at the resultant Texas State Aquarium reflect the distinctive environment of the Texas coast with its great temperature and salinity variations, its marshes and shallow bays and offshore habitats. The feature exhibit is a huge tank with a model of (what else?) an oil rig inhabited by large fish such as Gulf of Mexico snappers, groupers and sharks.

The shorefront location of the aquarium is excellent, being both close to nature and central to the city. The building design takes full advantage of the location. From lookout points you can watch the shrimp trawlers at work, and occasionally a pod of dolphins swims by just offshore. Great ships move slowly along the shipping canal next to the site.

## Animal husbandry

Japan is currently undergoing an aquarium revolution in which many new, strikingly different aquariums are being developed. The Japanese government has encouraged the construction of large aquariums as part of waterfront projects to attract more visitors and to increase domestic spending. At our symposium in 1990, director Yukiko Hori of the Enoshima Aquarium told us that over thirty aquariums were being planned. The Japan Aquarium Association has some sixty member institutions, and almost 40 million people visit Japanese aquariums each year.

One of the things I like about Japanese aquariums is their attention to husbandry. Breeding programs in aquariums are largely experimental and research-related, since so little is known about the reproductive requirements of most aquatic animals. With 20,000 species of fish and hundreds of thousands of different aquatic invertebrates, the scientific community has been able to focus on only a few species. The technical requirements of this important field are daunting because of the different environmental and nutritional needs of the individual species, and indeed of juvenile and adult animals of the same species. Newly hatched fish and invertebrates are mainly independent of their parents, feeding and facing the hazards of their environments alone.

There have been some particularly impressive husbandry programs in Japan for animals such as the manta rays and whale sharks, currently exhibited in the Okinawa Expo Aquarium and the Rim of Fire Aquarium in Osaka. These massive creatures have been captured in the ocean and now live in unbelievably huge tanks (almost one and a half million gallons at Osaka, for instance) created especially for them. The greatest problem is to get these specialized feeders to eat in the aquarium. Innovative feeding arrangements designed by Dr. Senzo Uchida of Okinawa are crucial to the success of the enterprise: special diets of planktonic krill, carefully introduced at just the right moment, fill the sharks' and rays' gaping mouths as the fish swim by the feeder.

The Enoshima Aquarium and the Ueno Aquarium in Tokyo developed techniques for propagating jellyfish. Jellyfish go through a strange life cycle where they alternate from asexual to sexual generation. The asexual polyp resembles a tiny anemone. It divides and splits off small medusae by asexual reproduction; these medusae swim off by themselves and feed on plankton until they grow into sizable jellyfish that are capable of producing polyps through sexual reproduction. At Enoshima I recently visited a behind-the-scenes area where polyps were being cultured and jellyfish reared. Again, sensitive understanding of the needs of the animals was crucial. For instance, because the polyps are so small and helpless, the sand placed on the tank bottoms is sterilized in a microwave oven to kill potential predators.

In October 1989, I flew with one of my staff members to Tokyo for the grand opening of the Tokyo Zoological Society's Sea Life Park. His Highness Prince Masahito (younger brother of the emperor) and Princess Hanako presided over the opening, and the prince gave an excellent talk emphasizing the importance of conservation and the saving of endangered species.

The park is located on filled land in Tokyo Bay and except for the glass dome of the entrance is largely underground. The reflecting pool on its roof is carefully situated so that a visitor has difficulty seeing where the pond ends and the bay begins. The central theme tank with its large acrylic panels contains bluefin and other species of tuna, the first successful presentation of live tuna in an aquarium. Tuna have very high oxygen requirements and generally die quickly after being captured or in transport. Success was only possible through co-operation with tuna farmers, the development of very special husbandry and transportation techniques, and much patient effort.

Tsunesuke Nakayama, with whom I toured European aquariums in 1988, was the first director of the Tokyo Sea Life Park. A year or so later he transferred to the Ueno Zoo in Tokyo and was replaced as director by Yoshitaka Abe, who had developed the tuna husbandry techniques.

Japanese aquariums compete with each other to have something unusual and, if possible, unique about them. Tokyo Sea Life Park has its tuna exhibit, Sunshine City Aquarium (located, amazingly, in an office building) has Commerson's dolphins and Okinawa Expo Aquarium specializes in large sharks. Toba has dugongs and finless porpoises, Kamogawa has the biggest marine mammal collection and Izu Mito Sea Paradise has the largest sea otter colony. The Port of Nagoya Public Aquarium has as its principal theme "A voyage to the Antarctic" and shares a wharf with the historic research icebreaker *Fuji*. The aquarium consists of a series of exhibits that follow the cruise track of the ship, revealing the marine life of Japan, the deep sea, the tropicals, Australia and the Antarctic. Dr. Itaru Uchida, a research scientist specializing in sea turtles, is the director.

The newest, and in some ways the most spectacular, of Japanese aquariums is the Aqua Museum, which opened in Yokohama in May 1993. Beneath a giant glass pyramid is a magnificent cetacean pool on one side and a sequential presentation of aquatic habitats on the other. Beginning with a mountain stream, visitors eventually find themselves on an escalator in a transparent acrylic tunnel, moving through an enormous tank representing the ocean habitat. Dr. Masayuki Nakajima of the Izu Mito Sea Paradise directed the development of this new institution.

I don't wish to give the impression that the Japanese have a monopoly on animal husbandry. Institutions like the Danmarks Akvarium have been quietly practising excellent animal care for years. This lovely aquarium was among the first to rear primitive, sturgeon-like paddlefish from the Mississippi River Basin. All in all, scientific husbandry is an extremely exciting field to work in and one that all aquariums are taking very seriously as they redefine their roles.

## Urban renewal, aquarium-style

As I know only too well from my own experience in Vancouver, not all aquariums have the luxury of space to expand into. This is especially true of urban aquariums. Paradoxically, aquariums are much sought after as motors of downtown revitalization since they are unbeatable attractions for locals and tourists. Architects have risen to the challenge with some highly interesting design solutions.

Peter Chermayeff of Cambridge Seven Associates in Boston has become the most prolific aquarium designer in the world. He began with the New England Aquarium in Boston. Built on a wharf, this aquarium didn't have space to spread out so Peter designed it vertically around a large central tank that rises in the middle of the building like a hotel atrium. His design was very successful, and the completed aquarium has become a completely self-supporting operation, attracting large numbers of visitors year after year.

Good ideas have a way of spreading, and the economic value of the New England Aquarium to downtown Boston impressed Mayor William Donald Schaefer of Baltimore, who was fighting to save his city from urban degeneration. Under his leadership the city sold its airport to the state of Maryland for $20 million, and it collected the remaining money by issuing bonds and obtaining federal funds. Despite criticism over issuing bonds for an aquarium rather than social projects, Schaefer persevered and appointed Peter Chermayeff and Cambridge Seven Associates to design the new facility. When it was completed, the building was turned over to a private, nonprofit organization that got the federal government to grant the institution a new title: the National Aquarium in Baltimore.

Like the New England Aquarium, the National Aquarium in Baltimore was a compact, downtown design that attracted millions of tourists into the central core of the city. Peter Chermayeff received calls from all over the world and ultimately built aquariums in Osaka, Genoa and Chattanooga, Tennessee.

The current director in Baltimore is retired U.S. Navy Captain Nicholas Brown, who gave a lively paper at our IUDZG Vancouver conference. In describing the history of the aquarium, he said, "When the National Aquarium in Baltimore began its operation, we were conceived chiefly as an economic motor for an urban area sorely in need of redevelopment. But we soon understood that we had a critically important mandate to educate our visitors as well as to entertain them."

Education has always been one of the most important values of the public aquarium. The difference between now and forty years ago is that today we are far more aware of our potential influence and more focussed in pursuing this mandate.

## Protection through interpretation

In New Zealand, Australia and Singapore, a new style of aquarium has been constructed that allows visitors to move through large exhibit tanks in acrylic tunnels, looking outward at the sea life all around them.

The Great Barrier Reef Wonderland in Townsville, on the northeastern coast of Australia, is one of the most interesting aquariums in the world. Among other innovative viewing facilities, it features one of these acrylic tunnels. However, what makes this public aquarium unique is its mission: it was built as an interpretation centre for the Great Barrier Reef, which is one of the natural wonders of the world. The concept came from Graeme Kelleher, chairman of the Great Barrier Reef Marine Park Authority.

The Great Barrier Reef aquarium was opened in June 1987, with funding from the city of Townsville and the Commonwealth and Queensland governments. Like so many modern aquariums, this self-supporting, nonprofit institution was a key part of a downtown waterfront development project.

It is an extraordinary place to visit. For one thing, it contains the world's second-largest aquarium tank (the largest is the Living Seas exhibit in Disney World's EPCOT). In this tank is housed a living coral reef system. Hard coral is very difficult to maintain alive in an aquarium because the chemistry, light and water movement of a coral reef are difficult to duplicate. Even in nature, hard coral grows well only at the outer edge of the reef at shallow depths on the windward side. In the Great Barrier Reef aquarium, the large coral reef tank is a closed system to allow for better chemical control. Water is pumped from the tank to the roof where it goes through trays of living algae. The nitrogen-rich animal waste in the tank water serves as a fertilizer for the algae. As the algae grows, using sunlight and artificial light from metal halogen lamps to drive the process of photosynthesis, it absorbs these wastes. The algae is continuously cropped and removed from the trays, thus taking these wastes out of the system. Conditions are further enhanced for the coral by water currents created by pumping water through large return pipes. Finally, waves are formed with the aid of an air pressure-driven wave machine at one end of the coral reef tank. This movement of water is essential for oxygenation and waste removal. The aquarium is designed specifically as an educational facility to encourage people to learn about the Barrier Reef and to support its conservation.

## To educate or to entertain . . . or both?

As any good teacher knows, education is helped immeasurably by a dash of drama or a good story line. Just because an exhibit is supposed to be educational doesn't mean it can't be captivating and attractive.

France's Centre National de la Mer, located at Boulogne-sur-Mer on the English Channel, is an excellent example of innovative exhibiting techniques. It does its job so well that it has become a cultural and tourist centre for the region. The centre's focus is on French seafaring and fisheries. The exhibits include the deck of a North Sea trawler and a great tank demonstrating the function of fishing gear. When I visited the aquarium with Sharon Proctor and Greg Davies before it opened in 1988, we were fascinated by some of their display ideas, particularly the integration of undersea sounds into exhibits, and we borrowed some of the ideas for our Arctic Gallery.

When it comes to using technology to create imaginative exhibitions, the Disney organization has few rivals. The EPCOT Center, which opened in 1986 at Disney World in Florida, is a sterling example of this. Walt Disney, many years before, had described EPCOT as his company's most important goal and greatest challenge for the future. At its core would be a series of pavilions highlighting science and technology and the human race's desire to develop solutions for a better tomorrow. In the early 1980s Kym Murphy invited me to join the advisory board for "Living Seas," a pavilion planned to focus on the world's oceans.

At the time of this invitation, Kym was the Disney organization's corporate manager, marine technology. His job was to develop the concepts and technology necessary for the maintenance of living animals in the new pavilion. I had met him in the late 1960s when he was working for Sea World. Like Earl Herald and Bill Kelley before him, Kym was interested in the technical side of water quality in aquariums.

When Kym first spoke to me about Living Seas, he named some other people who would be on the board. At that point they included Robert Ballard, senior scientist at the Woods Hole Oceanographic Institute; Sylvia Earle, a distinguished curator at the California Academy of Sciences, of which the Steinhart Aquarium is a part; and Gilbert Grosvenor, president of the National Geographic Society. Kym didn't have to ask me twice; I joined the group and enjoyed the experience greatly.

The Disney formula for exhibits hinges on creating a structured story and a feeling of adventure as visitors are transported through a colourful facility. In EPCOT, visitors receive an entertaining science experience as they visit different pavilions centred on various subjects or nations. Much of the information in Living Seas' exhibits is provided by interactive displays.

The first job of our meetings in Florida and California was to figure out a theme for the adventure. Robert Ballard became a central figure in this because of his underwater expeditions aboard the Navy's deep-sea submersible *Alvin*. Our discussions led to the creation of Jason, a talking submersible robot whose "personality" is designed to be attractive to children and who talks with a scientist.

Living Seas opened on a beautiful January day in 1986, and it now entertains millions of visitors each year. The colourfully painted building has spiralling, wavelike designs along its exterior. After you enter the pavilion, hydrolators (a kind of elevator that suggests movement down into the sea as it vibrates and releases bubbles alongside its windows) take you on a three-minute ride down to Seabase Alpha, a prototype undersea research facility in a Caribbean coral reef. The enormous size of the five-million-gallon tank and its round design contribute to the realism of the scene. Large acrylic windows afford an excellent look at a white sand lagoon floor, its coral heads inhabited by different kinds of fish. Dolphins swim through the ecological community, and occasionally you'll see a scientist in scuba gear working on the sea bottom. Once you disembark from the hydrolator you can walk around Seabase Alpha which, as an "outpost on the edge of discovery," is full of exhibits on ocean technology.

The Living Seas challenges the minds of young people to find out more about the oceans. In particular, the Seabase Alpha concept emphasizes exploration and reminds people that 67 per cent of the earth's surface is never exposed to sunlight.

## International teamwork

There has always been international co-operation in the aquarium community, but it has expanded to many new countries in recent years. I see this directly in my consulting work, which has taken me to Africa (where I worked with Dr. Richard Leakey on a proposed aquarium in Mombasa) and various parts of North America over the years. Most recently I've been involved with an international team engaged in creating an aquarium in Taiwan.

Late in 1991 I participated in a workshop on waterfront development at the Monterey Bay Aquarium. At the workshop I met Dr. Liangshiu Lee, a professor of chemistry at Sun Yat-Sen University in Kaohsiung, Taiwan, who told me that he was part of the group that was planning the National Museum of Marine Biology/Aquarium in southern Taiwan. The government of the Republic of China in Taiwan felt the country needed cultural and educational institutions, he said, and it wished to build a living museum concerned with the marine environment. We talked about the project, and in the end he invited me to come to Taiwan, see the site, give a few lectures and meet the planners. I agreed and soon found myself the overseas advisor to the project's preparatory office.

In Kaohsiung I met the director, Dr. L. S. Fang, a professor of marine biology in the Institute of Marine Resources at Sun Yat-Sen University. The dynamic Dr. Fang is an ichthyologist who was the last student of the great Carl Hubbs at the Scripps Institution in California. His goal is for the National Aquarium to become not only a state-of-the-art aquarium but a leading research institution of marine life in the waters of Taiwan and the South China Sea. Projected completion date is late 1997, and the cost will approach $200 million.

I very much like the site chosen for the project. It is about a hundred kilometres south of the large, industrial city of Kaohsiung inside the jurisdiction of the Kenting National Park. One of the charming features of the ninety-hectare grounds is a small hill that local legends say was once a living sea turtle; the hill is covered with ancient coral and marine fossils. Best of all are the site's 1700 metres of coastline facing the Taiwan Strait, which is full of living coral colonies. The climate and the size of the site make it possible to have both outdoor and indoor exhibitions.

I am pleased to find myself working with architect Chuck Davis of San Francisco and exhibit designer Joseph Wetzel of Boston. Overall co-ordination of the outside consultants is the responsibility of KCM International, the designers of the Seattle Aquarium. My role is to chair an advisory committee that includes directors Jurgen Lange of the Berlin Aquarium and Senzo Uchida of the Okinawa Expo Aquarium. We meet in Kaohsiung from time to time and review the work of the architects from the practical viewpoint of experienced aquarium operators. Our meetings include both foreign and local architects, Dr. Fang and the staff of the preparatory office. The latter are young men and women, many of whom have been Dr. Fang's students. Young and enthusiastic, they participate actively in the bilingual discussions. Dr. Lee interprets for those of us who need it, switching effortlessly between Mandarin and English.

The surrounding countryside has provided a good deal of inspiration for the exhibits. One day Dr. Lee took Joe Wetzel and me up into the misty mountains of the interior where we hiked along a stream to a magnificent waterfall. The scene was reminiscent of a delicate Chinese print. It appealed to Joe, who said he would like to design a similar waterfall for the entrance of the new aquarium.

Construction is to begin in 1994. The theme of the first phase will be the Waters of Taiwan, conceptually similar to the Vancouver Aquarium's Waters of Western Canada exhibit. Visitors will begin their tour of the aquarium at an exhibit representing a mountain stream containing *Oncorhynchus masou formosensis*, the Taiwan salmon, along with other mountain species. As the exhibits unfold, visitors will follow the various fish populations down to the mouth of the river through the estuary to a series of coastal habitats and finally to the South China Sea.

Besides exhibitions, the aquarium will include a major research division, breeding areas and hatcheries, and even facilities for international conferences. The aquarium, buildings, landscapes, research compound, conservation area and public recreation area are all conceived as integral parts of the museum.

I'm very much looking forward to the opening in 1997, when the people of Taiwan will be able to view their new and highly educational aquarium. I really believe that, as aquariums have done in so many other parts of the world, the National Aquarium may generate a higher level of appreciation for marine life in Taiwan and lead to sound conservation measures by the government.

# 25
# Looking Ahead

I've had a great deal of fun in my forty-odd years in the aquarium business. It remains a passion of mine, even now that I've handed over the administrative reins at the Vancouver Aquarium, and I continue to be interested in how the field develops.

As the directorial phase of my life ends, I can't resist the temptation to turn the fishbowl upside down and gaze into the resulting crystal ball. As a scientist, prediction is part of the game, and I think a number of developments can be predicted with some confidence.

As aquariums become more and more technically proficient, they will exhibit new and exciting species never displayed before. I think this will require them to be more flexibly designed than in the past in order to accommodate changing requirements. At the same time, they will become increasingly research-minded and educationally oriented. They will launch more expeditions into remote places, including the polar regions, the mid-ocean and the deepest waters of the planet. I also expect increasing mastery of the technology necessary for keeping and breeding rare species. The main focus of research for aquarists will continue to be the animals and species of animals that are displayed in our facilities. We are involved in whole animal biology and have an opportunity to see and observe aquatic creatures as few others are able. This original observation will continue to result in new scientific revelation.

In recent years, the Vancouver Aquarium has augmented its Van Dusen Science Centre with a research centre on Popham Island, created with the generous assistance of Rudy and Patricia North. Popham Island is in Howe Sound near Vancouver. This station, along with the new research vessel provided by Don and Margaret Garnett, allows us to carry out field studies on the life cycles of marine creatures exhibited in the aquarium. It also contributes greatly to our role as an interpretation centre for our region.

There are many ways to organize yourself for scientific research. Some aquariums have close relationships with university faculties. Examples are the Mystic Marinelife Aquarium's work with the University of Connecticut and the Miami Seaquarium's close association with the University of Miami. Others have set up their own affiliates or subsidiaries. In this category you find Sea World with its Carl Hubbs Sea World Research Institute, the New England Aquarium's Egerton Laboratories, New York's Osborn Laboratories and the International Marine Biological Research Institute at Kamogawa Sea World. At the Vancouver Aquarium we believe in having a small nucleus of independent researchers engaged in scientific natural history.

The necessity for aquariums to be self-supporting or profit-making means that they must continue to be fascinating to the public. New and exciting ways of exhibiting aquatic life will continue to be developed. You can be sure that acrylic windows will grow bigger, and acrylic tunnels and underwater rooms will be ever more spectacular. New technology will be developed to present crashing waves, tidal currents and torrential rivers.

On the other hand, I suspect it will continue to get harder for aquariums to capture animals in the wild, particularly dolphins and whales. That means we will have to rely on breeding those already in captivity and sharing specimens with other aquariums to maintain healthy gene pools. Future aquariums will be designed with facilities specifically for breeding and rearing important species. That will include husbandry laboratories and buildings, nursery pools and special holding areas. The nutritional and veterinary requirements of the animals will continue to be investigated and become better understood.

The primary objective of aquariums, I have always believed, is life science education. This must and will be accommodated in imaginative new facilities allowing students of all ages to come in close contact with the animals and learn from living organisms.

The importance of our educational role goes beyond the simple transfer of knowledge. There is a rapidly approaching world conservation crisis, that must become a major concern for aquariums. All aquariums must clearly explain, as part of their educational mandate, the serious environmental and population problems that exist in the aquatic world.

Most of all, they must continue to create basic appreciation for living aquatic animals, particularly among younger people. The terrible excesses of the whaling industry, the near-extermination of the sea otters and the destructiveness of the yellowfin tuna industry to dolphins must not be allowed to happen again. Everything we do comes back to this very simple role: through appreciation, people and communities develop ethical attitudes about animals. I am convinced of this every time I go to our student lab and watch the kids delightedly discovering the world of tiny intertidal creatures, every time I see children standing in wonder before a tropical fish tank or one of our arctic exhibits—and even when they ask me tough questions about our marine mammal program.

The delight and the wonder and the tough questions all mean that a connection has been made. You can watch all the films or educational videos or television shows you want, but there is no substitute for seeing the animals up close, watching gills move and hearing a seal's bark or the sharp exhalation as an orca surfaces to breathe. Since few people have the opportunity to visit actual habitats (and a good thing too, for the sake of the habitats!), aquariums are the best and in some cases the only way to provide that connection. In the end, that is why we are here.

# Notes

## The Biologist and the Businessman

I never met Ivar Hagland at the time, but some years later I tried to get him to donate $25,000 towards an exhibit on local marine life that would commemorate the bathhouse aquarium. The money was not forthcoming.

Members of the aquarium's technical committee included oceanography professor Bill Cameron, zoology professor Bill Hoar, architect Ron Nairne, Park Board Deputy Superintendent Stuart Lefeaux and UBC engineering professor Les Shemmilt.

I am indebted to Dr. W. M. Cameron for information about the meetings with government bodies to secure funding, as he participated in most of the important ones.

## Do You Know Anything about Cash Registers?

UBC scientists were to chase the riddle of trout migration for years, particularly Tom Northcote, who eventually demonstrated that water temperature had a dominant influence on the upstream or downstream migrations of young trout.

## Fish, Funds and Plumbing

Biologists at the Monterey Bay Aquarium in California, most particularly Dave Powell, the director of husbandry, are currently doing a great amount of research on the survival of deep-water fish and invertebrates. Cool temperatures and careful handling are imperative. Dave reports that creatures from the oxygen minimum layer (500–700 metres) require low oxygen, and this presents an interesting challenge to the aquarist.

## Octopus by Air Freight

One of Don Wilkie's most important contributions was to investigate the water conditions in First Narrows in order to provide a solution to the vexing problem of where to locate the aquarium's water intake. This he did with great thoroughness, including the organization of twenty-four-hour sampling series carried out with the help of volunteers.

## Shark Hunting and Politics and How To Tell the Difference

I was helped enormously during this period by a strong-minded young woman named Hannelore Karrer, who became my secretary, then bookkeeper and finally a kind of "vice-principal." Hannelore maintained an efficient operation for me through the 1960s while I turned to the problem of expanding the institution.

The outgoing president of the aquarium association was Dr. Ian McTaggart Cowan, a distinguished professor of zoology and chairman of the department at UBC. I had met him at Berkeley when he taught a summer course there in 1951 and thought he was one of the finest teachers I had ever seen in action. He had been involved with the aquarium from the start, and there was a nice symmetry in the fact that Bob McLaren, his replacement as president, was one of his former students.

With me on the *Comox Post* was a good friend named Jack Long, a superb photographer who freelanced for the National Film Board. Most of the expedition and what followed can be seen in Jack's film *Shark Hunt*, which premiered the following year.

Long before he arrived, John Widener had made inquiries about who in British Columbia had the equipment he needed to do his mouldings on site. He was directed to the Killam family, who owned Industrial Coatings. Bill Killam was happy to assist with the project and later became even more involved with the aquarium.

## A Bouquet of Orcas

Dr. Ian McTaggart Cowan was appointed chairman of the Ministry of Fisheries Committee on Whales and Whaling. At the end of the 1970s and during the 1980s, he and his committee were responsible for establishing the regulations pertaining to killer whales in captivity.

Pender Harbour was the launching pad for a number of commercial or scientific careers. A restaurant owner from Victoria named Bob Wright flew over to observe our station in the summer of 1968. He was so impressed that he went on to develop a killer whale exhibit known as Sealand at Oak Bay on Vancouver Island. It became a major tourist attraction, generating millions of dollars in the Victoria economy. Bob went on to become one of British Columbia's most successful businessmen, developing fishing resorts in various places on Vancouver Island and the Queen Charlottes.

Some young scientists were greatly stimulated by our killer whales. Young Michael Bigg, just completing his Ph.D., wanted to work at the aquarium and study killer whales. I didn't have a job for him at the time, but he ended up marrying an aquarium guide and devoting his life to determining the population size of B.C. killer whales. He was concerned about how many were being caught and early on advocated controls. Even younger was sixteen-year-old Graeme Ellis, the son of Pender Harbour's Anglican minister. He became a whale feeder for us, then worked for Bob Wright in Victoria and went on to become a leading field researcher of whales.

## More Than a Fishbowl

The uniforms were the creation of a clever artist named Walter Langdon who was working with designer Rudy Kovach. Walter was also the person who gave the belugas Bela and Lugosi their cinematic names.

Sharon Proctor's predecessor, Mical Middaugh, was our first professional educator in the aquarium. She worked with us in 1964 and 1965.

My long-suffering professor Bill Hoar once again found himself pressed into service in the planning of the "wet lab," which turned out to be very functional.

My wife, Kathy, and her friend Bays Blackhall were the docents for the killer whale program.

A successful Vancouver Corporation lawyer, David Lawson was one of the best governors we ever had on the board. He brought a number of important people into our activities, including the personable and extremely well-connected Senator Nichol. Dave became president when Ralph Shaw stepped down in 1972, then died in 1975 at the age of fifty.

A protégé of Bill Kelley's, Stephen Spotte is a scholarly aquariologist who has written many books, including *Seawater Aquariums: The Captive Environment* (1979), dedicated to Bill as his "teacher and friend."

## At Home with Skana and Hyak

Mike Bigg worked closely on the Canadian part of the killer whale project with Gordon Pike's associate, Ian MacAskie. Gordon, who had frequently lectured about whales in the aquarium and had assisted us with Moby Doll, had been in charge of whale research on the Canadian coast. When he died tragically, Mike Bigg assumed his mantle.

Mike Bigg, Ian MacAskie and, later, Graeme Ellis, who had worked with us in Pender Harbour, did the research that led to the discovery that there are two types of killer whale.

## Bringing the Amazon to Vancouver

Maury Young, Bert Hoffmeister, Ralph Shaw, Bob White and others, including me, formed the Tynehead Zoological Society to promote and implement the idea of a major zoo.

As usual Ralph Shaw was of great help in fund raising. Among the major donors to the Amazon Gallery were the Grahams, the City of Vancouver, MacMillan Bloedel, the W. J. Van Dusen Foundation and Jean Southam. We also got significant funding from the mining company Placer Development and from the Ruth and Vernon Taylor Foundation of Denver.

Our curator of education Dr. Sharon Proctor worked closely on the Amazon gallery with staff designer Greg Davies. The Unecon company designed the building and D. W. Thomson Consultants Ltd. developed the life support systems.

The rockwork was supervised by Glen Spicer of the Emily Carr School of Art, with the help of a number of art students. It was at that time a student named Peter Heiss distinguished himself, eventually becoming an invaluable member of the aquarium staff.

In October 1983, the Graham Amazon Gallery earned us the Tom R. Baines Award, the highest award of the Canadian Association of Zoological Parks and Aquariums.

## How To Blow-Dry an Otter

The sea otter story is presented in a beautifully illustrated book by Stefani Hewlett Paine called *The Nature of Sea Otters* published by Douglas & McIntyre.

There are currently two known groups of sea otters along the B.C. coast, one at the Bunsby Islands on the west coast of Vancouver Island (about 750 animals) and the other off the central coast near Namu (about 150 animals).

Design of the mechanical systems for the Finning Pool was done by our regular consultants Dave Leaney and Ted Maranda of D. W. Thomson. Most of the architects from the original design team of McCarter, Nairne had split off into a firm called the Unecon Company. Ron Nairne had gone back to school to get a law degree, but his main group was still doing our architectural work. Mrs. W. M. Young (Mary-Margaret) and her sister Mrs. William Barker (Joanne) are the daughters of the late Earl B. Finning, after whom the Finning Pool is named.

## The Reykjavik Affair

The director-general of fisheries (Pacific region) responded in a letter to our proposal to import two juvenile orcas, saying, "It is our feeling that display of such marine mammals is an exceedingly valuable educational asset for Canadian communities and that such displays stimulate public interest and awareness of marine resources and conservation concerns, consequently, our department position is supportive of such requests from highly reputable establishments such as the Vancouver Public Aquarium."

In his book on global small whale fisheries, Dr. Edward Mitchell states, "Evidently due to complaints about damage to fishing nets in Icelandic waters, the U.S. Navy was asked to rid the coastal area of killer whales." One year a U.S. Navy vessel operating in the North Atlantic was said to have destroyed hundreds of them with machine guns, rockets and depth charges.

I believe Jon Gunnarsson has since built a cover for his holding pool in Iceland.

Many months after the Supreme Court decision I had a meeting with Patrick Moore in the home of aquarium governor Denis Timmis. It was a good discussion, and while Patrick was opposed to the collection of whales from the wild, he was sympathetic to our efforts to create the best possible conditions for them in the aquarium.

The late Max Bell had been a chairman of FP Publications and publisher of the Calgary *Albertan*. I became acquainted with the foundation through its advisor, Donald Rickerd.

Although the government of Ottawa had changed, we still had friends there and were very pleased in April of 1985 when Pat Carney, the MP for Vancouver Centre (the constituency that includes Stanley Park) presented us with a cheque from the

new federal government for $500,000. The H. R. MacMillan Family Fund pledged $200,000 and the Vancouver Foundation pledged another $150,000.

I was particularly proud when our local scientists Mike Bigg, John Ford and Graeme Ellis presented a paper about the two types of killer whales in British Columbia waters, the residents and the transients. Mike Bigg died soon after from leukemia.

Overall organization of the complex opening event was done by Rhombus Media. The event was later broadcast across Canada as a one-hour special and sold to television networks around the world.

## Chief of the Undersea World

Jane Lawson van Roggen asked Elizabeth Nichol of the Equinox Gallery to become involved in the project, and her expertise was invaluable.

The assembly team included artists Jim Hart and George Rammell and carpentry assistant Jack Carson.

Maury and Mary-Margaret Young and Bill and Joanne Barker helped to fund the reflecting pool.

## Birth and Death

Dr. Sheila Innis, associate professor of nutritional biochemistry at the UBC Department of Pediatrics, who was also associated with the Vancouver Children's Hospital, monitored the calf's blood values and adjusted the formula accordingly. This individualized adjustment of formula feeding was new to marine mammal husbandry.

The head of our finance committee, Denis Timmis, was chosen by the board to chair the examination of our present and future policies, with long-time board member and past president Robert McLaren as his backup. Janet Atkinson-Grosjean, our manager of finance and administration, was also enlisted and wrote the extremely readable final report.

In the 1970s I had many talks with the head of Sea World of San Diego, George Millay, about the importance of breeding killer whales. As more and more restrictions were imposed on collecting whales, Sea World ultimately developed facilities for breeding them and now has achieved considerable success. Sea World had discovered in breeding dolphins that adult males become aggressive at the time of birth and calf mortality is higher when adult males are present.

Another factor, according to U.S. Navy veterinarian Sam Ridgeway, is that a nursing mother may go into estrus in the presence of a male and lose her milk. For these reasons Sea World began to move pregnant females into separate pools, usually together with other females. The Vancouver Aquarium must develop a system of doing this in the future if successful breeding is to take place among its killer whales.

As of 1993 twelve killer whale calves have survived in captivity, one in Marineland of Niagara Falls, one in France and ten in Sea World. One calf was born in Sea World to a seven-year-old mother also born in Sea World.

## Orphan Seals

The grandson of B.C. Sugar's founder, B. T. Rogers, Peter Cherniavsky had a family connection to the aquarium, for his uncle Forrest Rogers had served on our board of governors for many years.

Jean Southam, as always, was very important in speaking to MacMillan Bloedel and in helping us obtain the donation.

Mike McIntosh, the zoo's curator, took a strong interest in the seal pup nursery and was of great assistance.

## From the Land of the Midnight Sun

The Molson donation was made possible initially by our board member Lucile MacKay's connections in Montreal. This donation was then matched by Jean Southam and others.

## Return to the South Pacific

One of the board members who most supported me in my request for a leave was John Simpson, the Australian-born former head of the giant mining company Placer Development. Once it had been decided that I was going, he went so far as to contact Placer staff and business associates in Guadalcanal, Papua New Guinea and Australia to ensure that I would be well received.

The Marines had landed just east of the Tenaru River in August 1942. After fierce fighting they managed to hold Henderson Fields, the air field constructed by the Japanese. There had been great sea battles in the area, and so many warships were sunk between Guadalcanal, Savo and Gela that these waters became known as "Iron Bottom Bay."

Years later, I was invited to attend a ceremony organized by the Royal Canadian Life Saving Society in downtown Vancouver. David Lam was by this time lieutenant governor of British Columbia. The premier and members of Vancouver City Council were all in attendance. I was surprised but greatly honoured to receive a life saving medal from the society for my action during that difficult moment we had at the bottom of Truk Lagoon.

Longtime friend and aquarium member Ron Stokes established a reward fund for information leading to arrest but the culprit who had poisoned the tropical seawater system was never found.

Curator of Fishes Dr. Mark Graham, and aquarium member Wayne Etherington did most of the actual collecting on the trip to Truk, bringing in about 130 fish. Others on the trip included staff designer Greg Davies, Elin Kelsey from our education department and underwater photographer Doug Pemberton. Architect Nick Lozovsky also came along.

## Above, Below and Beyond the Fishbowl

Recently the distinguished zoologist (and marathon runner) Dr. Mitsuko Masui became director of Ueno Gardens, the senior organization in the Tokyo Zoological Society. Other new female stars in the aquarium firmament include Dr. Judith Wellington of the New Jersey State Aquarium and Phyllis Bell of the new Oregon Coast Aquarium.

Peter Chermayeff and his colleagues are currently designing large aquariums for Denver, Lisbon, Las Vegas and Kuwait. Smaller projects include Dana Point (California), Shaboygan (Wisconsin), Erie (Pennsylvania) and Seward (Alaska).

The system that allows a coral reef to be reproduced was developed first by Dr. Walter Adey at the Smithsonian Institution's Marine Systems Laboratory.

Kym Murphy conducted research on the use of ozone to oxidize nitrogenous wastes and microorganisms. The ozone itself, while very toxic, would quickly dissipate, leaving behind dissolved oxygen and crystal-clear water. During the same period, he worked on reverse-flow biofiltration, which not only complemented the ozonization process and supplied the surface area necessary for the removal of dissolved organics but also provided a "natural" self-cleaning substrate for the creatures being maintained.

# Presidents of
## the Vancouver Public Aquarium Association

| | |
|---|---|
| Carl L. A. Lietze | 1951–1955 |
| Dr. W. A. Clemens | 1956 |
| Harry Duker | 1957 |
| George T. Cunningham | 1958 |
| Frank R. Butler | 1959 |
| Dr. Ian McTaggart Cowan | 1960 |
| Robert E. McLaren | 1961–62, 1973 |
| AEneas Bell-Irving | 1963–66 |
| Ralph M. Shaw | 1967–71 |
| David A. Lawson | 1972 |
| Mye Wright | 1974–75 |
| Lawrence Dampier | 1976–78 |
| Dr. Glen H. Geen | 1979–80 |
| Joyce MacCrostie | 1981 |
| Hon. S. Ronald Basford | 1982–83 |
| Gordon F. MacFarlane | 1984–85 |
| Jane van Roggen | 1986–88 |
| Dr. Richard Hooper | 1989 |
| Dr. John M. Webster | 1990–91 |
| Lucile MacKay | 1992–93 |

# Acknowledgements

No aquarium director, even if he or she was there from the day the institution's doors opened as I was, can take even a tenth of the credit for how the aquarium turned out. I have tried to include the names of as many people who helped along the way as I could, but doing it properly would take another book. So I apologize to those whose names and stories deserve to be included but weren't for reasons of space and narrative.

Many people have contributed to the creation of this book by sharing their reminiscences (and in some cases their documents and photos) and kindly reviewing various parts of the manuscript. These include: F. S. Auger, William and Joanne Barker, Nancy Baron, Alan Best, William Braker, William Cameron, Mary Cashin, Peter Chermayeff, Peter Cherniavsky, William Conway, Ian McTaggart Cowan, Kenneth Dakin, Greg Davies, Charles M. Davis, Lee-shing Fang, Jeremy FitzGibbon, John Ford, Louis Garibaldi, Patricia Graffin, James and Isabelle Graham, Gilbey Hewlett, Sam Hinton, W. S. Hoar, Yukiko Hori, Aki Horii, B. M. Hoffmeister, David Huff, Ronald Jackson, Andrew Johnson, Robert M. Jordan, Graeme Kelleher, Himie Koshevoy, Andrew Lamb, Jurgen Lange, Stuart Lefeaux, Rachel Leger, C.C. Lindsey, Joyce MacCrostie, Lucile MacKay, Allan MacNeill, Ted Maranda, Jeff Marliave, Grace McCarthy, John McCosker, Patrick McGeer, Michelle McKay, Robert E. McLaren, Klaus Michaelis, Kym Murphy, Paul B. Newman, John Nightingale, Kenneth Norris, Julie Packard, Leslie Peterson, David Powell, John Prescott, Sharon Proctor, James T. B. Quayle, John Rawle, Arne Schiotz, Ralph M. Shaw, Jean Southam, Nancy Southam, Spencer Tinker, Jane van Roggen, Michael Waldichuck, John Webster, Donald Wilkie, Bill Wong, and Maurice and Mary-Margaret Young. Any errors that may have crept into this book, of course, are mine.

My editor, Andrew Wilson, has been of immense help in carving a book out of my first draft. The Vancouver Aquarium's librarian, Treva Ricou, has patiently assisted in searching for historical photographs. Mary McLeod did most of the typing of the final draft.

The H. R. MacMillan Family Fund, Enrico and Aline Dobrzensky, Ralph M. Shaw and Jean Southam have been of particular help with the book's creation.

Finally, I would like to mention with thanks the part my wife, Katherine Newman, has played as my companion in the adventure of establishing and developing the Vancouver Aquarium over the years. As a biology teacher and aquarium volunteer from the beginning, she has seen it all. Her insights have been of great help in writing the book.

# INDEX